Funeral Directing In the United States

A Guide for Funeral Service Students

Larry J. Cleveland

Funeral Service Educator and Instructor
Licensed Funeral Director

~ First Edition (2nd Revision) ~

Copyright 2019 by Larry J. Cleveland

First edition, second revision - January 2021

ISBN 978-0-998-2571-3-6

Published by Hudson Valley Professional Services
Queensbury, New York 12804
www.HudsonPros.com

Printed by Lightning Press
Totowa, New Jersey 07512
www.Lightning-Press.com

Disclaimer - The author of this book is not licensed to practice law and is not an attorney. The material provided herein has been developed from several sources, including: state and federal statutory, administrative, and case law; government agency advisory opinions, bulletins, and administrative orders; knowledgeable instructors and practitioners in the funeral service; and information available to the general public in various communication mediums. The content of this book is believed to be accurate and true; however, practitioners should always consult an attorney for legal advice on any question of law in funeral service matters.

Cover Photos - Presidential Funerals through the Decades

Front: *2004* - **President Ronald Reagan**
Members of the Armed Forces Honor Guard place his casket into a hearse, which will carry his remains to the grounds of the Washington National Cathedral for a State funeral service. Illustration courtesy of U.S. Navy. Photo by Photographer's Mate 3rd Class Todd Frantom.

Back: *1924* - **President Woodrow Wilson**
        1945 - **President Franklin D. Roosevelt**
        1963 - **President John F. Kennedy**

Table of Contents

PREFACE..Page 9

Book Introduction ....Page 11
Purpose and intent
Use of titles: funeral director, undertaker, and mortician
Definitions, notes, forms, and guides
Sources
Disclaimer

PART 1 - FUNERAL PROCEDURES

Chapter 1: Notification of Death...Page 13
Overview
Chapter definitions
Initial notification
Pricing inquiries
Telephone etiquette
Primary information needs
Secondary information and documentation

Chapter 2: Transfer (Removal) of Remains...Page 19
Overview
Chapter definitions
Vehicles
Equipment
Staff considerations
General transfer procedures
Home removals
Institution removals
Communicating with the family
The general price list (GPL)

Chapter 3: The Arrangement Conference ....Page 31
Overview
Chapter definitions
Purpose and preparation
Opening a dialogue with the family
Service options
Pallbearers
Preparation of a newspaper notice
Other arrangement considerations
Terms and methods of payment
Regulatory compliance

Chapter 4: Final Disposition Methods ....Page 43
    Overview
    Chapter definitions
    Cremation
    Earth burial (interment)
    Entombment
    Green (natural) burial
    Disposition at sea (burial at sea)
    Donation
    Cryonics
    Alkaline hydrolysis

Chapter 5: Death Reporting and Registration ....Page 51
    Overview
    Chapter definitions
    Death certificates - generally
    Death certificates - information needed
    Death certificates - importance, purpose, and use
    Electronic death certificates
    Fetal death certificates
    Disposition permits

Chapter 6: Government Benefits and Programs ....Page 57
    Overview
    Chapter definitions
    Social security benefits
    Veterans benefits - generally
    Burial allowances
    Tangible benefits
    Military funeral honors
    Military discharges
    National cemeteries
    Arlington National Cemetery
    Cemeteries in national parks
    State veterans' cemeteries
    Public assistance

Chapter 7: Funeral Goods and Services ....Page 71
    Overview
    Chapter definitions
    Goods and services - generally
    Funeral services - traditional
    Funeral services - innovative
    Funeral goods - traditional
    Funeral goods - innovative

Home funerals
Green (natural) burials
Third-party merchandise

Chapter 8: Documentation ....Page 87
Overview
Chapter definitions
Due diligence
Documenting due diligence
Documentation for laws, rules, and regulations
Documentation for financial accountability
Death case files
Professional liability
Archives

PART 2 - PRE-NEED FUNERAL CONTRACTS

Chapter 9: Prefunded Preneeds ....Page 93
Overview
Chapter definitions
Consumer awareness
Types of preneeds
Reasons for preneeds
Types of preneed contracts

Chapter 10: Preneed Arrangement Conferences..................................Page 97
Overview
Chapter definitions
Preneed arrangement conferences
The FTC and preneeds
Changes to prefunded preneeds
Other legal considerations
Preneed funding mechanisms

PART 3 - FUNERAL DIRECTING

Chapter 11: Preparing for Funeral Events ....Page 103
Overview
Chapter definitions
Lead director concept
Worksheets and checklists
Coordination with staff, allied professionals, and others
Providing goods and preparing service items
Identify and provide equipment
Finalizing preparations
Inspecting and approving funeral event sites
Preparing funeral event sites

Chapter 12: Supervising Funeral Events...Page 115
 Overview
 Chapter definitions
 Calling hours (visitation) event
 After calling hours
 Funeral service event
 Funeral processions
 Committal event

Chapter 13: Post-Funeral Follow-up and Aftercare...............................Page 129
 Overview
 Chapter definitions
 Post-funeral follow-up
 Direct aftercare
 Indirect aftercare

PART 4 - SHIPPING CONSIDERATIONS

Chapter 14: Shipping Cremated Remains...Page 133
 Overview
 Chapter definitions
 Domestic shipping
 Domestic transportation
 International shipping
 International transportation

Chapter 15: Shipping Human Remains..Page 139
 Overview
 Chapter definitions
 Domestic shipping
 International shipping
 Shipping by airline

Chapter 16: Shipping Containers..Page 145
 Overview
 Chapter definitions
 Transfer containers
 Miscellaneous containers

PART 5 - FORMS AND GUIDES

Forms
Form 1: New Case Intake Sheet..Page 151

Form 2: Arrangement Conference Handout ....Page 153

Form 3: Disposition Permits ....Page 157

Form 4: Statement of Death by Funeral Director (SSA-721)................................Page 161

Form 5: Claim for Standard Headstone or Marker (VA 40-1330) ....Page 163

Form 6: Claim for Government Medallion (VA 40-1330M)................................Page 167

Form 7: Application for U.S. Flag for Burial (VA 27-2008)................................Page 169

Form 8: Presidential Memorial Certificate Request (VA 40-0247)......................Page 171

Form 9: Certificate of Release or Discharge from Active Duty (DD-214) ....Page 173

Form 10: VA Before You Call Checklist ....Page 175

Form 11: Case Checklist and Worksheet..Page 177

Form 12: Staff Assignments ....Page 179

Form 13: Spring Burial Worksheet..Page 181

Guides
Guide 1: Environmental Protection Agency Burial at Sea Instructions ....Page 183

Guide 2: Typical Christian Church Interior Design..Page 185

Guide 3: Proper Way to Turn a Casket Around in a Church ....Page 187

Guide 4: USPS Guidelines for Shipping Cremated Remains ....Page 189

Guide 5: Typical Airline Shipping Requirements ....Page 191

GLOSSARY..Page 193

SOURCES CONSULTED..Page 203

ILLUSTRATIONS..Page 206

INDEX...Page 207

Preface

Funeral directing as a profession is a multi-faceted endeavor, one that requires a funeral director to simultaneously care and provide for the needs of the decedent, family, friends, and their community. They must be skilled planners and organizers, strong leaders, good communicators, and dedicated professionals capable of working collectively with support staff and allied professionals to achieve common goals.

Funeral directing covers a wide range of activities that encompass an even wider range of actions designed to offer a funeral service plan that carries out the wishes of the family with respect, dignity, and decorum. One textbook cannot adequately address all of these actions and activities, at least not at the level and depth needed to provide proper and suitable instruction to funeral service students. As such, many areas related to funeral directing are explored in textbooks focusing on a specific sub-topic or subject, such as cremation, embalming, regulatory compliance, or rites and customs; while core elements are provided in textbooks such as the one you are reading now. *Funeral Directing in the United States* explores these core elements:

- ➤ Notification of death and transfer (removal) of remains
- ➤ Arrangement conferences and death reporting
- ➤ Government benefits and programs
- ➤ Funeral goods and services (generally)
- ➤ Pre-need funeral service contracts
- ➤ Preparing for and supervising funeral service events
- ➤ Shipping human remains and cremated remains.

The content of this book has been identified by the American Board of Funeral Service Education (ABFSE) as being of importance in educating students about the funeral directing profession in the United States. This same ABFSE material is also the foundation for the development of questions on the national board examination. As such, this textbook provides both instructors and students with an up-to-date source of material designed to complement and enhance ABFSE educational mandates related to the fundamentals of funeral directing. The material is current, accurate, and essential to preparing prospective funeral directors for taking the two-part national board examination.

Larry Cleveland

Other Books by this Author

Funeral Service Marketing and Merchandise
ISBN: 978-0-998-2571-2-9

Funeral Service Rites and Customs
ISBN: 978-0-998-2571-4-3

Cremation in the United States
ISBN: 978-0-998-2571-7-4

Funeral Service Law in the United States
ISBN: 978-0-998-2571-6-7

New York State Mortuary Law
ISBN: 978-0-998-2571-5-0

Book Introduction

Purpose and Intent

Purpose - The purpose of this textbook is to assist and promote funeral service students as they pursue a career in the funeral service industry, as well as to provide support to the college-level faculty and staff members serving as student mentors and classroom instructors. The book has been developed by incorporating and integrating the educational material identified by the American Board of Funeral Service Education (ABFSE) as being of importance to the subject of funeral directing.

Intent - The intent of this textbook is to serve as a shared, common link between student and teacher; a link designed to serve both groups by presenting pertinent and relevant material in a consistent and organized style conducive to the learning environment. Integrating the information in this textbook with the skills and knowledge of the educator in the classroom is the formula to effectively preparing for and passing the two-part National Board Examination (NBE) at the conclusion of collegiate academic studies.

Use of Titles: Funeral Director, Undertaker, and Mortician

A cursory review of funeral service titles used by the fifty states reveals the vast majority have adopted the term *Funeral Director* to identify funeral service professionals. *Mortician* is still seen sporadically but now viewed by many within the service as sounding too morbid and gloomy. The term *Undertaker* is virtually non-existent, as state legislators have gradually phased this title out of the modern lexicon. Therefore, for the purposes of this book, the term *Funeral Director* will be used to represent all three titles equally.

Definitions, Notes, Forms, and Guides

Definitions - Where convenient for the reader, definitions are provided in the chapters and thereafter highlighted within the text with bold print. These definitions may also be repeated in subsequent chapters to provide prompt, easy access when of importance to the material being presented. All of the terms and definitions are compiled in a comprehensive glossary located in the back of this book, with each term cross-referenced to the chapters in which they appear.

Unless otherwise noted, the terms are definitions provided for use in accredited funeral service educational programs and therefore represent a potential source for test questions on the two-parts of the NBE. Some of the terms may be followed with a notation to identify their source from ABFSE glossaries, funeral service textbooks, legal statutes, research materials, the author, or other reliable authority. These notations and the sources they identify are as follows:

➢ FTC Guide - The information comes from the Federal Trade Commission publication titled, *Complying with the Funeral Rule*.

➢ [FTC 16 CFR 453] - Title 16, Code of Federal Regulations, part 453 (The Funeral Rule).

➢ [by Author] - The definition is of importance in understanding the material being presented.

➢ [FSL term] - *Funeral Service Law in the United States*, by Cleveland, © 2019.

➢ [MM term] - Funeral Service Marketing and Merchandise, by Cleveland, © 2018.

Notes - Notes are used in chapters to draw attention to material of specific interest or importance, or to provide additional clarification to a particular topic or subject of discussion. They are styled in the narrative as Note: with the additional information following immediately after the colon.

Forms - Sample forms and important documents are located in the Forms and Guides section of this book and identified in chapter narratives with a note. These forms and documents may be state specific, and readers are encouraged to research requirements in the states where they intend to practice to identify the proper forms in those states.

Guides - Guides to selected topics, such as the illustration depicting a Typical Christian Church Interior Design, are located in the Forms and Guides section of this book and identified with a note.

Sources
Sources of information are provided throughout the book and may be found in captions, annotations, or a specific attribution within the narrative. Each source includes the information or reference needed to quickly find them in the Sources Consulted section in the back of the book, where additional details and URLs (when available) are provided.

Disclaimer
The author of this book is not licensed to practice law and is not an attorney. The material provided herein has been developed from several sources, including: federal and state statutory, administrative, and case law; government agency advisory opinions, bulletins, and administrative orders; knowledgeable instructors and practitioners in the funeral service industry; and information available to the general public in various communication mediums. The content of this book is believed to be accurate and true; however, practitioners should always consult an attorney for legal advice on any question of law in funeral service matters.

Chapter 1: Notification of Death

Overview
This chapter reviews the proper procedures and recommended actions to be taken by funeral service professionals when they receive the first call reporting a death. Subsequent chapters expand on this to explore the transfer (removal) of remains, arrangement conference, and other progressive activities that follow the first call.

Chapter Definitions
At-need cases - when a death has occurred.

Coroner - usually an elected officer without medical training whose chief duty is to investigate questionable deaths.

Deceased - a dead human body.

First call - when the funeral establishment receives notification of death.

Initial notification of death - the first contact a funeral establishment receives regarding a death.

Medical examiner - a forensically-trained physician who investigates questionable or unattended deaths (has replaced the coroner in some jurisdictions).

Transfer of remains - the moving of the dead human body from the place of death to the funeral establishment or other designated place.

Initial Notification
When a funeral establishment receives the **initial notification of a death**, it may be referred to as **first call**; however, like much of the terminology used in the funeral service industry, this term has no official foundation or specific requirement for its use.

Some establishments prefer to call the initial notification a *death* call or *death* case. This is especially true when they utilize third-party answering and communication services during off-hours. With many of these providers now dispatching death calls by text message and email instead of direct voice communication, extra precautions are taken to ensure a clear distinction is established between non-emergent calls for service and immediate need calls for service. By including the word death in describing these immediate calls for service, there is less room for error and confusion.

The most common communication method across all spectrums is the telephone, and calls are usually answered directly by a funeral establishment when placed during regular business hours. For non-business hours, they often employ a third-party answering service to take the calls for them. In all cases, it is highly recommended a funeral service professional from the establishment speak to the family as soon as possible. For middle of the night calls from health care facilities, the best practice is to wait until the next morning to call the family. Cases where a death has just occurred and the family has requested the assistance of a funeral director are called **at-need cases** and require an immediate response.

Pricing Inquiries

On most occasions, individuals calling about an at-need case have already made the decision to use a specific funeral establishment, and the call is simply to formally request services. In less frequent cases, the caller is shopping for prices before selecting a funeral establishment. These shopper inquiries require special attention to ensure compliance with the Federal Trade Commission (FTC) Funeral Rule.

The Funeral Rule centers around the offering, display, pricing, and sale of funeral service goods and services. Within the Rule, the FTC has mandated three specific prices lists: General Price List, Casket Price List, and Outer Burial Container Price List. When a consumer inquires by telephone about prices for goods and services, they must be given any available information from the FTC required lists or any other available source which reasonably answers the question.

The FTC Guide states:

> *You must give consumers who telephone your place of business and ask about your prices or offerings accurate information from your General Price List, Casket Price List, and Outer Burial Container Price List. You also must answer any other questions about your offerings and prices with any readily available information that reasonably answers the question.*

> *Note: You cannot require callers to give their names, addresses, or phone numbers before you give them the requested information. You can ask callers to identify themselves, but you still must answer their questions even if they refuse to do so. You cannot require consumers to come to the funeral home in person to get price information.*

> *You can use an answering machine or answering service to record incoming calls. However, you must respond to questions from callers on an individual basis.*

> *Example: Your answering machine can have a message telling consumers to call a specified number during business hours for information about prices and offerings. You need to provide the requested information when consumers call during those hours, or, you can have an answering machine or answering service take consumers' names and phone numbers so that you can return the calls at your earliest convenience.*

> *You may have an employee answering your phones who can respond to easier questions regarding your offerings and prices by referring to the printed price lists, but who refers more difficult questions to you. If you are unavailable when the call comes in, the employee can take a message so that you can return the call later.*

You do not have to give price and other information after business hours if it is not your normal practice to do so. You can tell consumers who call during non-business hours that you will provide the information during regular business hours. However, if a consumer calls after hours to inquire about an at-need situation, and it is your practice to make funeral arrangements during non-business hours, you should provide price or other information the consumer requests.

There is no specific requirement in federal regulations for a person who provides price information over the telephone to be a licensed funeral practitioner. In fact, the FTC notes just the opposite, providing any employee must respond to price questions by referring to the printed price lists.

Note: Third-party answering staff members are not employees of the funeral establishment, and the Funeral Rules does not require them provide price information over the telephone.

When speaking with a consumer seeking pricing information, the best practice is to first inquire as to the types of goods and services being considered. This allows the funeral service professional to narrow the discussion to the desired items and tell the consumer about the available options. If unable to narrow the request, it is best to give a range of prices. If specific items are then selected, the Funeral Rule requires the prices for those specific items be stated individually, as listed on any of the three mandatory price lists.

Telephone Etiquette
Professionalism and compassion are two hallmarks of the funeral service industry and must be effectively employed when answering telephone calls coming into a funeral establishment. This is especially true when the call being received is one to make a death notification.

Note: The information that follows relates to those calls where the death notification is being made by a family member or other person with a close, personal connection to the decedent. For calls from other individuals or entities, such as another funeral establishment or a health care facility, the process will differ. The additional procedures to follow in those cases are provided later in this chapter.

Answering - All calls being received in a funeral establishment should be answered by announcing the names of the establishment and the staff member taking the call. Additional unnecessary information or greetings, such as 'good morning,' 'good afternoon,' 'Merry Christmas,' or 'happy holidays' should be avoided. There is nothing good, happy, or merry about the loss of a loved one, and the use of these greetings may cause additional stress and anxiety for a family already dealing with the death of a loved one. As soon as possible after confirmation a death has occurred, the funeral director should express condolences.

Care must be taken to use proper language and terminology at all times when receiving calls, while avoiding any slang or funeral industry jargon. As an example, a positive response to an inquiry should be acknowledged with a yes, not yea. Under no circumstance should a caller making a notification of death be placed on hold, told to call back at a later time, or be delayed. Death calls should and must take priority over all other activities.

Voice - It is important to speak in a voice that is both reassuring and comforting to a family member, friend, or other representative of a decedent. At this stage in the process, those individuals are looking for guidance – someone to give them direction and focus at a time when the world around them has suddenly become overwhelming, complicated, and unknown. First impressions are indeed lasting impressions.

A strong, reassuring, and comforting voice at the time of a death notification will include these qualities and assets:

> ➢ a conveyance of strength, confidence, and unqualified competence;

> ➢ a moderate tone, one not overly happy, cheerful, sorrowful, or sad;

> ➢ use of clear and concise diction (choice and use of words or phrases), speech, and pronunciation;

> ➢ a moderate volume, not too loud and not too soft;

> ➢ patience and understanding, with undivided attention to the current case; and

> ➢ use of common, simple language.

Closing - Closing out the death notification conversation is as important as answering the call itself, with the goal being to end the communication with the same professionalism and compassion. When possible, it is best to allow the caller to initiate the closing of the discussion to ensure they have been given the opportunity to ask the funeral director any last questions before ending the conversation.

When concluding the initial notification call, there are a few simple guidelines that will help provide a smooth transition. These include:

> ➢ Read back the information obtained from the caller to verify accuracy.

> ➢ Provide the caller with an estimated time of arrival, preferably in a specified time frame, such as minutes or hours; avoid the use of vague, abbreviated, or imprecise language, such as 'see you soon.'

> ➢ Consider avoiding any expression of thanks or appreciation for the call, as this may for some individuals have a negative or undesirable connotation or implication.

> ➢ Ensure contact information has been exchanged so both parties have avenues to reach each other quickly.

> ➢ Assure the caller the funeral establishment is fully prepared and competent to support and assist them throughout the forthcoming events they are facing.

➢ Inquire if the caller has any further questions, then again advise them they may call at any time with further questions or need for clarifications.

Primary Information Needs
While a significant amount of data will be accumulated as a death case progresses, there are certain pieces of information that should be collected at the time of a death notification to facilitate the actions needed to provide for the **transfer of remains**. The list of information needed is not absolute and, in all likelihood, will be subject to adjustments as necessary for a specific case. Primary information needs include:

➢ Name of the **deceased**.

➢ Location, including the street address and any specific place – such as outdoors, in a basement, on an upper floor, in an apartment, or in a vehicle.

➢ Caller name, including relationship to the deceased and callback numbers.

➢ Presence of any first responder personnel, such as police, fire, or EMS.

➢ Name and contact information for the medical certifier of death. If there is no medical certifier, the funeral director will need to contact a **coroner** or **medical examiner**.

➢ If known, the date and time of death.

➢ Information about conditions that may impede the actual transfer, including: obstructions – such as fences, narrow doorways, railings, and stairways; and physical characteristics of the decedent, such as overweight and or physical condition of importance.

➢ Confirmation the location where the transfer of remains will take place is ready for the funeral service to arrive.

In addition to the information listed above, a funeral director may want to know the method of final disposition and whether or not they have permission to embalm. However, these inquiries are usually better left until the time of the removal when the individual having the legal right to control the disposition has been clearly identified. In addition, questions of this nature are always easier for all parties concerned if they take place in-person, rather than by telephone or other means of communication.

Secondary Information and Documentation
Supplementary information - If the notification of death is made by a representative of the family – such as staff members in a hospital, nursing home, care facility, or other similar institution – it may be necessary to obtain secondary information, including:

➢ Name, address, and contact information for the person authorizing the funeral establishment to transfer the remains. In most cases, it would be advisable for the funeral director to contact this individual as soon as possible to reassure them the establishment has been notified and is fully prepared to assist during this time of need.

➤ The time when the facility will be ready for the arrival of the funeral establishment staff to carry out the transfer.

➤ Availability of refrigeration or other holding facilities where remains may be safeguarded until the funeral establishment can respond, if needed. This may be a consideration when the call is received during after-hours, and it would be more convenient for the funeral establishment or health care facility staff to wait until regular business hours.

➤ Instructions from the facility on the procedures to follow in making the removal, such as a preferred entrance, the location where paperwork will be exchanged, and any special restrictions, requirements, or requests.

➤ A confirmation as to whether or not family members or close friends of the decedent are or may be at the location of the transfer when the funeral establishment arrives.

Documentation - A record of all communications and actions taken with respect to the initial notification of a death should be memorialized in writing and maintained in the funeral establishment case file. It is recommended a standardized form be used to ensure all information, including authorizations, are properly recorded.

Note: See Form 1 to view a New Case Intake Sheet.

Chapter 2: Transfer (Removal) of Remains

Overview

This chapter reviews the proper procedures and actions to be taken to effectively accomplish the tasks associated with the transfer (removal) of human remains from the place of death. It includes information on vehicles, equipment, and staff requirements; as well as unique considerations when called upon to transfer a person from a home residence or institution. It also touches on the first steps to be taken in preparing the family for the arrangement conference, and the role played by a funeral director in providing a family with direction and guidance as they navigate the complexities of planning and executing a funeral service.

Chapter Definitions

Arrangement conference - the meeting between the funeral practitioner and the client family during which funeral arrangements are discussed; may refer to pre-need or at-need situations.

Cot - a portable stretcher commonly employed in a transfer vehicle for the moving of the deceased.

Death certificate - a legal document containing vital statistics, disposition, and final medical information pertaining to the deceased.

Dentures - false teeth.

Funeral coach (hearse) - specialty vehicle designed to transfer casketed remains.

General price list (GPL) - a printed list of goods and services offered for sale by funeral providers with retail prices. The GPL is considered the keystone of the Funeral Rule.

Officiant - one who conducts or leads a service or ceremony.

Pouch - a leak resistant, zippered bag designed to contain human remains and any body fluids; used primarily for the removal of human remains from the place of death.

Transfer of remains - the moving of the dead human body from the place of death to the funeral establishment or other designated place.

Transfer vehicle - the automobile generally used for transporting the uncasketed dead human body from the place of death to the mortuary.

Vital statistics - data concerning birth, marriage, divorce, sickness, and death.

Vehicles

For a **transfer vehicle**, the industry has seen a steady shift away from using a hearse or **funeral coach** for the transfer of human remains from the place of death. While a few journalists have decided to blame this shift on the greed of funeral directors seeking to reduce expenses, those working daily in the funeral service know the change has been overwhelmingly welcomed by the families they serve. In all but a very minimal number of cases, family and friends of a decedent are relieved and thankful when a funeral director does not arrive at the home in a hearse. This same sentiment is also being universally expressed by staff members of medical facilities and institutions requesting the services of a funeral service professional.

For many reasons, a hearse is not the ideal vehicle for making a transfer of remains, including:

> rollers built into a hearse bed and the internal devices used to secure a casket are not compatible with removal stretchers and cots;

> a hearse is a large vehicle and therefore more difficult to maneuver in tight quarters, such as residential neighborhoods and dense urban areas;

> transfer and removal equipment must be loaded and unloaded each time a hearse is needed for a removal;

> a hearse being used for a funeral may not be readily available for an at-need transfer; and

> as stated previously, consumers generally prefer a non-descript, less-obtrusive vehicle be seen at the home.

Funeral establishments may now purchase passenger vans and larger SUVs that have been customized by specialty auto dealerships for the **transfer of remains**. These companies also offer conversion options to take an existing fleet vehicle and renovate both the interior and exterior into a dedicated vehicle for the removal or transport of human remains.

In the image on the right, note the custom addition of a stretched 'S' on the rear side pillars. These decorations are called landau bars, a term derived from their use on landau top automobiles in the 1960s and now commonly seen on funeral coaches and customized transfer vehicles.

Regardless of the type vehicle chosen to handle transfers and removals, the best practice for a funeral establishment is to have a written policy on vehicle care, maintenance, and use. Such a policy could address these general requirements:

Alternative vehicle for the removal and transfer of human remains from a place of death.

Image courtesy of Tribute Enterprises.[1]

> A routine service and maintenance schedule.

> A 'no less than one-half tank' fuel policy.

> A routine schedule for cleaning the interior and exterior of the vehicle.

➢ Mandated replenishment of onboard supplies to a set minimum level.

➢ Paperwork required to be onboard at all times, such as a **general price list**, embalming authorization forms, and company business cards.

➢ A system to track staff use, accountability, and compliance with the written policy.

Equipment

One of the distinct advantages to using an alternative vehicle for the transfer of remains is it provides an opportunity to carry additional equipment and supplies. The primary piece of equipment is of course a mortuary **cot** or stretcher, often shortened in name to simply cot or stretcher. There is no universal agreement on the best terminology to employ and it varies dependent upon which region of the United States you happen to be in. Regardless of whether you call it a cot or a stretcher, the equipment is commonly employed in a transfer vehicle for the removal or transport of a decedent. They traditionally come with a decorative cot cover.

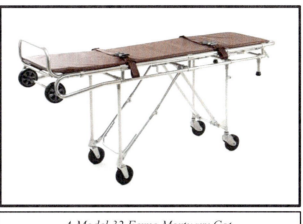
A Model 32 Ferno Mortuary Cot.

Unlike a medical stretcher for patients, a mortuary stretcher has two fixed and two swivel wheels, no side rails, and a bed that may be easily and quickly lowered to different elevations to facilitate the transfer of remains from various heights, including all the way down to the floor.

Flexible stretcher - A reeves' sleeve is a common flexible or collapsible stretcher that has been used for many years by the funeral service profession They are constructed of a light canvas material with several wood slats that run the length of the stretcher to provide for greater stability and strength, as well as anywhere from six to ten flexible handles or straps attached to the sides and ends for lifting and carrying.

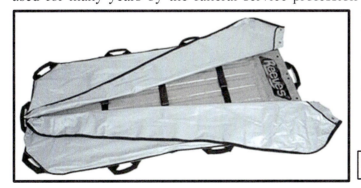

⟳ *A Reeves' sleeve stretcher.*

Evac stretcher - An evac stretcher is another common flexible carrying device. They are constructed of a rugged, heavy-duty canvas material with eight or ten canvas handles attached. Unlike the reeve's unit, the evac has no boards or slats, thus making them truly flexible. They are relatively new in the funeral service industry but receiving good reviews from professionals in the field who have found them especially helpful when used in tight quarters, such as up or down several flights of stairs with multiple landings and turns. These stretchers can be machine washed and take up very little space when folded.

Pillow - It is not uncommon for a family member to be in attendance when a decedent is being transferred to a stretcher. In other cases, family members may not observe the transfer but wish to see the decedent on the stretcher before being taken to the transfer vehicle. In both of these circumstances, consideration should be given to having the head of the decedent elevated and resting on a pillow, thereby ensuring a natural, comforting image for anyone observing the transfer or approaching to view the decedent on the stretcher prior to removal from the place of death.

Sheeting - Cloth sheets are a universal item that serve multiple purposes at the time of removal, from affording privacy to the decedent to a makeshift flexible stretcher. Rubber or plastic sheeting is important for cases in which the leakage of body fluids may be a concern.

Personal protective equipment (PPE) - The Occupational Safety and Health Administration (OSHA) defines PPE as:

> *Equipment worn to minimize exposure to a variety of hazards. Examples of PPE include such items as gloves, foot and eye protection, protective hearing devices (earplugs, muffs), hard hats, respirators, and full body suits.*

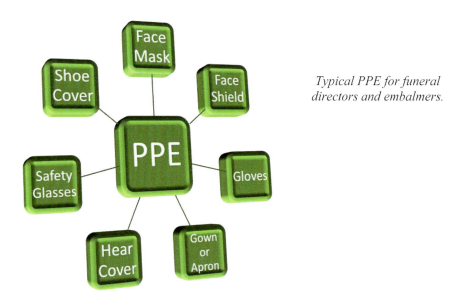

Typical PPE for funeral directors and embalmers.

Pouches - **Pouches**, also known as mortuary or disaster bags, are leak resistant, zippered bags designed to contain human remains and any body fluids. They provide important sanitary protections to those individuals tasked with handling human remains and ensure containment of any body fluids that may be present. They are made of a plastic-based material and available in a range of weight thicknesses, with heavy-duty disaster bags often used at the scene of a violent death, such as an automobile accident or suicide by firearm. Pouches also come in a range of sizes, and transfer vehicles should always be equipped to handle any case, including overweight, obese, infant, and children death events.

Note: To view images of pouches see the chapter titled, *Shipping Containers*.

Sanitary supplies - Supplies should include items needed to address and prevent unnecessary risks inherent to the funeral service, such as having hand sanitizer and disinfectant readily available and a supply of red bags for the proper disposal and containment of contaminated supplies, clothing, and bedding.

Special cases - A transfer vehicle should be equipped to handle any case they may encounter, including the appropriate equipment to provide for the removal of a deceased infant or child. This may include having smaller pouches and carrier devices in lieu of a full-size stretcher, as well as baby blankets and wraps.

Staff Considerations

Staff - The number of staff members needed to respond to a request for the transfer of human remains is dependent on the individual case and circumstances. Removals from a medical facility will usually only require one person, as these facilities are designed to accommodate stretchers by having elevators, ramps, wide entryways, and minimal obstructions. For other locations, the general rule is to have at least two people handle removals, including from:

> a home or private residence;

> the scene of a violent or intentional death;

> any facility or structure open to the general public; and

> any outdoor location.

There should always be at least one responder fully trained in proper removal and transportation procedures and, when legally required, possessing the government credentials and authority to perform these duties and tasks. Most states have laws that specify the licensing and registration requirements for the performance of funeral service tasks. Some may require a licensed funeral director personally appear and supervise a removal, while others have adopted legislation that provides for a lower level responder. For example, in addition to a funeral director being authorized to make a removal, the state of Vermont allows for the registration of 'removal personnel' for the sole purpose of making removals from a place of death.

Another consideration when responding to a first call is the potential availability of non-funeral service manpower. Law enforcement officials and other first responders are often at the location of a death that has resulted from an accidental or intentional act, and many of these officials will assist funeral staff members making a removal. This is especially true when police are maintaining a chain of custody record for evidentiary purposes in a criminal investigation. In these cases, it is not unusual for funeral service professionals to arrive at the scene and find the remains packaged for transportation in a container or pouch with a police seal attached.

Dress codes - Every funeral establishment must adopt a dress code for the various work tasks to be performed. For the transfer or remains, this may be a multi-level code that distinguishes between a residential or institution removal, or possibly the time of day or night. These levels may run anywhere from a formal business suit to business casual to something even less formal for specific circumstances. It is important staff be aware of the dress code they are expected to meet, and the code must be enforced consistently for all employees alike. Local customs and traditions have a powerful influence on these matters and should be taken into consideration when developing a dress code for a funeral establishment.

Training - The transfer of remains is not always a simple process, and an appropriate level of training should be given to all members assigned to performing these tasks. Instruction should be regularly updated, reviewed, and included in continuing education programs to support risk management initiatives in the workplace. At a minimum, training should include the review of:

➢ FTC Funeral Rule requirements;

➢ Occupational Safety and Health Administration (OSHA) standards as they apply to known workplace hazards;

➢ the proper use and operation of funeral establishment motor vehicles, equipment, and supplies;

➢ funeral establishment policies and procedures;

➢ techniques for the proper and safe transfer of human remains from a bed, floor, chair, or vehicle to a stretcher; and

➢ state or local laws, rules, and regulations specific to the removal, transfer, and transport of human remains.

General Transfer Procedures
There are certain general procedures recommended for the transfer of human remains, regardless of whether the removal is from a home, institution, accident location, crime scene, or other place of death.

These recommendations include:

➢ responding to the location in a prompt and safe manner;

➢ documenting all actions taken;

➢ verifying the identity of the deceased;

➢ checking for personal property, including medical devices, implants, **dentures** (false teeth), eyeglasses, and jewelry;

➢ documenting the disposition of personal property removed from the deceased by following chain of custody protocols;

➤ moving the deceased onto the mortuary cot or stretcher in a dignified and respectful manner;

➤ maintaining personal privacy by keeping the deceased obscured from view during and after the transfer;

➤ promptly take the decedent to the transfer vehicle once secured on the cot or stretcher; and

➤ safeguarding the human remains while in the transfer vehicle and going directly to the place of delivery with no unnecessary stops or detours.

Home Removals

For home removals, the following transfer steps are recommended. Staff should be mindful not all steps may be applicable to all cases, and the order they are carried out may change depending on the specific circumstances and needs of the family or others in attendance.

Step 1: Initial contact. Having verified the correct location and address at the time of the first call, respond to the location and make initial contact with the family. It is at this step staff should express personal condolences to the family and answer any immediate questions they may have. Always remember, family first.

Step 2: Legal considerations. Confirm legal requirements have been met before taking any action to transfer the remains. Each state has laws that regulate the removal and/or transportation of human remains from a place of death. Some states mandate a physician or other medical professional be contacted to confirm they are in a position to state the cause of death and willing to sign a death certificate. Other states require the prior approval or authorization of a coroner, medical examiner, or other specified public official before a removal may take place.

Note: In many cases, home hospice services or law enforcement officials make the legal notifications and secure the necessary authorizations before a funeral service is even contacted or arrives. Each state is different, and it is incumbent on funeral directors to be intimately familiar and in compliance with all legal mandates before making a removal.

Step 3: Planning for the transfer. It is important to formulate a plan on how to proceed with the transfer. By going with a family member to the location where the decedent is located and making practiced observations, the funeral director will be able to formulate a plan for the transfer with the least amount of disruption and distraction.

With a family member present, the funeral director will also be in a position to discuss any of the following issues that may be of concern:

➤ Permission to move furniture or other obstructions that may hamper the movement of the stretcher and funeral establishment staff in the home.

➤ Permission to take any bed linens or blankets with the decedent when used in making the transfer of the body to the stretcher or cot. Funeral directors frequently take the bottom sheet from a bed to move (slide) human remains onto a stretcher, and the family should be asked for permission to remove such items from the home. Many funeral establishments launder these items and return them to the family at the arrangement conference.

> Instructions on the disposition of personal property on or with the decedent, such as jewelry, blankets, mementos, or personalized items. This is especially important when dealing with a cremation case.

> Discussion on where the family wants to be seated or situated during the transfer. In most cases, a family will elect not to observe or participate in the transfer. However, the author is not aware of any state laws that prohibit a family from observing if they choose to do so, assuming the death is not the focus of a criminal matter or would create a hazard to first responders, the funeral staff, or the family.

During the walk-through, the director should be attentive and aware of the following conditions to assist them in developing a transfer plan:

> Identifying an entry way of sufficient width to enter and exit the home with a stretcher.

> Identify the proper orientation of the stretcher when entering (head or feet first), to then be in the correct position to make the transfer to the stretcher without the need to 'flip' the stretcher around to the proper orientation when in a confined space.

> Identifying furniture or other household items that may need to be temporarily moved to gain adequate access.

> Verifying adequate space to maneuver and accommodate a rigid stretcher, such as the space needed to make turns in a hallway or into a room off a hallway.

> Noting the position, height, and approximate weight of the deceased.

> Identifying any additional equipment or supplies needed to efficiently, promptly, and safely make the transfer, such as a flexible stretcher, leak-proof pouch, or personal protection equipment (PPE).

Step 4: Making the transfer. Prior to starting the transfer, staff members involved should be briefed on the aspects of the plan and informed of any specific duties or responsibilities. If the lead funeral director has been diligent in making observations and formulating a viable plan, the transfer of the remains should be a relatively smooth process.

The elements to a successful transfer plan are provided next; however, not all elements will present themselves in every transfer, and no two plans may be exactly alike. Funeral directors should always be prepared to amend a plan as needed to make the transfer quickly and quietly, with as little disruption as possible.

Elements of a plan may include:

- entering with the stretcher and any additional equipment needed, being mindful to remain quiet and respectful at all times;

- carefully moving any furniture or other obstacles, while exercising care to not damage walls, floors, furniture, or carpets with funeral service equipment or apparatus;

- properly positioning the stretcher in preparation for the transfer;

- wearing personal protection equipment (PPE);

- preparing the decedent for movement to the stretcher;

- carefully and respectfully transferring and securing the decedent to the stretcher;

- straightening and tidying the bed or other area where the decedent was located;

- gathering any funeral establishment equipment or supplies before exiting;

- if practical and safe to do so, removing PPE before passing by the family;

- exiting the home and placing the decedent into the transfer vehicle; and

- replacing any furniture or obstructions previously moved for access.

Step 5: After the transfer. Return to the family to advise them the transfer has been successfully completed and the location where the decedent will be taken. It is suggested the term 'care center' be substituted for morgue or preparation room when describing the location. Additional discussions and communications with the family at this time, such as requesting permission to embalm, are provided later in this chapter.

Institution Removals

For removals from an institution, such as a hospital or nursing home, consideration should be given to seeking answers to the following questions before responding to the place of death.

- Is there a specific entrance to use for the purpose of making the removal? Does it change based on the time of day or day of the week? Institutions frequently require funeral service providers use a delivery entrance or loading dock when making a removal during business hours and the main or front entrance during non-business hours.

- Does the facility provide an escort for the funeral service? Larger institutions with security staff on duty 24-hours a day often escort funeral establishment staff while on the property. Smaller operations may ask the funeral director to come to a specified floor or wing of the building and meet someone at a nurse's station or central location.

> Have the remains been released by the institution for pick-up by the funeral service? Is the facility ready for the arrival of the funeral establishment?

> Are there now or are there expected be family or friends of the deceased at the facility at the time of the removal?

> Is there any paperwork the funeral establishment should bring with them at the time of the removal? Where will any paperwork the funeral director must sign or pickup be located?

> Are there any known hazardous conditions or special precautions with respect to this particular case for which the funeral director should be made aware, such as a contagious disease, radioactive implants or treatments, or overweight concerns?

Communicating with the Family

When the family of a decedent is present at the place of death where the removal is going to take place – home, institution, or otherwise – the funeral director should be prepared to meet briefly with them to discuss any immediate needs before the transfer takes place. After the decedent is ready for transportation and in the transfer vehicle, the funeral director should briefly meet with the family again to update them.

There are three primary goals to be achieved when meeting with a family at the place of death. They have no preferred order and, in some cases, may not be relative or appropriate to the case being handled at that time.

Goal 1: Permission to embalm. The Federal Trade Commission, within the language of the Funeral Rule, identifies three circumstances under which a funeral establishment may charge a family for embalming:

1. State or local law requires embalming under the particular circumstances regardless of any wishes the family might have.

2. The funeral director has obtained prior approval for embalming from a family member or other authorized person.

3. The funeral director is unable to contact a family member or other authorized person after exercising due diligence; has no reason to believe the family does not want embalming performed; and, after embalming the body, obtains subsequent approval from the family for the embalming.

Therefore, with very limited exceptions, the FTC Funeral Rule mandates obtaining permission prior to the embalming of human remains. This leaves the funeral director with no option but to broach this sensitive topic with the family as soon as possible. General inquiries about the type of disposition and services being considered by the family will usually get the answer without undue emotional stress, but the funeral director must have express permission to embalm, not an implied or assumed consent.

Note: Every state, in addition to a few larger municipalities, have laws or requirements regulating the embalming of human remains, and some require the approval for embalming be in writing. Funeral directors must therefore be familiar with the state and local laws regarding embalming where they practice, as well as applicable federal law. For instance, there are states where embalming *is not required by law* under any circumstance, thereby completely eliminating the first scenario under the FTC Rule provided in Goal 1 above.

Goal 2: Schedule the arrangement conference. The **arrangement conference**, defined as the meeting between the funeral practitioner and the client family during which funeral arrangements are discussed, is explored in depth in the next chapter. However, one of the goals at the time of the removal is to get the conference scheduled, as the need to coordinate with other allied professions, such as clergy and cemetery officials, cannot take place until the family has expressed their needs and wishes at the arrangement conference.

Goal 3: Prepare the family for the arrangement conference. Many families are not familiar with the complexities involved in the planning, preparation, and direction of a funeral service. To prepare for the intensity of the arrangement conference, it is recommended they be given some general instructions on what to expect, what to bring with them, and the questions they may need to answer. Ideally, the funeral director will have a handout for the consumer that provides a listing of topics to be discussed and handled at the conference, including these matters:

➤ disposition preference (burial, cremation, natural, etc.);

➤ event preferences (visitation/calling hours, funeral service, memorial service, etc.);

➤ the social security number of the decedent and record of any benefits being received;

➤ if a veteran, military service discharge papers and available specifics on the time period and location of service;

➤ **vital statistics** of the decedent, including the information needed to comply with legal requirements to report a death and file a **death certificate** with government agencies;

➤ clothing and clothing accessories, as needed;

➤ a recent photograph for newspaper notices, online obituaries, visitation hours, and funeral ceremonies;

➤ life insurance policies, documents, and related information;

➤ **officiant** preferences, including name, affiliation, and contact information;

➤ obituary information, including proper names, spellings, and familial relationships;

➤ any preferences for a hairdresser or beautician, including contact information; and

➢ cemetery information, including a copy of the deed and plot location, if known.

Note: To view an Arrangement Conference Handout, see Form 2.

<u>The General Price List (GPL)</u>
As noted in the previous chapter, the FTC Funeral Rule mandates the use of three specific price lists: General Price List, Casket Price List, and Outer Burial Container Price List. While these lists play a significant role during the arrangement conference, funeral directors should be aware any discussion with the family at the time of the removal may trigger the requirement to provide a copy of the General Price List to the consumer.

The FTC Guide states:

> *You do not have to hand out the General Price List as soon as someone walks into your business. But you must offer the price list when you begin to discuss any of the following:*
>
> - *the type of funeral or disposition that you can arrange;*
>
> - *the specific goods and services that you offer; or*
>
> - *the prices of your goods and services.*
>
> *Before giving a GPL to a bereaved individual, you may offer your condolences and discuss preliminary matters like veteran's benefits or death certificates.*
>
> *The triggering event for giving out the GPL is a face-to-face meeting. The face-to-face meeting can occur anywhere, not just at the funeral home. For example, you must give out a General Price List even if the discussion of prices or arrangements **takes place in the family's home or while removing the deceased from a hospital or a nursing home.*** [Bold emphasis added.]

Therefore, if discussion on scheduling and preparing the consumer for the arrangement conference strays into any of the FTC points bulleted above, the law requires the consumer be given a copy of the current General Price List. While this does not usually occur, staff members performing removal and transfer duties should always have a copy of the current funeral establishment GPL with them for possible distribution to a consumer to comply with the FTC Funeral Rule.

Chapter 3: The Arrangement Conference

Overview
Several chapters in this book relate to the arrangement conference, and this chapter provides a general outline of the duties and responsibilities of the funeral director. The following chapters explore final disposition options; reporting a death to government authorities; and the government benefits and programs to which a family may be entitled. All of the activities described in these chapters relate to the collaborative efforts of the funeral establishment staff and the family as they strive to develop the service events that together become a funeral service plan.

Chapter Definitions
Acknowledgment cards - thank you cards.

Arrangement conference - the meeting between the funeral practitioner and the client family during which funeral arrangements are discussed; may refer to pre-need or at-need situations.

Cash advance - any item of service or merchandise described to a purchaser as a 'cash advance,' 'accommodation,' 'cash disbursement,' or similar term. A cash advance item is also any item obtained from a third party and paid for by the funeral provider on the purchaser's behalf. Cash advance items may include but are not limited to: cemetery or crematory services; pallbearers; public transportation; clergy honoraria; flowers; musicians or singers; nurses; obituary notices; gratuities; and death certificates.

Casketbearer (pallbearer) - one who actively bears or carries the casket during the funeral service and at the committal service.

Certified copy of a death certificate - a legal copy of the original death certificate.

Death certificate - a legal document containing vital statistics, disposition, and final medical information pertaining to the deceased.

Death notice - a newspaper item publicizing the death of a person and giving service details. In some parts of the United States, can contain the same information as an obituary.

Funeral goods - means all products sold directly to the public in connection with funeral services [by FTC].

Funeral services - means services used to care for and prepare bodies for burial, cremation, or other final disposition; and services used to arrange, supervise, or conduct the funeral ceremony or final disposition of human remains [by FTC].

Honorary casketbearers (Honorary pallbearers) - friends of the family or members of an organization or group who act as an escort or honor guard for the deceased. They do not carry the casket.

Memorial book (register book) - a book signed by those attending a visitation or service.

Memorial folder (service folder) - a pamphlet made available at the funeral service giving details about the deceased and the funeral arrangements. (Chapter 5)

Memorial gathering - a scheduled assembly of family and friends following a death without the deceased present.

Memorial service - funeral rites without the remains present.

Obituary - traditionally, a news item concerning the death of a person which usually contains a biographical sketch. Can appear in media other than newspapers such as online sources and service programs. Is sometimes used interchangeably with death notice or funeral notice.

Prayer card - a card with the name of the decedent and a prayer or verse, which may or may not include the dates of birth and death.

Survivor(s) - one who outlives another person or event.

Vital statistics - data concerning birth, marriage, divorce, sickness, and death.

Purpose and Preparation

The **arrangement conference** is a sit-down meeting between the funeral director and the family of a decedent to organize and plan funeral events. It may refer to an at-need or pre-need case.

Purpose - There are a wide range of options available in planning events to celebrate the loss of a family member and the life they lived, and it is important to clearly identify the wishes and needs of the family with respect to those activities and events they desire to include for the funeral they envision. Sorting through all of these options and making selections is the primary task at hand and the very purpose for which the parties gather for an arrangement conference.

Once the core elements of the funeral service have been identified, the funeral director can begin to coordinate the staff members and allied professionals who will be preparing for and executing the various events. When doing so, care must always be taken to coordinate family wishes with religious requirements or restrictions, legal mandates, and local customs or rites.

Preparation - In preparing for the conference to take place, funeral directors should:

➤ review prior cases handled for this same family, if any, to get a sense of what events, goods, and services were chosen previously and may therefore be requested again (i.e., similar casket, same calling hours, etc.);

➤ gather and prepare the forms, documentation, and handouts that will or may be needed during the conference;

➤ verify support staff have been scheduled and are prepared to attend at the designated time, date, and place;

➤ inspect the conference room to ensure it is clean, has adequate seating, and the lights are turned on prior to the family arriving;

➤ inspect the casket selection showroom to ensure it is in proper order and suitable for the family to enter, including lights turned on and funeral goods carefully arranged and presentable;

➤ prepare the Federal Trade Commission mandatory price lists for distribution, retention, or review, as required in the Funeral Rule; and

➤ familiarize themselves with the condition and physical characteristics of the decedents' remains, to determine if there are any factors or peculiarities that might present an impediment to the preparation, embalming, dressing, casketing, or viewing of the body, such as size, weight, facial injuries, or body decomposition.

Opening a Dialog with the Family

Arrangement conferences should be held in a place conducive to creating a warm and welcoming environment. The room itself should have furniture and fixtures consistent with a typical home-style living room, such as comfortable chairs for seating, wall decorations, carpeting, and good lighting. These provide a more comfortable and familiar setting for the family and thereby add to a calming and stress-free environment.

The centerpiece of the conference room should be one large table with the participants seated all around it. This preferred option sends an implicit message to each of the attendees of being equal in their expected participation and contribution to the planning of the funeral service. A traditional office setting, with the funeral director seated behind a desk in a position of leadership and authority, tends to diminish the role played by the family and may create a barrier to open communication and discussion.

Following expressions of sympathy and condolences, an informal approach is recommended during the initial stages as a means to keep the discussion moving and promote participation by all parties. It is important for a funeral director to develop a strong working relationship with the family during these early planning steps, as it sets the stage for future communications as the process progresses through the planning and presentation of the funeral events.

In conversations with the family, a funeral director should focus on certain key points and strategies to inspire more discussion and openness, with the intention being to learn more about the decedent and the family that could then be beneficial in planning unique, meaningful, and personalized funeral events. Toward that end, funeral directors should:

➤ ask open-ended questions, thus encouraging others to speak and elaborate on their personal knowledge and facts about the decedent;

➤ be vigilant for verbal and non-verbal clues into the personal interests, ambitions, accomplishments, likes, and dislikes of the deceased;

➢ focus attention on items, ideas, and concepts that may lend themselves in contributing to a personalized and customized funeral event, such as the utilization of non-traditional venues, goods, and services; and

➢ provide a broad outline of the potential events available, and explain how those events may affect each other.

Service Options

The FTC categorizes funeral items as being either goods or services. **Funeral goods** are products sold directly to the public in connection with funeral services. They are usually tangible items. **Funeral services** are to care for and prepare human remains for burial, cremation, or other final disposition, as well as services used to arrange, supervise, or conduct the funeral ceremony or final disposition of human remains. They are usually intangible items.

Identifying the funeral goods and funeral services a consumer wishes to include are two of the most important components of the arrangement conference. For service items, this may include services related to the preparation of human remains, such as embalming, applying cosmetics, dressing, and casketing. It may also include funeral related services, such as visitation hours, a funeral ceremony, graveside services, or the inclusion of military honors. In addition to these traditional service items, the industry has expanded to offer and accommodate a wide range of special and unique services, such as balloon releases, theme-oriented funerals, live-stream ceremonies, executive coach transportation, DNA preservation, food and beverage services, and kinetic photo presentations.

The funeral director must be the facilitator and coordinator of the service items chosen by the family. For those involving third-parties – such as a clergy member, cemetery superintendent, food caterer, or transportation specialist – the director must align dates, times, and locations to ensure a smooth and error-free program of events. It is very important after the arrangement conference to verify and confirm all of the persons and entities involved are committed on the date and time specified and ready to provide the services and equipment needed to fulfill the needs of the family.

In recent years, the funeral industry has also started to lend their proven expertise in organizing and planning to include events formerly left to the family, especially those centered around **memorial services** and **memorial gatherings**. Unique locations – such as on a cruise boat or in a state park – may require permits, advance notice, and substantial planning. Funeral directors that offer to coordinate these events as a part of the overall funeral experience for a family have opened new sources of revenue and enhanced the relationship between the survivors they serve.

Pallbearers

A **casketbearer (pallbearer)** is defined as one who actively bears or carries the casket during the funeral service and at the committal service. There are several factors to take into consideration when pallbearers are needed to accommodate funeral events chosen by the family. Some of these considerations may need to be discussed at the arrangement conference when the family is selecting who they would like to serve as bearers, especially as they relate to the stamina and strength of the individuals chosen.

Stamina - Pallbearers are not simply ceremonial positions. They must have the stamina and strength to lift and carry an often-heavy casket up and down stairs, over uneven ground, around cemetery monuments, and onto relatively narrow wooden planks placed alongside an open grave.

Number - The number of bearers required may vary anywhere from four to nine based on the combined weight of the container and decedent, in addition to the physical locations they may need to enter and exit. These may include buildings where the width of a door is not sufficient to allow a casket with the bearers alongside to pass, or facilities with a significant number of steps. Each case is unique, and pallbearer issues must be addressed accordingly.

As an example, in June 2004, when the casket holding the remains of the 40th President of the United States, Ronald W. Reagan, needed to be carried up the Capitol steps, it required two teams of nine military pallbearers. The significant number of steps to climb and the weight of the solid Mahogany Marsellus casket required these pallbearers to change teams at the midpoint of the steps to successfully accomplish the task.

Members of the Armed Forces Honor Guard place the casket of President Ronald Reagan into a hearse for transfer to the Washington National Cathedral for a State funeral service.

Image courtesy U.S. Navy. Photo by Photographer's Mate 3rd Class Todd Frantom.

Honorary - In some cases, a family may wish to have individuals serve as pallbearers that are not physically capable of performing the duties required. To accommodate these requests, a funeral director may suggest they have two sets of pallbearers: one for carrying the casket and the other as **honorary pallbearers** to lead the casket in a ceremonial capacity.

Preparation of a Newspaper Notice

The written notice of death placed in public media outlets and on funeral establishment websites may be called a death notice, obituary, memorial notice, or funeral notice. There is no uniformity in the terms one might run across in the United States, and variations on definitions exist in different regional locations. The ABFSE has however undertaken to identify the two most common terms used: death notice and obituary.

A **death notice** is defined as a newspaper item publicizing the death of a person and giving service details. They are often referred to as a short notice and used in the funeral service industry to provide basic service information in advance of a more detailed obituary, thus giving readers an opportunity to make advance plans if they wish to attend.

An **obituary** is defined traditionally as a news item concerning the death of a person which often includes a biographical sketch. They may appear in media formats other than newspapers, such as a funeral establishment website.

As noted, there are vagaries in the use and definition of these terms. A death notice in one geographical region may have the very same information found in an obituary in a different location. Funeral directors must acquaint themselves with the options available in the communities they serve, and have a current list of all applicable fees readily available at the time of the arrangement conference. There are a range of fee schedules used by media outlets, with some offering to publish a short death notice at no charge if a paid obituary will follow on a subsequent day, while others may charge a separate fee for each.

Vital statistics - Obituaries will usually include certain decedent **vital statistic** information, such as dates of birth, marriage, and death; as well as the parents' names.

Survivors - **Survivors** are defined as those who outlive another person, and one paragraph of an obituary is usually dedicated to those individuals. Immediate relatives are often listed specifically by name and relationship, such as 'his sister, Susan Jones'; while distant relatives may be identified by relationship groups with no specific names, such as 'many aunts and uncles.'

Predeceased - Similar to survivors, one paragraph in an obituary will usually list those immediate relatives that have passed away prior to the decedent. This section most often includes the names of direct descendants, including parents, siblings, spouses, and children.

Biographical information - This is a short synopsis of a person's life and may include information about occupations, religious affiliations, social memberships, fraternal organizations, education, military service, marriages, and life enjoyments. On occasion, a family member may elect to write the life enjoyments paragraph themselves for the obituary.

Special acknowledgements - With the increased number of people utilizing hospice care services and long-term nursing facilities, there has been a corresponding increase in recognizing the caregivers who provide these services. It is not uncommon to see the names of doctors, nurses, close friends, and neighbors acknowledged in an obituary or death notice for care and compassion shown during a time of special need for the decedent.

Service details - Funeral events open to the public should be listed in the newspaper notice with dates, times, and locations. This would include visitation hours, funeral or memorial services, graveside ceremonies, and after-service gatherings. In some circumstances, it may be advantageous to acknowledge non-public events without providing specific dates or times, such as stating burial will take place at the convenience of the family. This gives advance notice to those planning to attend the funeral service there will be no procession or need to go the cemetery. Without this statement, some attendees may think burial information was erroneously omitted and start calling the family and/or funeral establishment to ask about a burial service.

Photograph - It has become customary to include a photo of the deceased with an obituary or death notice for publication in the local newspaper and on funeral establishment websites.

Advisements - Families may also use an obituary to advise friends and relatives they may make donations in memory of the deceased to a charitable group, such as an organ or tissue donor program, disease research organization, or animal rights advocate.

Other Arrangement Considerations

There are other topics of discussion that may be encountered at the time of the arrangement conference, and funeral directors should be prepared to respond to inquiries about the different topics listed below. These items are the most common, but the list of inquiries one might expect to receive from a family are far too numerous to fully enumerate here.

Flowers - In most states, funeral establishments may assist consumers with the purchase of funeral flowers and receive a fee for their services. This arrangement makes it convenient and appealing for both parties, as the family needs not deal with the supplier, pick up the product, or deliver it to the funeral establishment. On the other hand, the funeral director has an additional source of revenue and can have the flowers arranged and displayed before the family and guests arrive.

Death certificates - **Death certificates** are legal documents containing vital statistics, disposition, and final medical information pertaining to the deceased, and **certified copies** *may* be needed to settle the estate. Certified *transcripts* of a death certificate do not include final medical information, cause of death, or manner of death and, in many cases, serve the same purpose as a death certificate. For example, a transcript may be used to transfer the title on a motor vehicle. Using certified transcripts can protect sensitive and personal information, such as when the manner of death is suicide. Both documents are available from state and local vital statistics offices.

Hair stylist/barber - While funeral directors are trained to apply cosmetics and prepare a decedent for viewing and calling hours, there may be times when a specialist will be requested to stylize the hair of a decedent. Families may have their own personal choice on who they would like to perform this task or, as an alternative, request the funeral director to assist them.

Memorial book (Register book) - **Memorial books** are signed by those attending a visitation or service to record their attendance. They may have a unique theme, such as a military branch or specific occupation. Knowing the options available will arm the astute funeral director with the information needed to make helpful suggestions to the family.

Acknowledgment cards - **Acknowledgment cards** are thank-you cards a family may use to acknowledge an act of kindness or other expression of support, such as a food dish brought to the family home or basket of flowers sent to the funeral establishment for calling hours. They usually come in packs of 50 or 100 and include: the cards, a short inscription, room to write a personal note, and envelopes.

Prayer cards - **Prayer cards** are small, palm-sized cards with the name of the decedent, date of death, date of birth, and a prayer or verse on one side and an image or illustration on the opposing side. There are a number of themes and images, as well as multiple verses and other passages from which to choose, and funeral directors should familiarize themselves with the various options. As an example, if a family has characterized the decedent as someone who loved the outdoors, the director with a good working knowledge of prayer card options would know if there is a nature-themed prayer card available. A personal photograph may also be substituted for a stock image.

Prayer cards with nature-themed images.

Memorial folder (service folder) - **Memorial folders** are printed programs or pamphlets handed out at the funeral providing details about the deceased and an outline of the service ceremony. Some churches routinely offer to gather the information and print the folders for distribution at the church at the time of the funeral. In other cases, a funeral establishment may offer these as an item to purchase during the arrangement conference.

Terms and Methods of Payment
Terms - Business is business and funeral establishment owners must be consistent in verifying the method and terms of payment agreed upon by the parties at the conclusion of arrangements. Some establishments have a standard written payment policy provided to the family at the start of the conference, while others make the terms of payment decision on a case-by-case basis. In either option, it is important the consumer understand and expressly acknowledge the terms, in writing, before they leave the funeral establishment. Failure to address this issue at the time of arrangements can lead to contentious legal consequences, misunderstandings, and adversarial relationships. All staff employees should be given concise written instructions on how these matters are to be handled.

Methods - There are six typical methods of payment once the terms have been agreed upon:

1. Cash, or checks. These payments are called cash with order (CWO), meaning payment must be received at the time the services and goods are ordered and the contractual agreement is signed by the parties. In other words, at the conclusion of arrangements.

2. Credit. The credit method is an agreement that payment will be made at some later date. When this is the chosen method, it is usually further identified as one of the following:

   MOM - Payment must be made by the middle of the month.

   EOM - Payment must be made by the end of the month.

   CBD - Payment must be made by cash before delivery of services or goods.

   COD - Payment must be made by cash on delivery of the services and goods.

3. Credit card. In these cases, the funeral establishment owner may be required to pay a fee to a financial institution to process the credit card payment. Funeral establishment owners should be aware a limited number of states prohibit sellers from imposing a surcharge or fee to use a credit card in lieu of payment by cash, check, or other similar means.

4. Insurance assignment. Consumers may have a life insurance policy, the proceeds from which they intend to use for payment of the funeral bill. The beneficiary on an insurance policy may assign the proceeds directly to the funeral establishment by executing the proper documents with the insurance company. Funeral establishments usually accept assignments for payment, but should verify with the insurance company there are sufficient funds available to cover the full amount due. If funds are not sufficient, an additional payment method must be agreed upon by the parties to pay for the remaining balance. In addition, as many states regulate life insurance policies as they relate to funeral establishments and funeral directors, it is important to ensure compliance with any applicable state laws when dealing with life insurance assignments.

5. Prefunded funeral proceeds. The money in a preplanned and prefunded pre-need account is most often held in trust for the purchaser by a financial institution and paid to the funeral establishment following the provision of services and goods at the time death. These accounts represent a secure, guaranteed payment for the funeral establishment. There are no federal laws specifically regulating prefunded preneeds, but they are almost always heavily regulated and monitored by state banking and business laws.

6. Other benefits. Consumers may be eligible for funeral and burial benefits from federal or state government programs, such as Social Security and Medicaid. As with insurance assignments, funeral directors should verify there are sufficient benefit funds available to cover the full amount due. If funds are not sufficient, an additional payment method must be agreed upon by the parties to pay for the remaining balance.

Regulatory Compliance

Another important component of the arrangement conference is ensuring compliance with regulatory requirements and associated paperwork or documentation.

General Price List - A copy of the current funeral establishment General Price List (GPL) must be given to a consumer whenever there is any discussion about:

> the type of funerals or dispositions the establishment can provide;

> the specific goods and services they offer; or

> the prices of goods and services.

All three of these items will be part of the conversation during the arrangement conference, and the funeral director must ensure the consumer promptly receives a copy of the GPL when the discussion begins. A GPL must be given to the consumer for *retention* (to keep).

The GPL must contain FTC mandatory disclosures as they relate to:

> a consumer's right to select only the goods and services desired;

> embalming is not usually required by law; and

> alternative containers must be available when direct cremation services are offered.

*Non-declinable fee*s - Consumers must be made aware of the one non-declinable fee on a GPL. This fee may be listed as a separate line item, called a Basic Services Fee, or included in the price of the casket. The majority of establishments use the separate line item option, although some states have chosen to call it an arrangement fee instead of basic services fee. This charge to pay for basic services and overhead is added to the total cost of the funeral arrangements, and this section on a GPL also has an FTC mandatory disclosure.

Cash advances - Another area on the GPL that may need explanation is **cash advances**, defined briefly as any item obtained from a third party and paid for by the funeral provider on the purchaser's behalf. Cash advance items *may* include: cemetery or crematory fees, public transportation, clergy honoraria, obituary notices, gratuities, and death certificates.

The FTC Funeral Rule does not require any specific goods or services be listed as a cash advance, nor does it prohibit a funeral establishment from making a profit on a cash advance purchase. However, individual states have passed a plethora of legislative initiatives to regulate how cash advances are handled. Some have requirements mandating certain items be offered *only* as cash advances, such as crematory fees and certified copies of death certificates. Others totally prohibit funeral establishments from making any profit whatsoever on cash advances. Practitioners are therefore advised to research all state and local laws with respect to cash advance funeral charges before developing and distributing a GPL.

Other price lists - In addition to the GPL, a funeral director should be prepared at the arrangement conference to provide a Casket Price List and/or Outer Burial Container Price List, if any items on these lists are going to be purchased. Unlike a GPL, these lists are given to a consumer to *review* while making a selection and then returned to the funeral establishment when they leave. The FTC does not mandate they be given these lists to keep. It is also a requirement these lists be given to the consumer *before* they enter a selection room and see prices on individual caskets or are orally given pricing information by the funeral director.

Itemized statements - In addition to price lists, the FTC requires a Statement of Funeral Goods and Services Selected (Statement) be provided to every consumer. The Funeral Rule states:

> *Licensed funeral directors and funeral firms must furnish, at the time funeral arrangements are made for the care and disposition of the body of a deceased person, a written statement showing thereon the price of the funeral, which shall include an itemized list of the services and merchandise to be furnished for such price and a statement of the cash advances and expenditures to be advanced.*

And further, the FTC states the purpose of the statement is to allow, "*… consumers to evaluate their selections and to make any desired changes.*"

While the FTC does not require any specific form, heading, or caption on a Statement, individual states have enacted a wide range of legislation related to this all-important document. Some require a format similar to a contract, while others require funeral establishments use an official state form designed to comply with the FTC requirement. One such state, after creating a state form, went on in the narrative of the legislation to note the form, "*… shall be limited to the statements, language, titles, and numerical order contained in said section.*" It is therefore important for funeral directors to familiarize themselves with how their state has addressed the FTC mandate for a Statement.

In virtually all states, the FTC Statement will require the signatures of a funeral establishment representative and the consumer attending the funeral arrangements with the priority right to control the final disposition of human remains.

Embalming - Consumers must be given written notice the law does not usually require embalming. This is accomplished by including the mandatory FTC embalming disclosure in immediate conjunction with the price for embalming on the GPL.

Additionally, when making funeral arrangements that include an embalming charge, the Funeral Rule mandates prior approval for the embalming. Some state or local governments may require embalming in certain circumstances and, in these cases, further permission to embalm from the family is not necessary. In those jurisdictions or circumstances where embalming is optional, the funeral director must have the express permission of the family or other authorized person to carry out the procedure. It cannot be an implied consent; it must be an express consent or permission.

Note: Some states and jurisdictions have expanded on the Funeral Rule permission to embalm requirement by enacting legislation requiring the actual authorization be in writing.

Cremation - Another area of concern in regulatory compliance centers around the use of cremation as a final disposition. Once again, there is a wide range of laws, rules, and regulations that have been enacted in the states and, in some cases, within a state by a local government. Some of the more prevalent areas to be aware of include:

➢ waiting periods of anywhere between 24 and 72 hours after death before human remains may be cremated;

➢ clearance (approval) for cremation by a coroner, medical examiner, or other public official;

➢ specific written authorization for cremation from the person(s) with the right to control the final disposition;

➢ obtaining a government issued cremation permit or other similarly named authorization;

➢ the need for a consensus or unanimous agreement of the parties to authorize cremation for a final disposition when more than one person has an equal right to control a final disposition, such as three adult children of the deceased; and

➢ cemetery rules regarding outer burial containers for urns.

Note: The author has not reviewed the FTC Funeral Rule here in great detail as it goes beyond the scope of this book. The topic is explored extensively in college textbooks adopted for use in law courses of instruction found in funeral service programs across the nation. *Funeral Service Law in the United States*, published in 2019, is one such source. Additional information about this book may be found in the Sources Consulted listing.

State and local laws - In all cases, state and local laws, rules, and regulations may further restrict or amplify the provisions of federal law. Funeral directors must therefore familiarize themselves with all sources of law in their home state to maintain compliance.

Right to control - Individual states set the criteria for making a determination on who has the priority right to control the final disposition of human remains. In some states, the person presenting themselves as having the priority right must execute a statement attesting to this fact, and stipulating they have no knowledge of anyone holding a higher priority position. These statements, in those states that require them, often include language that provides liability protections for the consumer, funeral director, and funeral establishment. This assumes of course the parties have taken actions both reasonably and in good faith.

The need to determine with a high degree of certainty who has the priority right to control the final disposition of human remains is a critical component at the time of the arrangement conference. Once this person has been identified, the control they exercise will usually include the care, disposal, transportation, burial, cremation, or embalming of the body of a deceased person and all other associated measures to complete these tasks. Funeral directors must therefore be cautious and deliberate in ensuring they have exercised due diligence in making this determination. The best practice is to have the person execute a statement attesting to their priority right to control the disposition.

Chapter 4: Final Disposition Methods

Overview
Another component of the arrangement conference will be a discussion on the method of final disposition, and funeral directors must be familiar with the available options in the communities they serve. This chapter reviews the eight final dispositions currently existing in the United States; however, not all dispositions are available in all 50 states.

Chapter Definitions
Alkaline hydrolysis - a process that uses water, alkaline chemicals, heat and sometimes pressure and agitation to accelerate natural decomposition, leaving bone fragments.

Block - a subdivision of a cemetery containing several lots.

Burial (interment) - the act of placing a dead human body in the ground.

Cemetery - an area of ground set aside and dedicated for the final disposition of dead human remains.

Columbarium - a structure, room or space in a mausoleum or other building containing niches or recesses used to hold cremated remains.

Couch crypt - a crypt in which the casket likes parallel to the crypt face. (Chapter 4)

Cremated remains - the result of the reduction of a dead body to inorganic bone fragments by intense heat.

Cremation - the reduction of a dead human body to inorganic bone fragments by intense heat in a specifically designed retort or chamber.

Crypt - a chamber in a mausoleum, of sufficient size, generally used to contain the casketed remains of a deceased person.

Entombment - the placing of remains in a crypt in a mausoleum.

Grave - an excavation in the earth as a place for interment.

Green burial - disposition without the use of toxic chemicals or materials that are not readily biodegradable.

Green cemetery - a place of interment that bans the use of metal caskets, toxic embalming, and concrete vaults and may also require the use of aesthetically natural monuments.

Inter - to bury in the ground.

Inurnment - placing cremated remains in an urn or placing cremated remains in a niche or grave.

Lot - a subdivision in a cemetery which consists of several graves or interment spaces.

Mausoleum - a building containing crypts or vaults for entombment.

Memorial park - a cemetery, or section of a cemetery, with only flush to the ground type markers.

Niche - a recess or space in a columbarium used for the permanent placing of cremated remains.

Outer burial container - any container designed for placement in the grave around the casket.

Receiving vault - a structure designed for the temporary storage of bodies not to be immediately interred.

Retort - the burning chamber in a crematory, also referred to as the cremator; the total mechanical unit for the cremation process.

Section - the largest subdivision of a cemetery.

Temporary container - a receptacle for cremated remains, usually made of cardboard, plastic, or similar materials designed to hold cremated remains until an urn, other permanent container is acquired, or other disposition is made.

Tomb - a general term designating those places suitable for the reception of a dead human body.

Urn - permanent container for cremated remains meant for decorative or inurnment purposes.

Cremation
In 2016, according to the Cremation Association of North American, **cremation** surpassed burial as the most preferred choice for the disposition of human remains in North America. Future projections call for the cremation rate to exceed 75% by the year 2040.

Cremation is the reduction of a dead human body to inorganic bone fragments by intense heat in a specifically designed retort or cremator. The **retort** is the burning chamber in a crematory and may be referred to as the cremator or combustion chamber.

After the cremation process, cremated remains are secured in a **temporary container**. These are most often plain boxes made of corrugated cardboard, rigid plastic, or light-duty tin. The cremated remains and some form of durable identification, such as a numbered brass tag, are usually packaged in a heavy-duty plastic bag to make them sift proof and then placed in the temporary container. The container is typically sealed with shipping quality tape and may be mailed to the intended recipient or retrieved at the crematory by an authorized person. Funeral directors may retrieve cremated remains and transfer the contents into an **urn** or other permanent container.

Inurnment - A graveside service for the burial of cremated remains may be called an **inurnment**. The origin of this term is thought to have been an attempt to distinguish between the burial of human remains in a grave (interment) and the burial of cremated remains in a grave (inurnment). Later, as cremation became more widely chosen, the definition of inurnment was expanded to include non-burial options, such as placement in a columbarium niche for safekeeping. Today, the ABFSE defines inurnment as: *the act of placing cremated remains in a niche or grave*, which extends the definition well beyond a simple burial option.

Other dispositions - An urn may be placed in a **columbarium**, which is a structure, room or space in a **mausoleum** or other building containing **niches** (rhymes with witches) or recesses used to hold cremated remains. Niches are an opening or space in a columbarium used for the permanent placing of cremated remains and, when located inside a mausoleum, may have a glass face so the urn is visible from the exterior of the niche.

A columbarium may also be a separate structure set apart from a mausoleum. Many of these are located outdoors and incorporate multiple niches in a cascading series of columbarium walls. They may be designed to hold more than one urn or container, similar to a family burial lot having more than one grave.

Earth Burial (interment)

Burial is the act of placing a dead human body in the ground. A burial in the funeral service industry is formally called an interment, derived from the word **inter**, meaning to bury in the ground. These two words – inter<u>ment</u> and inter<u>n</u>ment – are frequently confused. An internment is a state of confinement, such as a prisoner of war being interned in an internment camp. The professional practitioner will be careful to use the proper pronunciation of the word interment when speaking about the burial of human remains.

Burial is currently the second most preferred choice for the disposition of human remains in the United States. Other methods may use the word burial in their title, but a traditional burial takes place in a traditional cemetery, as compared to a burial at sea in the ocean or a green burial in a **green cemetery**. These additional 'burial' methods are described later in this chapter.

A traditional **cemetery** is an area of ground set aside and dedicated for the final disposition of human remains, while a **memorial park** is a cemetery or section of a cemetery with only flush to the ground markers.

Outer burial containers - Caskets are usually protected in the grave by an **outer burial container**, defined as any container designed for placement in the grave around the casket. They are more commonly known in the industry as a burial vault or simply vault.

At the very minimum, the purpose of a vault is to prevent the dirt on top of the grave from collapsing into or on top of the casket, if and when it deteriorates. Vaults may have other qualities, such as limiting the intrusion of outside materials and protecting the casket. Beyond that, they contribute to the attractiveness of a cemetery, memorial park, or other burial location by preventing the ground from settling.

Temporary holding - In states with low winter temperatures sufficient to freeze the ground, casketed human remains awaiting burial in the spring may be placed in a **receiving vault**, a structure designed for the temporary storage of bodies not to be immediately interred or held until the condition of the ground permits the burial to take place.

Sections, blocks, lots, and graves - Both cemeteries and memorial parks use the terms section, block, lot, and grave to identify where individual burial spaces are located. Each subsequent term defines a more specific cemetery location than the preceding term, making section the largest area and grave the smallest.

In other words, a **section** is a subdivision containing several blocks; a **block,** a subdivision containing several lots; a **lot,** a subdivision containing several graves; and a **grave,** an excavation in the earth for a single casket or urn.

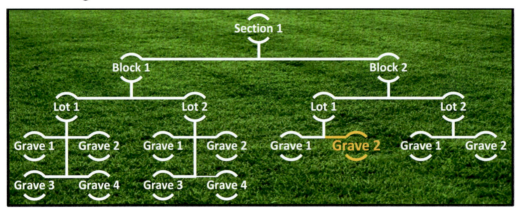

Using this schematic as an example, human remains buried in GRAVE 2 would be recorded in cemetery records as being located in Section 1, Block 2, Lot 1, Grave 2.

Entombment

Entombment is defined as the placing of human remains in a crypt in a mausoleum. This provides for safeguarding them above ground in a building or structure designed specifically for this purpose. When considering this option, funeral directors should inquire about mausoleum rules that may impact overall expenses associated with entombment, such as mandatory embalming or specific requirements on the type, make, model, or characteristics of the casket.

Crypts are similar to graves and defined as a chamber in a mausoleum. They are used to safeguard the casketed remains of a decedent. The majority of crypts are designed to have the casket placed inside feet first, with the head of the decedent located directly behind the face plate that covers the front of the crypt when closed. A limited number may be designed to have the casket placed inside widthwise, with the side of the casket directly behind the face plate. A chamber with this orientation is called a **couch crypt**.

Mausoleums vary in size from privately owned edifices designed to safeguard and protect a limited number of casketed remains, such as a family; to large public structures designed to hold hundreds of casketed remains. Private mausoleums are sometimes called **tombs**, a general term designating those places suitable for the reception of a dead human body but more accurately defined as large *underground* vaults capable of holding the remains of several people.

Similar sized crypts in the same mausoleum may vary in price based on any of these variables:

- availability of a couch crypt that takes up more of the premium 'front' crypt space;

- crypts may be stacked four or five high, with the eye level units demanding a higher price than those located closer to the floor or ceiling;

- crypts may be located on the first floor or a lower or upper level, with those levels offering easier access and no stairs to climb usually priced higher; and

- some crypts may be located closer to a chapel area, have alluring exterior views, or possess some other oddity or uniqueness making them more attractive to certain customers.

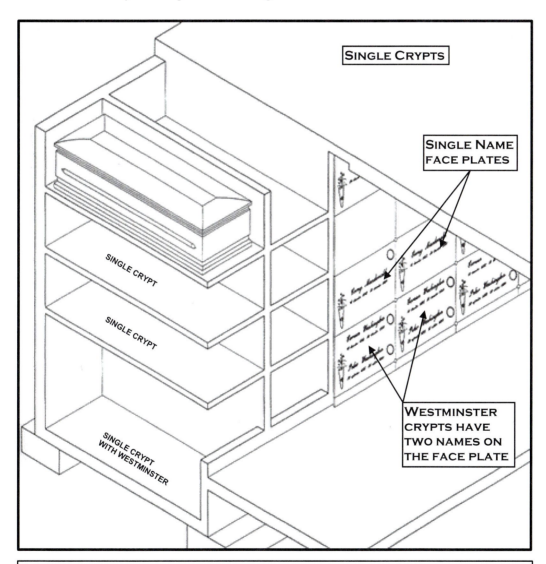

Each single crypt has its own face plate for memorialization information. Some floor level crypts may have the Westminster option, which allows for two entombments, with one below floor level as shown in the lower left corner of the illustration. Note the face plates on the Westminster crypts have two names engraved on them.[2]

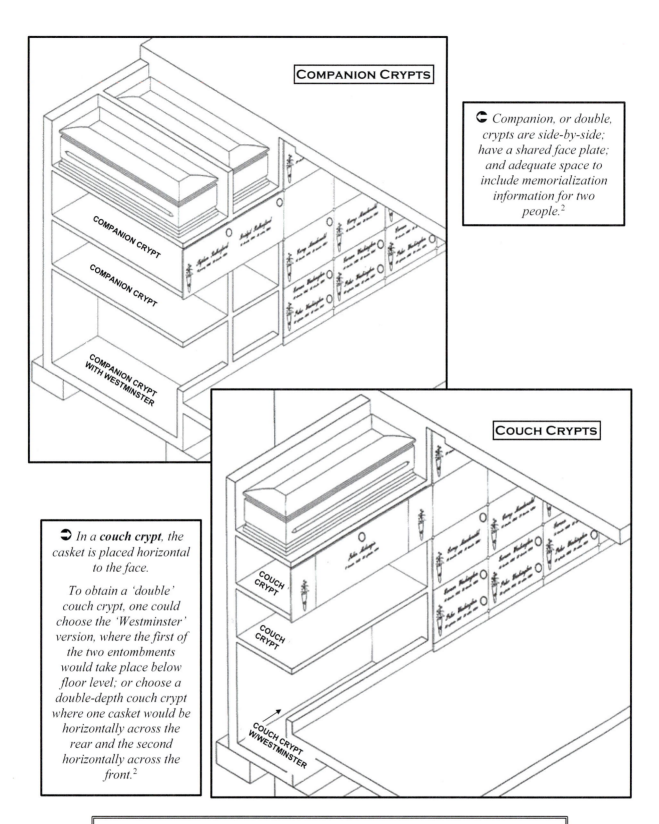

COMPANION CRYPTS

COMPANION CRYPT

COMPANION CRYPT

COMPANION CRYPT
WITH WESTMINSTER

☞ *Companion, or double, crypts are side-by-side; have a shared face plate; and adequate space to include memorialization information for two people.*[2]

COUCH CRYPTS

COUCH
CRYPT

COUCH
CRYPT

COUCH CRYPT
W/WESTMINSTER

➲ *In a* **couch crypt***, the casket is placed horizontal to the face.*

To obtain a 'double' couch crypt, one could choose the 'Westminster' version, where the first of the two entombments would take place below floor level; or choose a double-depth couch crypt where one casket would be horizontally across the rear and the second horizontally across the front.[2]

Crypt descriptions and images located on this and the previous page are courtesy of North Bay Roman Catholic Cemeteries in North Bay, Ontario, Canada, and Carrier Mausoleums Construction, Inc., Saint-Laurent, Quebec, Canada.[2]

Green (Natural) Burial

A **green burial** is the disposition of human remains without the use of toxic chemicals or materials that are not readily biodegradable. Also known as a natural burial, this eco-friendly approach to a final disposition utilizes products, services, and merchandise that are free of toxic/hazardous materials, biodegradable, and minimize the use of energy. The concept of a natural burial has been around for centuries. Habenstein notes the Greeks, as far distant as 1600 BC, prepared the deceased by anointing the body with, "*… oils, perfumes and spice,* [but] … *made no serious attempt at embalming.*"

Green burial is a relative newcomer to funeral services in the United States in its present iteration but has seen a steady growth in recent years. A funeral director planning to offer a green burial option must first acquaint themselves with the tenets and beliefs behind the movement and educate themselves to the unique goods and services this option demands. These include the rapid development of special containers and designated cemeteries. For example, a green cemetery is a place of interment that bans the use of metal caskets, toxic embalming, and concrete vaults. They may also require the use of aesthetically pleasing natural monuments.

Note: See the chapter titled, *Funeral Goods and Services*, for more information on natural burials.

Disposition at Sea (Burial at Sea)

Dispositions at sea are regulated by the U.S. Environmental Protection Agency (EPA). The EPA requires the burial at sea of human remains take place at least three nautical miles from land and in water at least 600 feet deep, and funeral directors must comply with all EPA rules and regulations with respect to preparing the human remains and container for the burial at sea. As this is a unique method of disposition requiring a suitable vessel for transportation, there are private companies that offer burial at sea services to funeral establishments, similar to companies that offer burial vaults and interment service equipment at the time of a traditional burial.

Note: See Guide 1 for EPA Burial at Sea Instructions.

Donation

Medical colleges and universities, as well as scientific research and testing facilities, regularly need sources to supply cadavers for use in their respective studies and programs. One such source are those individuals that make preneed arrangements and therein provide for their remains to be donated upon the occasion of their death. Family members are another source, as those holding the right to control a final disposition may elect to choose donation at the time of an at-need arrangement conference.

Note: While the donation option is listed here as a disposition for the purposes of an arrangement conference, it should be noted many of these facilities provide for the further disposition of human remains once no longer suited to research and education purposes. The preferred option is cremation, with the cremated remains being returned to the family. For unclaimed cremated remains, the facilities usually schedule a brief remembrance service to ensure a dignified and proper burial. The author is familiar with one such medical college that annually sponsors a brief memorial service and invites students from the local funeral service program to attend.

Cryonics

This involves the freezing of human remains immediately after death in the belief they may be revived in the future when medical advances have the capacity to restore health and sustain life. Remains are frozen at temperatures lower than minus 380 degrees Fahrenheit and safeguarded in specially constructed storage facilities. As of this writing, only California, Arizona, Oregon, and Michigan have cryonics facilities where human remains may be legally preserved.

Alkaline Hydrolysis

This disposition method is defined as a process that uses water, alkaline chemicals, heat, and sometimes pressure and agitation, to accelerate natural decomposition, leaving only bone fragments. Jonah Engel Bromwich, in an October 2017 New York Times article, chose to describe **alkaline hydrolysis** somewhat more vividly in stating:

> *A machine uses a chemical bath to dissolve protein, blood, and fat, leaving only a coffee-colored liquid, powdery bone, and any metal implants, like dental fillings.*

The liquid and metal implant waste products Bromwich describes are properly discarded, while the bone fragments are ground into a white powdery ash and returned to the family. These ashes are very similar in appearance and consistency to the ashes that make up cremated remains, although fire-based cremation residue is gray in color instead of white. Because of these similarities and shared goals, the hydrolysis process is alternatively known as bio-cremation, flameless cremation, aqua-cremation, or water cremation.

Bones and bone fragments after alkaline hydrolysis process completion.

Chapter 5: Death Reporting and Registration

Overview

One of the most important roles of a funeral service practitioner is working cooperatively with medical certifiers of death to gather the information and data needed to complete and file a certificate of death with government officials.

This chapter reviews the types of information that must be on a death certificate; the purpose and use of the data collected by state and federal agencies; the emergence of electronic filings; and the legal parameters surrounding the issuance of a permit to provide for the final disposition of human remains.

Chapter Definitions

Burial-transit permit (disposition permit) - a legal document, issued by a governmental agency, authorizing transportation and/or disposition of a dead human body.

Cause of death - diseases, injuries, or complications that resulted in death [by Author].

Certified copy of a death certificate - a legal copy of the original death certificate.

Death certificate - a legal document containing vital statistics, disposition, and final medical information pertaining to the deceased.

Informant - one who supplies vital statistics information about the deceased.

Manner of death - the mode of death, such as accident, homicide, natural, or suicide [by Author].

Registrar - means a public official responsible for keeping official records on births, deaths, and marriages.

Vital statistics - data concerning birth, marriage, divorce, sickness, and death.

Death Certificates - Generally

The U.S. Department of Health and Human Services (DHHS), Centers for Disease Control (CDC) is responsible for developing and defining the information required for death registrations in the United States. The individual states then use the CDC guidelines to enact laws, rules, and regulations to formalize the information required on a death certificate and mandate the reporting and registration of all deaths within the state jurisdiction.

Using the CDC national standards for **death certificates**, each state has created forms to use for death reporting and registration. The name of the form may vary slightly by state, but the information they contain must adhere to national standards by including certain required data, such as whether or not a work injury contributed to the death. In addition, some states may require data or information they deem of importance beyond those items required by the CDC. Once a properly completed report has been presented to a designated government agency or office for filing, a permit is issued authorizing the final disposition of the human remains.

Death Certificates - Information Needed

A certificate of death that meets the requirements of the CDC will have several sections of required data and information that must be completed by funeral service practitioners, medical certifiers, and state officials to create a permanent government record of a death. All of the required information and data needs to be gathered and verified before a certificate may be submitted and accepted for filing and registration.

The five most common sections on a certificate of death include:

1. Biographical and vital statistic data on the decedent.

2. Funeral service provider and practitioner information.

3. Final disposition method and location.

4. Certification as to cause and manner of death by a medical certifier.

5. Government authorizations.

Biographical and vital statistic data - This includes the **vital statistics** associated with the decedent, as well as select biographical and major life event facts.

One of the sources for this information is an **informant**, a person who supplies vital statistics information about the deceased. The items the CDC requires in this section include:

Legal name (first, middle, last)	Gender	Date of birth
Social security number	Age[1]	Marital status
Residence at time of death	Service in the US armed forces?	Birthplace[2]
Surviving spouse (if any)	Informant's name and address	Usual occupation[3]
Father's name	Place of death[4]	Education
Mother's maiden name	Hispanic origin? Yes or no	Race

[1] Broken down by months and days for under one year old, and hours and minutes for under one day old
[2] City and state, or foreign country
[3] Including the kind of business or industry
[4] Including the municipality, county, state, and zip code

Funeral provider and practitioner information - This section requires information to identify both the funeral service provider and funeral service practitioner associated with the case. The provider may be called a funeral firm, establishment, home, or other similar name; while the practitioner may be called a funeral director, embalmer, undertaker, mortician, or other similar title. For the provider, the name, address, and unique government identifier (such as a license or registration number) must be included. For the practitioner, the name and unique government identifier must be included.

Final disposition method and location - This section must provide pertinent information with respect to the final disposition of the human remains, including the date, method, and location. The method options on a certificate are specific to each individual state government, as not all methods are permitted in all states. The most common methods are burial, cremation, entombment, and donation (for medical research and education purposes). In consultation with the family of the decedent, the funeral director identifies the method of disposition and enters this information on the certificate.

Certification as to cause and manner of death - In discussing the medical certification section, it is important to understand the distinction between the *cause* of death and the *manner* of death. **Cause of death** is used to identify the medical reasons, such as diseases, injuries, or complications that resulted in death. The **manner of death** is the mode, such as accident, homicide, natural, or suicide. Both of these items are identified and recorded on a death certificate by the certifier of death.

Depending on the requirements of each state, the individuals authorized to serve as a certifier of death may include medical examiners, coroners, attending physicians, affiliated (covering) physicians, physician assistants, and nurse practitioners. In all these cases, the certifier is usually a licensed physician acting individually or a non-physician acting jointly with, and under the supervision of, a licensed physician. Funeral directors are not responsible for the completion of any part of the medical certification section.

At a minimum, the information in this section will include:

➢ the actual or estimated date and time of death;

➢ the date and time death were pronounced;

➢ the cause and manner of death;

➢ whether or not an autopsy was performed;

➢ contributing factors, such as being a smoker or illicit drug user; and

➢ the name, license number, and signature of the certifier of death.

Government authorizations - A **registrar** is a public official responsible for maintaining records on births, deaths, and marriages. They are the official to whom a death certificate is submitted or filed for registration with a state government. The role of a registrar is to review the certificate when it is presented to them for filing by the funeral director and, when in an acceptable form, issue a **burial-transit or disposition permit** authorizing the transportation and/or disposition of the human remains.

Registrars authorize the disposition method, date, and location, as entered in the final disposition section of the certificate by the funeral service practitioner. After the filing and registration process has been completed, the registrar has the authority to issue copies of the original death certificate, known as **certified copies**. Funeral directors are not responsible for completing any part of the government authorization section.

Death Certificates - Importance, Purpose, and Use

Permanent record - As stated in the CDC Handbook, *"The death certificate is a permanent legal record of the fact of death of an individual."* As such, this record is of importance to the family of the decedent for the purposes of providing for final disposition, settling the estate, and closing out the life affairs of the decedent. A certificate or transcript of death may be needed when dealing with any of these issues:

> ➢ requesting death benefits from government programs;

> ➢ applying for life insurance proceeds;

> ➢ transferring real estate, stocks, bonds, and other financial assets;

> ➢ settling pension benefit matters; and

> ➢ transferring vehicle titles.

Research needs - Beyond the significant importance to the survivors of the decedent, the information recorded on a death certificate is a valuable resource for a variety of medical and health-related research efforts. As an example, the examination and review of death certificates played a role in the discovery of a correlation between early-age deaths and individuals working in certain construction industries. This ultimately resulted in the identification of the toxic dangers associated with asbestos inhalation in the workplace and the implementation of mandatory health protections for laborers using materials containing asbestos. The CDC has stated statistical data compiled from death certificates is:

> *... of considerable value to individual physicians and medical science because they can be used to identify disease etiologies and evaluate diagnostic techniques* [and the information may be used]... *to estimate and project population sizes, which are important in forecasting and program planning.*

Electronic Death Certificates

The use of electronic filing systems for the recording of vital statistics has been sweeping across the United States at a steady pace, with one state after another adopting software programs capable of managing data related to births, deaths, marriages, and divorces. Each of these states have agreements with the CDC to forward this information for inclusion in the national database. It is from these records the medical and health service communities cull the information they need to further their research.

This evolution from a hardcopy paper registration system to an electronic system has been described as enabling funeral directors, medical certifiers, and government registrars to:

> ➢ streamline the death registration process;

- improve the quality and timeliness of the data collected;

- reduce the time it takes to file death records; and

- improve communication among those responsible for filing.

It is expected all of the states will complete this transition to electronic filings for death registrations in the very near future.

Fetal Death Certificates

In addition to the standard death certificate, states often have special filing requirements and distinctly different fetal death certificates for the reporting and registering of fetal deaths. The regulations and parameters under which filings are mandated vary significantly from state to state but are frequently based on the length of the gestation period at the time of the fetal death.

The wide disparity in state requirements makes it difficult to identify the specific duties and responsibilities of the funeral director handling a fetal death case. Some states place the onus of completing the vital statistics, biographical, and life event information on the medical certifier instead of the funeral director. In other cases, depending on the length of the gestation period, states may provide for the filing and registration of fetal death cases without any interaction or participation from within the funeral service community. It is therefore the responsibility of funeral service practitioners to familiarize themselves with the laws, rules, and regulations concerning fetal death registration requirements in the states where they practice to ensure full compliance is achieved.

Disposition Permits

The immediate purpose in filing a death certificate is to obtain the necessary authorization to go forward with the final disposition of human remains. This may also include the need to have the legal authority to transport human remains outside the state where death occurred.

The documents used to record authorizations for disposition and/or transportation are generically called disposition permits; however, some states have alternative names depending on the method of final disposition or transportation. Such terms may include:

- cremation permit;

- burial permit;

- transit permit; and

- anatomical or donation permit.

In those cases where the manner of death is something other than natural, it may be necessary to have a coroner or medical examiner 'clear' or sign off on the filing of a death certificate before a permit will be issued. In addition, there are some states (and select counties within some states) that mandate a coroner or medical examiner sign off on all cremation or alkaline hydrolysis dispositions, including a natural death, when these specific final disposition methods are chosen.

Finally, the disposition permit provides a permanent record of the final disposition, as the permit requires the signature of all the parties involved in the process, including:

➢ cemetery officials for burials;

➢ crematory operators for cremations;

➢ mausoleum managers for entombments; and

➢ authorized persons at medical and research institutions for donations.

These endorsed permits must then be recorded in the office of vital records with jurisdiction over the place of disposition. These local municipal offices then forward the original to the state vital records office where the document becomes a permanent legal record of the final disposition.

Form of authorization - The CDC Funeral Directors' Handbook on Death Registration and Fetal Death Reporting provides the following information concerning the form of authorization for the final disposition of a dead body or fetus:

> *The form of authorization for final disposition varies by state. In some states, the authorization is issued by the local registrar when a properly completed death certificate or fetal death report is presented. In other states, the authorization is issued over the signature of the attending physician or the medical examiner or coroner. The signature is obtained at the time the cause-of-death and certifier portions of the death certificate or fetal death report are completed. Several states require no authorization form for the disposition of the body or fetus, or they require one only under certain specified circumstances (e.g., when the body is to be removed from the state).*

> *Still other states require only that the funeral director send a notification to the proper registration official indicating that a death or fetal death has occurred and that the body or fetus is being disposed of. States that have adopted systems to electronically register and file death certificates can also generate authorization forms for final dispositions through this electronic death registration process.*

Note: See Form 3 to view a selection of state disposition permits.

Chapter 6: Government Benefits and Programs

Overview

Both federal and state governments have a number of benefits and programs for eligible survivors of a decedent. The three most well-known agencies in the federal government that administer death benefits are the Social Security Administration (SSA), Department of Veterans Affairs (VA), and Department of Health and Human Services (DHHS). Funeral directors play a significant role in working with these agencies and assisting families to obtain benefits. This chapter will explore the available benefits and programs as they relate to interaction with the funeral service industry.

Note: The government websites for the departments listed above are the sources of the material in this chapter. It has been condensed and abbreviated to create a workable summary for this book. For detailed and current information about death benefit programs, readers should explore the websites in more detail, and contact agency officials with any inquiries. The website addresses for the federal agencies are provided in the Sources Consulted listing.

Chapter Definitions

Department of Veterans Affairs (VA) (previously known as Veterans Administration) - a federal agency that administers benefits provided for veterans of the armed forces.

National cemetery - a cemetery created and maintained under an act of Congress for burial of veterans of military service and their eligible family members.

Perpetual care - an arrangement made by the cemetery whereby funds are set aside, the income from which is used to maintain the cemetery indefinitely.

Social Security Administration (SSA) - a branch of the U. S. Department of Health and Human Services which provides benefits for retirement, survivors, and disability; and includes Supplemental Security Income (SSI) and Medicare.

Social Security Benefits

The **Social Security Administration (SSA) is** an independent agency of the federal government. Among other duties and responsibilities, it is tasked with managing social security benefits as they relate to survivors. There are two primary benefits available dependent on a determination of eligibility.

Lump-sum payment - A one-time payment of $255 may be made to a surviving spouse if they were living with the decedent at the time of death. If they were living apart, the spouse may still be entitled to this one-time benefit if they are eligible for other social security benefits based on the employment record of the decedent. If there is no surviving spouse, a child eligible for benefits based on the record of the deceased in the month of death may also qualify.

Monthly payments - If a decedent worked during their lifetime and contributed to the social security system through payroll deductions or self-employment payments, survivors *may* be eligible for social security benefits. Meeting the criteria to establish eligibility is dependent on several factors, such as age and marital status at the time of death and whether or not there are dependent children, parents, or others.

The abundance and assortment of eligibility requirements renders a quick assessment of social security benefits impossible for those not intimately familiar with the criteria. Family members should therefore be directed to local social security officials for direction and guidance on SSA matters, and funeral directors should have the location and address of a local social security office readily available to give to a family when needed.

Notifying Social Security of a death - For every death handled by a funeral establishment, the funeral director is responsible for notifying the SSA. The one-page form for this purpose, Statement of Death by Funeral Director, may be mailed or faxed to a local or district SSA office. This notification meets one of the requirements for the family when applying for survivor benefits and assists the SSA in making a determination on eligibility.

Many of the electronic death registration systems being implemented in the states have the capability to electronically verify a social security number directly with the SSA when a death certificate is being completed. If the number is verified by the SSA, the funeral director is then not required to complete or file the paper Statement of Death.

Note: See Form 4 to view an SSA Statement of Death by Funeral Director.

Veterans Benefits - Generally
The U.S. **Department of Veterans Affairs (VA)** offers several benefits to survivors upon the death of an eligible veteran of the armed services, and the information that follows provides a brief summary of the benefits available to survivors as of June 2020. Funeral directors should always verify any information provided to survivors is not only accurate but current, as government rules and regulations are amended and updated frequency.

Burial Allowances
Eligibility - Survivors of a deceased veteran may be eligible for a monetary burial allowance. To qualify, the veteran must have been discharged under conditions other than dishonorable.

In addition to the required honorable discharge, the veteran must meet at least one of these conditions:

> ➢ died as a result of a service-connected disability;

> ➢ was receiving a VA pension or compensation at the time of death;

> ➢ was entitled to receive a VA pension or compensation, but decided instead to receive his or her full military retirement or disability pay;

> ➢ died while hospitalized by the VA, or while receiving care under VA contract at a non-VA facility;

> ➢ died while traveling under proper authorization and at VA expense, to or from a specified place for the purpose of examination, treatment, or care;

> ➢ had an original or reopened claim for VA compensation or pension pending at the time of death and would have been entitled to benefits from a date prior to date of death; or

> ➢ died on or after October 9, 1996, while a patient at a VA approved state nursing home.

Compensation - Prior to 2014, the VA paid for burial and funeral expenses on a reimbursement basis, which required survivors to submit receipts for relatively small one-time payments that the VA generally pays at the maximum amount permitted by law. The VA has since made significant changes to the monetary burial benefits regulation to simplify the program and pay eligible survivors more quickly and efficiently. Those new regulations became effective on July 7, 2014, and authorize the VA to pay, without a written application, most eligible surviving spouse's basic monetary burial benefits at the maximum amount authorized by law. This is accomplished through the use of automated systems rather than reimbursing them for actual costs incurred.

For a service-related death, the VA will pay up to $2,000 toward burial expenses for deaths on or after September 11, 2001, or up to $1,500 for deaths prior to September 11, 2001. If the veteran is buried in a VA **national cemetery**, some of the cost of transporting the deceased may be reimbursed.

For a non-service-related death, the VA will pay up to $762 toward burial and funeral expenses for deaths on or after October 1, 2017 (if hospitalized by the VA at time of death), or $300 toward burial and funeral expenses (if not hospitalized by the VA at time of death), and a $762 plot-interment allowance (if not buried in a national cemetery).

Tangible Benefits

Upright headstones and flat markers - The VA will provide a government headstone or marker for the unmarked grave of any deceased eligible veteran in any cemetery around the world, regardless of the date of death. A headstone or marker may also be provided for eligible veterans who died on or after November 1, 1990, and whose grave is marked with a privately purchased headstone.

Upright headstones are available in granite or marble, while flat markers are available in granite, marble, and bronze.

Cemetery staff in national, military post, and military base cemeteries are responsible for setting a VA headstone or marker at no charge; however, some state veterans' cemeteries may charge an applicant a nominal fee. Arrangements for setting a government headstone or marker in a private cemetery is the responsibility of the applicant and all placement costs are at private expense.

In addition to the name, date of birth, date of death, and military service information, a cemetery headstone or marker may display an approved emblem of belief. No other graphics, logos, symbols, or depictions are permitted, other than authorized emblems of belief; the Civil War Union Shield; the Civil War Confederate Southern Cross of Honor; and the Medal of Honor.

This VA granite marker has been set parallel to the ground as a footstone in a private cemetery.

Belief emblem
Veteran name
Home state
Rank and military branch
Periods of conflict served (if any)
Dates of birth and death

An emblem of belief for placement on a government headstone or marker is an emblem or symbol that: represents the sincerely held belief of the decedent; constituted a religion or the functional equivalent of religion; and was believed and/or accepted as true by that individual during his or her life. The belief represented by an emblem need not be associated with or endorsed by any group or organization.

The VA also offers niche markers to identify columbaria used for the inurnment of cremated remains.

Note: See Form 5 to view a VA Claim for Standard Headstone or Marker and illustrations of the belief emblems available.

Memorial items - The VA provides *memorial* headstones and markers for eligible deceased active duty service members and veterans whose remains have not been recovered or identified; buried at sea; donated to science; or whose cremated remains have been scattered. They may also be furnished in national, military base, or state veterans' cemeteries to eligible spouses whose remains are unavailable for interment, whether or not they predecease the eligible veteran.

These headstones and markers bear an, 'IN MEMORY OF' inscription as their first line. They must be placed in a recognized cemetery and are not available for placement in private cemeteries for spouses or other dependents.

Medallions - The VA will provide a government medallion for eligible veterans who served on or after April 6, 1917, and whose grave is marked with a privately purchased headstone or marker.

Bronze medallions are durable and can be easily affixed to privately purchased headstones, thereby avoiding any headstone or marker setting fees. The medallion also offers a way to identify a grave as that of a veteran when a cemetery prohibits placing a standard VA marker as a footstone because of cemetery rules limiting the number of stone markers to one per grave.

Note: See Form 6 to view a VA Claim for Government Medallion.

Flag - A United States flag is provided to the survivors of a deceased veteran who served honorably in the U.S. Armed Forces and may be used to drape a casket or accompany an urn. They are furnished to honor the memory of a veterans' military service to his or her country. An application to receive a flag may be submitted to the VA on a form available online as a form-fill document; however, funeral directors customarily assist survivors in completing the form and submitting it to a local VA facility or United States Postal Service office. These agencies are authorized to accept applications and provide a flag to the funeral director for use at the time of the funeral.

Note: See Form 7 to view a United States Flag for Burial Purposes application and review the order of precedence for who may receive the burial flag.

Presidential memorial certificate - A Presidential Memorial Certificate (PMC) is an engraved paper certificate, signed by the current President of the United States, to honor the memory of deceased veterans who are eligible for burial in a national cemetery. More than one PMC may be requested by mailing a completed application and supporting documentation to the National Cemetery Administration.

Note: See Form 8 to view a Presidential Memorial Certificate Request application.

Gold Star Lapel Button - The Gold Star Lapel Pin Program has its origins in the First World War when families with members in the armed forces would fly or hang a flag outside their home or place it in a window visible from the exterior of the home. The flag would have a blue star on it for each family member serving in the military. If the family service member lost their life during the conflict, the blue star would be replaced with a gold star, letting the community know the price the family paid for the cause of freedom.

Federal law stipulates a Gold Star Lapel Button may be awarded to identify widows, parents, and next of kin of members of the armed forces:

➢ who lost their lives during World War I, World War II, or during any period of armed hostilities in which the United States was engaged before July 1, 1958;

➢ who lost or lose their lives after June 30, 1958…

   ✓ while engaged in an action against an enemy of the United States,

   ✓ while engaged in military operations involving conflict with an opposing foreign force, or

- ✓ while serving with friendly foreign forces engaged in an armed conflict in which the United States is not a belligerent party against an opposing armed force; or

- ➤ who lost or lose their lives after March 28, 1973, as a result of…

  - ✓ an international terrorist attack against the United States or a foreign nation friendly to the United States, recognized as such an attack by the Secretary of Defense, or

  - ✓ military operations while serving outside the United States (including the commonwealths, territories, and possessions of the United States) as part of a peacekeeping force.

The Secretary of Defense will furnish one gold star lapel button without cost to the widow and each parent and next of kin of a member who lost or loses his or her life under any circumstances as provided above. In such case, no more than one gold star lapel button may be furnished to any one individual. When making a Gold Star Button determination:

- ➤ The term 'widow' includes widower.

- ➤ The term 'parents' includes mother, father, stepmother, stepfather, mother through adoption, father through adoption, and foster parents who stood in loco parentis.

- ➤ The term 'next of kin' includes only children, brothers, sisters, half-brothers, and half-sisters.

- ➤ The term 'children' includes stepchildren and children through adoption.

- ➤ the term 'World War I' includes the period from April 6, 1917, to March 3, 1921.

- ➤ The term 'World War II' includes the period from September 8, 1939, to July 25, 1947, at 12 o'clock noon.

- ➤ The term 'military operations' includes those operations involving members of the armed forces assisting in United States Government sponsored training of military personnel of a foreign nation. The term 'peacekeeping force' includes those personnel assigned to a force engaged in a peacekeeping operation authorized by the United Nations Security Council.

The program described above is administered by the United States government, and funeral directors can easily assist a family in obtaining this benefit by completing a simple application online. There are several other gold star programs that are not affiliated with the government, such as American Gold Star Mothers, Inc. and Operation Never Forgotten.

Military Funeral Honors
Honoring Those Who Served is the Department of Defense (DOD) program for providing dignified military funeral honors to veterans who have defended our nation. Upon the request of a family, federal law requires every eligible veteran receive a military funeral honors ceremony, to include

folding and presenting the United States burial flag and the playing of taps. The law defines a military funeral honors detail as consisting of two or more uniformed military persons, with at least one being a member of the veterans' parent service of the armed forces.

The DOD program calls for funeral service providers to request military funeral honors on behalf of the family of a veteran. The VA National Cemetery Administration cemetery staff can also assist with arranging military funeral honors at VA national cemeteries. In addition, private veteran organizations may assist in providing military funeral honors when needed.

Military Discharges

Many of the benefits offered by the VA are dependent on the veteran having been, "*discharged under conditions other than dishonorable*." Funeral directors should be aware there are currently five military discharge classifications:

1. Honorable discharge.
2. General discharge under honorable conditions.
3. Other than honorable discharge.
4. Bad conduct discharge.
5. Dishonorable discharge.

The first two classifications automatically grant veteran benefits upon separation from service, including survivor death benefits. The remaining three generally do not grant any veteran benefits; however, a family may request the VA review a discharge classification and therefore eligibility to receive any particular benefit.

The type of discharge afforded to a veteran is recorded on military discharge paperwork. Commonly referred to in the funeral service industry by the current form number, DD-214, the document will clearly state the discharge classification in a section called *Character of Service*. The form is formally titled a Certificate of Release or Discharge from Active Duty, and the DD-214 form number has been used by all of the military branches since January 1, 1950. Prior to that date, other forms with different form numbers, in addition to the DD-214, were used by the various armed service branches.

Note: See Form 9 to view a DD-214 Certificate of Release or Discharge from Active Duty.

National Cemeteries

National cemeteries - As of August 2020, there were 160 national cemeteries and 33 soldier's lots and monuments, including:

- The 144 national cemeteries in 40 states and Puerto Rico, as well as the 33 soldier's lots and monument sites, all maintained by the Department of Veterans Affairs, National Cemetery Administration.

- The two national cemeteries maintained by the Department of the Army: Arlington National Cemetery and the U.S. Soldiers' & Airmen's Home National Cemetery, both located in Washington, D.C.

- The 14 cemeteries associated with historic sites and battlefields maintained by the National Park Service, Department of the Interior. All but two of these are now closed to new interments.

Veterans may be buried at no cost in any of the VA national cemeteries that has open space. Veteran benefits include opening and closing the grave, **perpetual care**, a government headstone or marker, a burial flag, and a Presidential Memorial Certificate. Cremated remains are also acceptable and either buried or inurned with honors in the same manner as casketed remains.

Spouses and certain dependents of a veteran may also be buried in a national cemetery, even if they predecease the veteran. They are buried with the veteran; receive perpetual care; and have their name, date of birth, and date of death inscribed on the reverse side of the veterans' headstone.

Committal services in a VA cemetery are conducted in an outdoor, covered shelter on a strictly-scheduled and orchestrated basis, usually at 30-minute intervals. Late arrivals may be required to wait until there is an unscheduled opening, as the staff will not usually allow those who are late to inconvenience those who are on time. It is the funeral director's responsibility to inform the family of the absolute need to be prompt, and ensure the procession arrives in a timely fashion.

Funeral and graveside services are not permitted on the grounds of a VA national cemetery, although a family may in some cases, with prior approval, witness an inurnment.

Note: The general procedures described above are for VA cemeteries, they do not apply to Arlington National Cemetery operated by the U.S. Army in Washington, D.C. Information about services in Arlington is provided later in this chapter.

National cemetery eligibility - The VA publishes a wealth of information and eligibility criteria online; however, funeral directors should *never speculate* or inform a family any particular individual is eligible for burial in a national cemetery until after receiving an official notification from the National Cemetery Scheduling Office (NCSO). The NCSO has the primary responsibility for verifying eligibility and makes a case-by-case determination in response to every request for burial in a VA cemetery. There are five categories of individuals potentially eligible for burial in a national cemetery.

1. Active members. Members of the armed forces that die on active duty are eligible for burial in a national cemetery.

2. Veterans. A veteran discharged under conditions other than dishonorable is, with certain exceptions, eligible to be buried in a national cemetery. The exceptions are for service beginning after September 7, 1980, as an enlisted person; and service after October 16, 1981, as an officer. For these exceptions, at the time of death, these individuals must have completed a minimum of 24 continuous months service or the full period for which the person was called to active duty, such as a reservist called to active duty for a limited duration.

3. Spouses. The spouse of an eligible veteran or member may be eligible for burial in a national cemetery even if the veteran is not buried or memorialized in a national cemetery. The surviving spouse of an eligible veteran who had a subsequent remarriage to a non-veteran and whose death occurred after January 1, 2000, is eligible for burial based on their marriage to an eligible veteran. A former spouse of an eligible service member whose marriage to that service member has been terminated by annulment or divorce is not eligible.

4. Dependent children. Dependent minor children of an eligible veteran are also eligible for benefits. A minor child for these purposes is defined as a child who is unmarried and under 21 years of age, or 23 years of age and pursuing a full-time course of instruction at an approved educational institution.

   The unmarried adult child of a veteran of any age may be eligible. In these cases, the adult child must have become permanently physically or mentally disabled and incapable of self-support before reaching 21 years of age, or before reaching 23 years of age if pursuing a full-time course of instruction at an approved educational institution.

5. Others. Members of the following groups may also be eligible for burial in a national cemetery:

   ➢ Military reserve units, such as the National Guard and reserve officers' training corps.

   ➢ U.S. citizens who served in the armed forces of a government during any war in which the United States has or may be engaged.

   ➢ Commissioned officers of the National Oceanic Atmospheric Administration.

   ➢ Commissioned officers of the regular or reserve corps of the Public Health Service who served on full-time duty on or after July 29, 1945.

   ➢ World War II Merchant Mariners.

> ➤ Philippine Armed Forces who served in the organized military services of the Government of the Commonwealth of the Philippines prior to July 1, 1946.

> ➤ Parents of the veteran.

> ➤ Other persons or classes of persons as designated by the Secretary of Veterans Affairs.

All of these remaining groups have specific criteria and conditions that must be met to qualify for burial, and any question of eligibility should be directed to the NCSO.

VA National Cemetery Scheduling Office (NCSO) - The scheduling office of the VA National Cemetery Administration processes and schedules all requests for burial or inurnment in the cemeteries maintained by the Department of Veterans Affairs. They do not handle scheduling for Arlington National Cemetery or any of the cemeteries maintained by the National Park Service. Individual national cemeteries do not schedule burials, as all requests must go through the NCSO.

The NCSO is open seven days a week from 8:00 a.m. to 7:30 p.m. ET, with the exceptions of being closed on Thanksgiving Day, Christmas Day, and New Year's Day. Burials at national cemeteries take place Monday through Friday. When there is a federal holiday on a Monday or Friday, cemeteries may schedule burials either on the actual holiday or on one of the days over the holiday weekend. The NCSO always has the currently available burial times for every cemetery.

For funeral directors scheduling a burial or inurnment in a VA national cemetery, these are the recommended steps to follow:

Step 1: In consultation with the family: select the cemetery, and the preferred date and time for the committal service. Do not commit or make plans for any specific date until it has been confirmed by the VA.

Step 2: Gather information to fill out and complete the VA Before You Call Checklist (Checklist), and secure a copy of the discharge papers (DD-214) for the veteran, as well as any additional records and documentation needed to complete the request.

Step 3: Fax or email the Checklist and support documents to the NCSO, and then call them on their toll-free number to go over the request. With all of the information they need in hand, the NCSO will often be in a position to determine eligibility and, if eligible, schedule the service at the cemetery. If the date and time are not available, they will provide alternate dates and times for the chosen cemetery. For this reason, it is important for the call to the NCSO be made during the arrangement conference or other time when the family is readily available to accept or decline an alternate date and time, as well as answer any questions.

Step 4: If a funeral director has all of the information needed for the Checklist and a copy of the DD-2014, the determination on eligibility and confirmation of a scheduled service in a national cemetery will be completed during the initial phone call. The NCSO will provide the funeral director with a unique case number and follow-up with an email confirmation of the scheduled service. If there are any issues or problems to address, they will advise the funeral director during the initial call and place a hold on the request until resolved.

Note: See Form 10 to view the VA Before You Call Checklist.

Arlington National Cemetery

The United States Army maintains Arlington National Cemetery (Arlington) in Washington, D.C., and the cemetery website has information on the eligibility, requirements, and procedures for scheduling an interment or inurnment.

As noted by the Army, the process to schedule a burial at Arlington can be complex, and the length of time it takes for scheduling *standard* military honors is typically several weeks to several months. *Full* military honors can take longer to schedule because of the need for additional military resources, such as escorts and a caisson; while requests for chapel services can extend the wait time by an additional two months. To reduce wait time in the scheduling process, Arlington recommends requesting the use of the chapel only if a funeral service has not been previously conducted. If a family is seeking to schedule a specific date for an interment after their loved one has passed, Arlington recommends they be contacted four months prior to the desired interment date.

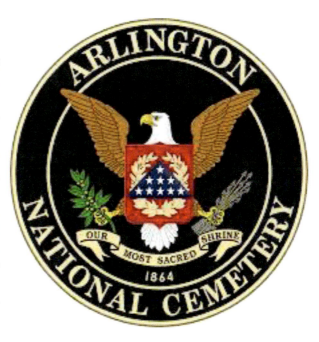

Requesting services - A funeral director initiates a request for services in Arlington by calling the customer care center toll-free telephone number. At the time of the initial call, the center will issue the funeral director a unique case number and request all required documents be emailed for review. In addition to the data on the VA Before You Call Checklist, Arlington requires funeral directors provide information regarding unusually heavy caskets, oversize caskets, or any other item or condition which could impact the handling of the remains on the day of the service.

The actual scheduling of a service will not take place until the customer care center works through a checklist of requirements, including such items as establishing who has the legal right to control the final disposition; confirming the service member (or dependent) eligibility for burial or inurnment; and contacting the Primary Next-of-Kin (PNOK) or Person Authorized to Direct Disposition (PADD). Arlington recommends the funeral director provide them with multiple ways to contact the funeral establishment and the PNOK or PADD to help ensure the cemetery reaches someone when the scheduler calls to set a date.

Arlington schedules services based on available cemetery and military resources. On average, they conduct between 27 and 30 funeral services each weekday, eight of which are services with full military honors. There are up to six committal services an hour, five times a day. Saturday services are also available for placements (inurnments) and services for cremated remains that do not require military honors or military chaplain support. On average, the cemetery conducts between six and eight services on Saturdays.

Documentation - There are several documents required to complete the application process and successfully schedule a burial, including a DD-214 Military Discharge record; death certificate; and certificate of cremation (if applicable). As the process continues, there are other documents that will require a signature before the service takes place.

Services for cremated remains - With respect to services for cremated remains, Arlington:

➢ requires certification of 100% of the cremated remains;

➢ requires a cremated remains certificate;

➢ supports the industry best practice of including the cremation identification number associated with the remains and annotated on the cremation certificate;

➢ does not accept cremated remains by mail; and

➢ provides urns should be no larger than 9x9x9 inches and, if the urn purchased by the family exceeds this size, Arlington staff must be notified prior to the interment date.

Military honors - The decedent's branch of service provides the respective military honors, with the level of honors received depending on the rank of the deceased. The three levels are:

1. Standard Military Honors - provided for enlisted service members and include a casket team (pall bearers), firing party, and bugler.

2. Full Military Honors - provided for commissioned officers, warrant officers and senior non-commissioned officers, and include a casket team (pall bearers), firing party, and bugler; and *may* include an escort platoon (size varies according to the rank of the deceased) and a military band.

3. Armed Forces Honors - these are the same as full military honors, except escort platoons from each of the armed services participate. These funerals are reserved for the President of the United States (as commander-in-chief), Secretary of Defense, Chairman of the Joint Chiefs of Staff, or officers granted multiple-service command duties.

Exception: All service members who die from wounds received as result of enemy action and are being interred, inurned, or memorialized at Arlington National Cemetery are eligible to receive full military honors.

U.S. Navy firing party for Full military honors.

Other benefits - Burial flags, presidential memorial certificates, headstones, and markers for use in Arlington may be obtained from the VA using the same procedures as described previously for VA maintained national cemeteries.

Cemeteries in National Parks

The National Park Service (NPS) maintains 14 national cemeteries. These represent a continuum of use dating to a period before the establishment of the historical parks of which they are an integral part. These are administered to preserve the historic character, uniqueness, and solemn nature of both the cemeteries and the historical parks where they are located.

National cemeteries administered by the NPS are classified as either active or closed. Active cemeteries have casket or cremation gravesites available for the initial burial of human remains or cremated remains following the death of the individual. Closed cemeteries have no available unreserved gravesites for either casket or cremation first interments but may inter eligible family members in the same gravesite as previously interred individuals.

As of this writing, there are two active national cemeteries administered by the NPS:

➢ Andersonville National Cemetery in Andersonville, Georgia; and

➢ Andrew Johnson National Cemetery in Greenville, Tennessee.

The remaining 12: Antietam, Battleground, Chalmette, Custer, Fort Donelson, Fredericksburg, Gettysburg, Poplar Grove, Shiloh, Stones River, Vicksburg, and Yorktown are closed.

Funeral directors must contact an NPS cemetery directly to determine availability, eligibility, and procedures for requesting a burial.

State Veterans' Cemeteries

Many states also operate and maintain cemeteries for veterans. These are often established and improved using federal funds and have eligibility requirements similar to VA national cemeteries. One notable requirement for eligibility may be for the decedent to have been a legal resident of the state at the time of death.

State cemeteries are operated solely by state governments with no direct VA oversight. As of this writing, there are four states with no state veterans' cemeteries: Alaska, Florida, New York, and Oregon. A complete listing of all national and state cemeteries for veterans, together with addresses and contact information may be found on the VA National Cemetery Administration website.

Funeral directors seeking to use a state veterans cemetery must contact the individual burial sites directly to determine specific requirements, eligibility criteria, and benefits.

Public Assistance

Many state and county governments administer programs providing public assistance to individuals and families living below the poverty level or having special needs, such as the aged, blind, and disabled. These programs may alternatively be known as welfare benefits or social service benefits for indigents or needy persons.

Each state or county government designates an office or department to administer these public assistance programs. They in turn define the available benefits; set rules for eligibility; process applications for assistance; and supervise those admitted to the programs.

Burial programs for indigents vary widely, but eligibility is often based on financial assets (or lack thereof), there being no known next-of-kin, or the next-of-kin is unwilling or incapable of providing a decent burial. Assistance may include funding for such goods and services as: the purchase of a burial container, crematory fees, visitation, and a grave. The limits of the benefits these programs provide vary significantly from one jurisdiction to the next.

Funeral directors must familiarize themselves with the public assistance programs available in the communities they serve and establish working relationships with the agencies tasked with administering the programs.

Chapter 7: Funeral Goods and Services

Overview
This chapter reviews funeral goods and services available to consumers for funeral service events. It includes information on two relatively new funeral types: green (natural) burial funerals and home funerals. The chapter concludes with a review of FTC advisory opinions related to third-party merchandise.

Chapter Definitions
Adaptive funeral rite - a funeral rite that is adjusted to the needs and wants of those directly involved.

Alternative container - an unfinished wood box or other non-metal receptacle or enclosure, without ornamentation or a fixed interior lining, which is designed for the encasement of human remains and which is made of fiberboard, pressed-wood, composition materials (with or without an outside covering) or like materials.

Calling hours - (visitation, visiting hours) - time set aside for friends and relatives to pay respect for the deceased prior to the funeral service.

Celebrant - a person who designs and officiates a personalized ceremony or rite; the officiant who celebrates the Mass in the Roman Catholic Church.

Celebrant funeral - a funeral service not focused on any specific religion, belief, faith, or rite; officiated by a trained and qualified, non-clergy official [by Author].

Cremated remains – the result of the reduction of a dead body to inorganic bone fragments by intense heat.

Direct cremation - disposition of human remains by cremation, with no formal viewing, visitation, or ceremony with the deceased present.

Direct disposition - any method of disposition of the human remains without formal viewing, visitation, or ceremony with the deceased present.

Funeral goods - means all products sold directly to the public in connection with funeral services [by FTC].

Funeral services - means services used to care for and prepare bodies for burial, cremation, or other final disposition; and services used to arrange, supervise, or conduct the funeral ceremony or final disposition of human remains [by FTC].

Graveside service - a ceremony or ritual, religious or otherwise, conducted at the grave.

Green burial - disposition without the use of toxic chemicals or materials that are not readily biodegradable.

Green cemetery - a place of interment that bans the use of metal caskets, toxic embalming, and concrete vaults and may also require the use of aesthetically natural monuments.

Green funeral - death care that minimizes the use of energy in service offerings/products and that bans the use of toxic/hazardous materials.

Home funeral - one that takes place within the residence of the deceased as was commonly done in the United States until the mid-20th century.

Humanist funeral - a funeral rite that is in essence devoid of religious connotation.

Immediate burial - disposition of human remains by burial, with no formal viewing, visitation, or ceremony with the deceased present, except for a graveside service.

Inurnment - placing cremated remains in an urn or placing cremated remains in a niche or grave.

Memorial gathering - a scheduled assembly of family and friends following a death without the deceased present.

Memorial service - funeral rites without the remains present.

Goods and Services - Generally
Goods and services shape and focus the funeral experience for the family and friends of the deceased. In addition to a number of traditional items, there are many innovative goods and services a funeral establishment may elect to offer. The traditional items are the foundation for making funeral arrangements, while the innovative, optional items are quite often designed to deliver additional personalization and customization to funeral service events.

Services - The FTC has identified **funeral services** as those services used to care for and prepare bodies for burial, cremation, or other final disposition; and services used to arrange, supervise, or conduct the funeral ceremony or final disposition of human remains. They generally are non-tangible items *provided* to a consumer for a fee, such as the use of the funeral establishment for calling hours or the presence of a funeral director to supervise a graveside committal service.

Goods - The FTC has identified **funeral goods** as all products sold directly to the public in connection with funeral services. They generally are tangible merchandise items *purchased* by the consumer, such as a register book or flag case.

The next four sections will explore: 1) traditional funeral services, 2) innovative funeral services, 3) traditional funeral goods, and 4) innovative funeral goods.

Funeral Services - Traditional
Many of the traditional service items offered to a consumer during the arrangement conference are based on the type of funeral service chosen and funeral events to be included. All of the service

options may not be applicable to all of the funeral types and events, but traditional services may include any of the following:

Transfer (removal) of remains	Supervision of funeral service events
Arrangement conference	Embalming and preparation of remains
Reporting the death to government officials	Payments for cash advances
Obtaining a burial (disposition) permit	Dressing and casketing
Coordination with allied professionals	Use of funeral establishment facilities
Writing death notice and obituaries	Use of funeral establishment vehicles
Coordination of related events	Transportation of human remains

As noted earlier, many of the traditional service items are dependent on the type of funeral service chosen. Funeral types include:

➤ Traditional funeral - A traditional funeral is one in which remains are embalmed and prepared for presentation at a public viewing. This is followed by **calling hours**; a formal, often religious funeral service; and concludes with burial in a cemetery.

➤ Cremation funeral - The cremation funeral follows essentially the same path as a traditional funeral, with the exception being the remains are held for cremation after the funeral service instead of being buried. An **inurnment** or other method of disposition for **cremated remains** takes place on a later date.

➤ Memorial service - A **memorial service** is one dedicated to remembrance of the decedent and conducted without the body being present. When the final disposition is cremation, a memorial service may be called a full cremation service, one that includes visitation, a formal service, and a graveside ceremony; with the one notable exception being the body is not present for any of the events.

➤ Adaptive funeral - An **adaptive funeral rite** is defined as a funeral adjusted to the needs and wants of those directly involved. They have many of the same elements as a traditional funeral service but include some unique or specific need for the family, such as the venue location for calling hours.

➤ Humanistic funeral - The **humanistic funeral** is defined as a funeral rite that is, in essence, devoid of religious connotation. These non-denominational services often have family members or close friends as speakers. They focus on the life, personality, and character of the decedent and often reflect on their personal interactions, fond memories, and humorous encounters with the decedent over a period of many years.

➤ Memorial gathering - A **memorial gathering** is a scheduled assembly of family and friends following a death without the deceased present. These have become very popular with the escalating number of cremations taking place in the United States. In some cases, a memorial gathering may be held in addition to one of the other funeral service types. As an example, a family may schedule a traditional funeral service to take place immediately after death, followed by a memorial gathering several days, weeks, or months later. These gatherings may take place in locations and settings not usually associated with funeral celebrations, such as a restaurant or a public park.

➢ Graveside service - A **graveside service** is a ceremony or ritual, religious or otherwise, conducted at the grave site. In most cases, a graveside service is considered to be a stand-alone option but may be used in conjunction with one of the other funeral types, such as an immediate burial. Graveside services are also common in areas where winter burials are not possible and the final disposition of human remains takes place in the spring.

➢ Immediate burial - The **immediate burial** is defined as the disposition of human remains by burial, with no formal viewing, visitation, or ceremony with the deceased present, except for the graveside service.

➢ Direct cremation - A **direct cremation** is defined as the disposition of human remains by cremation, with no formal viewing, visitation, or ceremony with the deceased present.

Note: Any funeral type providing for the disposition of human remains without a formal viewing, visitation, or ceremony with the deceased present is a **direct disposition**.

➢ Celebrant funeral - To fully comprehend **celebrant funerals**, it becomes necessary to first understand variations in the use of the word **celebrant**. The traditional definition of celebrant includes any individual that formally presides over any kind of celebration. As such, a clergy member officiating at a funeral service or marriage ceremony would fit the traditional definition of a celebrant. However, when used to describe a celebrant funeral, a celebrant is defined as a trained and qualified *non-clergy* official that conducts a funeral service which is not focused on any specific religion, belief, faith, or rite.

Many funeral establishments are now training staff members to serve as celebrants and offering celebrant funerals as an option to consumers. Celebrant funerals are relative new-comers as a funeral type but share many of the same characteristics and attributes found in the funeral types described earlier. As such, there is some debate in the funeral service community as to whether they are more properly defined as a stand-alone funeral type or simply a modification or addition that may be applied to any other type.

Funeral Services - Innovative

Innovative services offer opportunities to customize and personalize a funeral without sacrificing the solemn and respectful customs and decorum expected on the occasion of a death. It is the provision of these optional services funeral directors need to continually monitor to keep current with industry trends. This is becoming even more important as traditional full-service cases are being replaced by millennials seeking a remembrance service that injects a large dose of individuality and personalization. Innovative services include such items as:

Live streaming services - Using streaming services is becoming more and more popular as the ease of mobility in our society provides the means for families to move all over the world to pursue their dreams. Those family members, coupled with the elderly and mobility challenged, represent a segment of society that may derive a substantial benefit in being able to view and, in some cases, participate in a funeral service over the internet. Several companies offer streaming services that provide feeds directly from the funeral establishment so others can view the service in real time.

Themed funerals - Popular with millennials, themed funerals offer the means to style a funeral service to represent the individual. They may be as simple as the color and materials used to prepare the background for the calling hours. For example: a bier, flower racks, kneeler, sympathy card stand, lectern, and wall decorations could all be coordinated to present a nature theme.

➲ *This Blue Midnight casket display is a typical themed funeral set-up for a visitation and funeral service. Note the backdrop, light torchiers, flower stands and casket bier are all the same red oak wood theme. Even the nature photograph on the wall complements the natural wood theme*

Illustration courtesy of Northwoods Casket Company.[3]

Having ready-to-go alternative themes also affords greater flexibility in ensuring each funeral service experience is special and unique. A more complex theme, such as one for a decedent that treasured his motorcycle, might include a display of his motorcycle jacket, helmet, and gloves; a map of his road trips; and a slideshow of photos taken during his rides. If at all practical, the motorcycle could even be positioned near the casket in the funeral establishment.

➲ *This themed funeral set-up for a cremation case is centered around the decedents' life in her quilting workshop. Her quilts were used to decorate the chapel, and remnants of fabric from her shop were affixed to each of her prayer cards. An image of the cards is shown in the Funeral Goods section of this chapter.*

Photo courtesy of Wilson Funeral Home.[5]

The opportunities and ideas for creating a themed funeral are only restricted by the imagination of the funeral director. Funeral establishments that want to offer a special one-of-a-kind themed funeral must be creative and prepared to think outside the box. Those that do will quickly gain a positive reputation in their community and enjoy a loyal following from those individuals who crave and will pay for a service to remember.

Transportation services - Previously limited to a few large sedans or mid-size limousines, in recent years the idea of having transportation accommodations to easily move a large group of people in a comfortable and often luxurious manner have become more popular. These conveyances may be described by some as high-end buses, but those who operate these services refer to them as executive coaches or VIP limousines, a far more accurate description once anyone has an opportunity to actually board and inspect one.

These elite transportation services allow families to remain together in one vehicle as they move to and from funeral event locations, and also offer transportation to a family gathering after formal services conclude. Funeral establishments that have used these transportation services note the added convenience they provide to them as well, by eliminating the need to organize and then continuously monitor and corral several vehicles in a funeral procession.

Many families are not aware of the availability of these conveniences and opportunities, and funeral establishments that partner with livery service professionals may offer yet another service to those they serve. Although not a common appearance yet, there are companies now experimenting with executive coaches that have a dedicated bay for loading casketed remains into the same vehicle with the family.

The interior of a 2016 Mercedes-Benz, Executive Coach, owned and operated by Premier Plus Travel and Tours in Queensbury, NY.[7]

DNA preservation - This is one of the newer innovative services being offered by funeral establishments and is an option that lends itself well to both interment and cremation final dispositions. Global Genetic Health, a company located in Thunder Bay, Ontario, Canada, and a current leader in this endeavor, states on their DNA Memorial website:

> *DNA allows heirs the opportunity to track, diagnose, and prevent everything from simple skin disorders to terminal cancer. The more familial DNA that is preserved, the more doctors have to work with in genetic medicine. A family's genetic legacy is valuable in this era of genetics.*

As of April 2020, DNA Memorial was offering preservation services to funeral establishments in Canada, the United States, the United Kingdom, Israel, Brazil, The Netherlands, and Sweden; and had over 700 U.S. funeral establishments participating. Global Genetic Health also provides their DNA services to other companies for scientific purposes in over 40 countries worldwide.

The role a funeral director plays in the process includes: offering the service to the families they serve, collecting a DNA sample from the decedent, and coordinating with the laboratory handling the preservation of the DNA. The collection of the sample itself is a simple matter of obtaining a cheek swab from the decedent, which can take place before or after sterilization or embalming.

In explaining the DNA preservation concept, Ryan Letho, PhD (Biotechnology), CEO and Founder of DNA Memorial, stated:

The DNA is extracted, purified, and then stabilized by attaching it to microscopic beads. It is then stored under an inert gas. It is this stabilization step that allows the DNA to be stored at room temperature in the safety of one's own home. Since cremation destroys all DNA, and the interment of a body will break down the DNA over time, the funeral director is the family's last chance to save their loved one's DNA for a future generation.

After processing, the DNA material is similar in appearance to cremated remains, and a small portion may be placed inside a piece of jewelry; stored in a keepsake container; or mixed with other materials, such as paint. The DNA can be used over and over again for testing and, if kept sealed, will remain viable indefinitely. DNA ancestry testing, previously unavailable for testing decedent remains, is now an option through funeral establishments.

Image courtesy of DNA Memorial (Global Genetic Health, Inc.), Thunder Bay, Ontario, Canada.[8]

By all indications, the movement to include DNA preservation as a service option is gaining remarkable momentum and, because of the potential medical and social impact these samples hold for the future, it is a service many will seek for forthcoming family generations.

Photo presentations - Photo presentations have gone well beyond the simple use of picture boards and homemade collages on easel stands. Funeral establishments can now offer a wide-range of diverse services to deliver a visual representation of a decedent's life. They can convert family photos from original hard copies into digital formats and then arrange them for a slide show presentation on one or more monitors. There are companies with software programs – such as Microsoft PowerPoint – designed specifically for these purposes and capable of creating slides with custom borders, captions, animations, transitions, music, and an audio narrative.

Food and beverages - Food and beverage items have been a part of funeral services in some form or another for centuries, dating back to the earliest Greek cultures of record and the first colonial settlers in America. Those services today, in those states that do not prohibit such activities in a funeral establishment, have evolved into primarily a light buffet or the offering of snack foods. For funeral establishments with the necessary space requirements to seat and feed a group of people, food services can generate a significant income. However, funeral directors should be aware the preparation and serving of food is a notoriously difficult business, often tightly regulated by state public health authorities.

Video programs - Videos may be added to a static visual presentation or offered as a separate service to families wishing to use multiple audio-video mediums. Service fees for photo presentations may be based on the number of pictures, with additional fees and options for the purchase of duplicate copies. For a nominal fee, some funeral establishments offer to direct mail 'remembrance' copies of audio and video tributes to those not able to attend, or to those who expressed a desire at the service to have a copy for themselves.

Funeral Goods - Traditional
Traditional tangible goods purchased by the consumer may include such items as:

Alternative containers	Memorial items	Flag case	Burial clothing
Burial plots and graves	Acknowledgement cards	Prayer cards	Cross or crucifix
Burial containers (casket, urn, etc.)	Outer burial containers (vaults, sectionals, etc.)	Headstones and markers	Register book

These long-time traditional best-sellers should not be taken for granted, as there are always ways to increase the appeal and value of any item. Themes, colors, materials, and designs should all be reviewed on a periodic basis to ensure the traditional funeral goods being offered are consistent with modern trends in the industry.

Traditional prayer cards personalized with strips of fabric to reflect the decedent's love for quilting.

Photo courtesy of Wilson Funeral Home.[5]

Personalizing traditional funeral goods is a proven way to attract more families and business. As described earlier, one funeral director chose to theme a funeral after a quilting workshop owned by the decedent. He used her quilts to decorate the chapel for calling hours and personalized a traditional item (prayer cards) by affixing a piece of fabric from her workshop to each card. These two, simple, innovative actions to enhance a traditional funeral service and a traditional funeral good added a very personal and intimate touch to this case.

Funeral Goods - Innovative
There are an infinite number of funeral goods beyond those traditional items listed above that may be offered to a family to further the celebration and recognition of the life of a loved one. Whether or not these are offered is at the discretion of each individual funeral establishment owner, who must first carefully evaluate the options to determine if they represent the character and nature of the community they serve. There should also be an analysis of the cost-to-benefit ratio for both the consumer and the business before the adoption of any specialty items.

Many innovative goods offer exceptional opportunities to customize and personalize a service and deliver a funeral experience that is not just good but great. The benefits of offering a range of special goods goes far beyond a simple profit margin. They pave the path to a reputation that may make the difference between a family going to Business A or Business B in the future. The single, most cost-effective advertisement for any business are unsolicited words of appreciation and praise spoken by recent customers to their network of family, friends, and co-workers. Innovative goods include such items as:

Jewelry - Pendants, charms, rings, pins, cuff links, and key fobs are just a few of the jewelry items that offer a unique, intimate, and personal way to remember a loved one. These items lend themselves well to other special offerings, such as taking an imprint of the decedents' fingerprints (or infant footprints) and having them engraved on the jewelry. Some jewelry items have a cavity built into them specifically for the purpose of holding a small quantity of cremated remains. These items offer an intimate and personal way to remember a loved one.

Tapestry - A tapestry is a thick textile fabric with a weaved photo or image imprint. They may be hung on a wall, used as a furniture covering, draped on a stand near the casket, or placed on an urn table during a visitation or funeral. Some directors purchase a tapestry imprinted with the photo from the newspaper notice and hang it in the chapel for the family when they arrive for calling hours. The family appreciates the director took the time and effort to give them a personal and thoughtful gift, and relatives and friends may wish to purchase one following the service.

Memory candles - Memory candles offer another opportunity to personalize goods, as they may include the name, relevant dates, and a recent photograph of the deceased. As with the tapestry item, others in the family may want to have one for themselves after services have concluded.

Giveaways - Giveaways take place at a visitation or graveside service and involve giving family and friends an item they will recognize as being associated with the deceased, such as a personalized golf ball, wristband, baseball cap, lanyard, bookmark, key tag, candy bar, or lapel pin. These recall pleasant memories, spark conversations, and inspire others to be active in expressing themselves, making the event a more personal and joyful celebration of a life.

Balloons and sky candles - A balloon release presents an opportunity to ensure a burial or graveside service is one to remember. These releases are especially appropriate for infant or child funeral services, or cases where there are a number of young children attending that need a physical outlet to express feelings for the loss of an older relative, friend, or maybe a school teacher. Helium balloon kits designed exclusively for graveside services are available with overnight delivery. Akin to a balloon release are sky candle releases for evening memorial services.

Monograming and embroidery - Fabrics may have a design or lettering embroidered on them, and there are endless options to personalize casket pillows, extendovers, overlays, and head cap panels. The addition of monogrammed initials to the portion of the overlay that drapes down the front of a casket is an ideal location, with the inner panel on the head cap another prominent location. Casket companies are now designing these cap spaces to hang or display pictures, knick-knacks, and other personalized mementos.

Photo courtesy of Matthews International.[6]

In summary, there are an endless number of ways to offer goods that personalize a funeral and make the experience one to be remembered for years to come. These goods motivate others to use the same funeral home, thus increasing sales and exposure to even more potential consumers.

Home Funerals

In addition to the funeral types listed previously, there are two additional types gaining a foothold in the funeral service industry. These special funerals have unique needs and requirements when it comes to goods and services that require a more detailed explanation. The first of these is a **home funeral**. A home funeral is one that takes place within the residence of the deceased, as was commonly done in the United States until the mid-20th century.

The National Home Funeral Alliance describes a home funeral as follows:

> *A home funeral happens when a loved one is cared for at home or in a sacred space after death, giving family and friends time to prepare the body, file legal paperwork, and gather and grieve in private.*

> *Home funerals can be held at the family home or not. Some nursing homes, church community groups and funeral homes may allow the family to care for the deceased after death. The emphasis is on minimal, non-invasive, and environmentally friendly care of the body.*

> *Support and assistance to carry out after-death care may come from home funeral educators and guides, but their goal is to facilitate maximum involvement of the family in charge of the funeral process, and their social network.*

There are similarities in the goals and objectives of a home funeral, natural (green) funeral, and a direct (immediate) burial. The one common factor they all share is a continuing trend to return to the funeral customs and rites experienced in early America. These customs included many of the tasks associated with a home funeral today, including:

➢ preparation of the remains by family members and friends, including washing, disinfection, dressing, and presentation for viewing;

➢ personal notification of the death to family and friends (often using social media);

➢ crafting and display of personal items, photographs, and memorabilia in the home;

➢ organizing and supervising a remembrance service, often led by an elder of the family with the participation of several generations of the family;

➢ transportation of the deceased to the place of final disposition in a common vehicle;

➢ preparation of the gravesite for the burial; and

➢ performing a suitable burial or graveside service.

The role of a funeral director in a home funeral may be limited to assisting a family in complying with legal requirements; or a much more extensive role providing direction, guidance, goods, and services. The depth of involvement is dependent on two factors: 1) the legal requirements in the community where death occurs; and, 2) the level of assistance a family may wish to have from a funeral service professional.

Legal considerations - As of this writing, there are nine states with regulations that require the assistance of a funeral director at some level: Alabama, Connecticut, Illinois, Indiana, Louisiana, Michigan, Nebraska, New Jersey, and New York. The extent of those regulations varies widely and may include such state-mandated funeral director duties and responsibilities as:

➢ removing human remains from the place of death;

➢ ensuring proper medical authorities certify as to the cause and manner of death;

➢ gathering information and data to complete and file death reports and certificates with applicable state agencies;

➢ supervision of funeral services where human remains are present;

➢ supervision of the interment of human remains when chosen for the final disposition;

➢ obtaining state permits to authorize a cremation disposition; and

➢ preparation of human remains for transportation, either domestically or internationally.

In addition to state laws specific to funeral directors that may influence the home funeral concept, there are other potential sources of regulatory compliance that may apply, including:

➢ counties, cities, towns, and villages may legislate ordinances or local laws to regulate funeral service related activities in residential homes;

➢ privately operated cemeteries and crematories may control activities on their premises and in their facilities by having written rules and regulations;

➢ family and private cemeteries may have requirements related to public health and safety, such as their proximity to clean water sources; and

➢ the FTC Funeral Rule, as it relates to what constitutes a funeral service provider and the legal ramifications if a provider is involved in any of the home funeral events.

Family requests - There are currently no states that prohibit a home funeral, as it is defined above, nor are there any states that prohibit having any other funeral types in a home, such as a humanistic or natural funeral. The distinctions between a *home funeral* and a *funeral in a home* do not present themselves as a bright line. Therefore, families may desire a home funeral but wish to include elements from other funeral types. The range of combinations is limitless and funeral directors must be prepared to provide guidance, direction, services, and goods when families make inquiries.

<u>Green (Natural) Burials</u>
A **green (natural) burial** is another new emerging funeral type. Alternatively called eco-friendly burials, they utilize products, services, and merchandise free of toxic and hazardous materials. **Green funerals** minimize the use of energy in service offerings, and goods must be biodegradable.

The fundamental aspects of a natural burial have existed for several years in the form of immediate burials, as introduced by the Federal Trade Commission when the funeral rule was adopted in 1984. An immediate burial is very similar to a natural burial; however, a true natural funeral includes all of these elements:

> ➢ interment of the remains in the earth;

> ➢ no embalming or other preservation that might inhibit decomposition;

> ➢ remains allowed to recycle back into the earth naturally;

> ➢ disposition of remains not preceded by cremation;

> ➢ eco-friendly and biodegradable materials, containers, and products;

> ➢ interment in protected or designated space, specific to natural dispositions;

> ➢ designated burial spaces dedicated to preserving the environment and nature; and

> ➢ utilization of natural grave markers, such as plants, trees, and rocks (no concrete).

The natural burial movement has progressed well beyond the basic immediate burial to the point where there are now several professional associations dedicated to educating the public and natural burial providers, as well as promoting the natural burial choice as an option for the disposition of human remains. These groups offer special support services and educational opportunities for funeral service providers.

Many of the services associated with traditional and cremation funerals are, in concept, compatible with a natural burial funeral, such as the transfer of remains, use of facilities, livery items, and supervision of related events. However, there may be a need to expand or scale back these same service offerings to complement the green burial experience. As an example, many funeral establishments serving the natural funeral community now offer a special livery item that provides for the movement of the decedent to a green burial space. This transportation may take such forms as a hand-pulled, decorative cart or wagon, thus maintaining the goal for all of the elements of the funeral service to be eco-friendly.

The preparation of the remains for a viewing is another area with alternative service opportunities. Topical disinfection, washing, grooming, dressing, and placement in a conveyance device or other container are a few of the preparation options available.

There are opportunities and, in many cases, necessities for funeral establishments that desire to offer a natural burial funeral. Consideration must be given to: burial containers, burial cemeteries, burial garments, and conveyance devices.

Burial containers - A consequence of the natural burial movement has been an uptick in the use of the word coffin in the American vernacular, as some manufacturers have taken to describing natural burial products as green coffins or e-coffins. This is perhaps a symbolic representation reflective of a return to colonial times when human remains were buried without preservation in six-sided, anthropoid shaped coffins. In fact, it could be argued colonial burials were the birth of the current movement, understanding of course the objectives consistent with a natural burial today are not the same objectives necessitating a timely burial in the 1700s.

This Simple Pine Box is made for natural burials. The pine is cut to provide for tongue and groove construction and uses no metal components. Not shown here is the interior, comprised of three cushions and a pillow stuffed with natural cotton.

Courtesy of Northwoods Casket Company, Beaver Dam, Wisconsin.[3]

Fully enclosed containers (caskets) for natural burials are manufactured using any number of different wood species and wood by-products. In addition, construction materials may include bamboo, banana leaves, seagrass, rattan, willow, and teak plants. All the components of these containers must of course meet the criteria for being environmentally friendly.

Burial cemeteries - A **green cemetery** is a place of interment that bans the use of metal caskets, toxic embalming, and concrete vaults. They may also limit monuments or markers to natural materials that complement and protect the environment and, in some cases, require natural markers of any kind be set flush to the ground. Natural green burial spaces and cemeteries are growing in popularity as the green burial movement has slowly but steadily advanced over the last two decades, as well as the fact more and more cemeteries have embraced this method of disposition as one deserving consideration.

Burial garments - Green burials require garments and clothing items that are consistent with the eco-friendly aspects of the service. In many cases, these are nothing more than a shroud, wrapping cloth, or similar garment or cloth in which human remains are wrapped or dressed for burial.

Shrouds have become very popular for these funeral services and several companies have found a niche in offering exquisite shrouds made of 100% cotton or other all-natural materials. Shrouds may also be personalized in a number of different ways, such as with the addition of flowers, photographs, memory notes, or art work.

Conveyance devices - Natural burial conveyances are designed to meet several purposes and needs, and may serve one function or several, including as a container to:

> ➤ position and display human remains for a viewing or funeral service;

> ➤ protect human remains when being moved to and from modes of transportation;

> ➤ provide a convenient method to convey remains to the gravesite with dignity and respect;

> ➤ facilitate the lowering of human remains into the grave; and

> ➤ serve as the final burial device in the earth.

These devices usually consist of a rigid or robust wooden base or tray. They may be called: body, shrouding, or trundle boards; burial platforms or trays; trundle coffins; or simply carriers.

This is a Burial Trundle Combo with a 100% organic cotton burial shroud and securing straps. The trundle is made of Wisconsin pine with an all-natural Tung oil finish. This combination unit is employed to both safeguard and transport human remains.

Courtesy of Northwoods Casket Company, Beaver Dam, Wisconsin.[3]

Regulatory considerations for green burials - The federal government has no regulations specific to natural green burials; however, there are several states that have adopted legislation to ensure protection of both the environment and the public health. Many laws focus on the physical location where burials will occur, taking into consideration any evidence of underground water supplies or the potential for any ground contamination. A funeral establishment intent on offering and conducting natural burials should consult with state and local officials to determine what requirements or restrictions, if any, apply in the communities they serve.

The transportation of a deceased person for a natural burial is another area of regulatory concern. Crossing state and municipal boundaries, as well as national borders, must be taken into consideration when transporting human remains that have not been embalmed. Unfortunately, the many differences from one state or one country to the next makes it all but impossible to compile, and include in this text, all the information needed to make an informed legal decision about transporting human remains that have not been embalmed. Therefore, once again, it is the responsibility of the funeral director to consult with the state and local government agencies they work with to ensure compliance.

Third-Party Merchandise

When the FTC Funeral Rule was implemented over 30-years ago, the issue of third-party caskets was not of much interest to the funeral establishments of that era. Today, with the proliferation of third-party casket vendors and fierce competition in selling caskets to an ever more cost-conscious and skeptical consumer, the issue is one of great interest to the funeral service industry. As a result, the FTC has issued several advisory opinion letters related to third-party caskets.

It should be noted a good share of the FTC opinion letters on third-party caskets center around one specific section of the Funeral Rule, that in part states:

In selling or offering to sell funeral goods or funeral services, it is an unfair or deceptive act or practice for a funeral provider to: condition the furnishing of any funeral good or funeral service to a person arranging a funeral upon the purchase of any other funeral good or funeral service...

The collective opinions expressed in the FTC advisory letters *prohibit* certain activities related to third-party caskets, including:

1. A funeral establishment may not refuse the delivery of a third-party casket. To do so would set a condition for the consumer whereby they would have to buy a casket from the funeral home if they want the funeral home to provide other services and merchandise.

2. A funeral establishment may not require a family's presence for the delivery of a third-party casket. This would place an unreasonable burden on a consumer's choice to purchase a casket from a third-party seller.

3. A funeral establishment may not refuse to sign for the merchandise or acknowledge delivery of a third-party casket.

4. A funeral establishment may not refuse to use third party merchandise until the consumer inspects it.

5. A funeral establishment may not charge any additional fees for handling a third-party casket. These prohibited charges include fees for: receiving the casket; disposing of the container or packaging in which it is shipped; storage when delivered in advance of time needed; inspection; and preparation for use.

6. A funeral establishment may not refuse the delivery of a third-party casket under any conditions applied *exclusively* to third-party casket retailers, including:

  ➤ a refusal to accept delivery: more than a specified number of days in advance of its use;

  ➤ less than a specified number of days in advance of its use;

  ➤ during regular business hours, except by prior appointment; and

  ➤ during regular business hours at a particular date and time, unless the funeral home is unable to accept caskets from *any supplier* at that date and time.

7. A funeral establishment may not withhold the use of standard equipment, such as a utility or church truck, to assist in bringing a casket into the funeral home at the time of delivery. Such equipment is part of a funeral establishment's overhead costs charged to and paid by consumers in the form of the non-declinable arrangements fee. It would be an unreasonable burden to deny consumers the benefit of the equipment for which they must pay simply because they have exercised their right to purchase a casket from a third party.

In reading the FTC advisory opinion letters it becomes abundantly clear third-party casket vendors must be treated *exactly* the same as a funeral establishment's regular wholesale casket vendors. Any special requirements or treatment in the delivery or handling of a third-party casket could subject a funeral establishment to potential enforcement action by the FTC based on the 'unreasonable burden' prohibition.

Chapter 8: Documentation

<u>Overview</u>

Funeral establishments create and maintain records to monitor and manage their businesses. Documentation may include papers common to all enterprises, such as insurance documents and bank statements. Other records will be unique to the management and operation of funeral establishments, such as maintaining individual death case files that contain multiple documents and records specific to that case. This chapter will review the importance of documentation in the funeral service industry.

<u>Chapter Definitions</u>

Due diligence - the attention reasonably expected from, and ordinarily exercised by, a person who seeks to satisfy a legal requirement or to discharge an obligation.

Malpractice - failure to perform a professional service with the ability and care generally exercised by others in the profession.

<u>Due Diligence</u>

In meeting the standards of due diligence in the funeral service industry, practitioners must be thoughtful, genuine, and determined in exercising fore-thought, good judgment, care, and prudence in providing funeral goods and services to families. This includes:

➤ Taking reasonable and prudent actions. The ordinary conduct of the practitioner must be such that no reasonable person would have an objection; find such conduct to be overbearing; or perceive the conduct to be anything less than satisfactory and acceptable under the circumstances.

➤ Following standards of care. Standard of care is that degree or level of care a reasonable person would exercise under similar circumstances. By its very nature, a funeral establishment business has an inherent duty to provide for the safeguarding, care, preparation, and final disposition of human remains. The level and quality of suitable care to be taken to perform these duties must be clearly defined by funeral service management and communicated to staff members charged with the duty to meet the standards of care.

➤ Maintaining job skill levels. Licensed staff members must maintain a high level of skill and ability to be able to carry out their duties proficiently and competently. The recognized need to maintain personal skills is underscored by the vast number of states that require annual continuing education on all aspects of funeral service.

➤ Practicing risk management. The importance of exercising risk management in the workplace is evident by the common practice of insurance companies requiring risk management programs in the organizations they insure. These programs identify exposures in the work environment and then require proactive steps be taken to diminish the potential for these known risks to cause any injury or loss. Initiating a risk management program can reduce the possibility of a costly lawsuit or legal claim against the establishment.

For example, a funeral establishment owner may identify 'slip and fall' incidents in the facility restrooms as a potential risk to those who visit the establishment. To manage this known risk, the owner could implement a policy that requires staff members to inspect all restrooms for any hazardous condition on a scheduled basis during those times when visitation or funerals are taking place. This policy would then need to be personally communicated to all staff members, with supervisors being held responsible for verifying compliance on a case-by-case basis.

Documenting Due Diligence

When performing duties and tasks that demonstrate and support due diligence efforts, it is important all related records and documentation associated with the actions and activities undertaken by staff members is properly maintained. While preserving documentation cannot prevent the filing of a claim, it may serve to mitigate (lessen) any damage awards when defending a civil claim in court.

Using our 'slip and fall' example, if a visitor were to fall on a wet floor in a restroom and injury themselves, it would be very beneficial to be able to submit documentation that supports the efforts taken by the funeral establishment to prevent such an incident. This may include the risk management plan; proof of implementation; proof of staff training; and records specific to the claim. The records may include a log of the restroom inspections performed by staff on the day of the incident, and many establishments require an 'incident report' be completed whenever any unusual activity takes place, such as a person suffering an injury inside the facility. These reports may also be used to demonstrate due diligence.

In-house documents and forms - Funeral establishment owners and operators should develop in-house documents and forms to further the efforts to support and demonstrate the exercise of due diligence, especially in having:

> ➤ written policies and procedures on all tasks and duties performed in the funeral establishment, such as the proper care and maintenance of the preparation room and safe methods to move human remains during a first call;

> ➤ checklists to guide staff on the required activities to complete a task, such as the proper methods to receive, prioritize, and set floral arrangements for calling hours ; and

> ➤ a record system to track human remains and cremated remains from the time of the first call to final disposition, including the use of tracking tags on the body and a log for making written entries on all changes in status.

The table that follows lists some of the documents and forms being used in funeral establishments today to demonstrate, promote, and provide a written record of due diligence practices. These include forms created by a funeral establishment specific to their operations, or others gathered by the establishment from outside sources, such as government applications and OSHA compliance standards.

Inventory of personal property	Written authorizations and releases	Vehicle maintenance records
Body tracking reports	Scheduled facility inspections	Applications for survivor benefits
Embalming case report	Cremation case tracking	Facility maintenance records
Custom merchandise orders	Third-party crematory inspections	Staff training records
Designation of intentions for disposal of cremated remains	Identification of person w/right to control final disposition	Statement of priority right to control the final disposition
Authorization to embalm	Positive ID of the decedent	Staff assignments
Case checklist and worksheet	New case intake worksheet	Arrangement conference guide
Request to witness cremation with indemnification clause	Request to divide or commingle cremated remains	OSHA hazard communication policy

Documentation for Laws, Rules, and Regulations

Federal - The FTC Funeral Rule is designed to afford certain protections and rights to consumers when they engage funeral service professionals in a business relationship. As such, it is important for funeral establishment to maintain any records that demonstrate compliance with the Rule, should the need arise. These may include:

> ➤ A record of the publication and effective dates for the general, casket, and outer burial container prices lists the Funeral Rule mandates, along with maintaining hard copies of the lists themselves.

> ➤ Copies of the mandatory *Statement of Funeral Goods and Services Selected* documents provided to consumers for each death case handled by the funeral establishment.

The copies of the price lists and statements provide written documentation of compliance with the Rule, and proof that the mandatory FTC disclosures and statements were on these documents in the proper form and location.

State and local - State and local administrative agencies also exercise considerable authority over the activities of funeral establishments. While each state is slightly different, many regulate these areas of funeral service practice:

> ➤ licensure and registration of funeral directors and funeral establishments;

> ➤ operation of preparation and embalming rooms;

> ➤ facility requirements, such as signage, seating capacity, and access for disabled persons;

> ➤ authorizations to perform certain tasks, such as a removal, an embalming, or a cremation;

> ➤ continuing education requirements; and

> ➤ regulation of price lists above and beyond FTC requirements.

Documentation and records that show proof of compliance with these regulations should be maintained and archived by the funeral establishment. These documents should also include copies of any records held by employees, such as government issued licenses and registrations, as well as certificates or credentials received to substantiate compliance with continuing education and training requirements.

Documentation for Financial Accountability

Death cases - Separate account ledgers should be maintained for each death case to record all financial transactions, and each transaction should have written support documentation, such as: invoices, receipts, statements, cancelled checks, or credit card slips. These records should be in sufficient detail to quickly resolve any issue that may arise concerning billing and payments. This brings a high degree of accountability to the business and provides a clear understanding between the parties of the financial commitments and responsibilities they each hold.

Tax purposes - All income and expenses should be carefully documented to provide the information and data needed to accurately prepare and file mandatory business tax filings. All records related to sales, property, school, corporate, business, or other tax assessments should be maintained in archival records based on government requirements.

Prepaid preneed accounts - The funds in these accounts, as will be described in later chapters, are often controlled by state business and financial laws that address the unique characteristics of these contractual agreements. A record should be maintained of all actions taken with respect to any funds received, including where and when they were initially deposited and an accounting for any funds added or withdrawn from the account.

Death Case Files

Each death case handled by a funeral establishment should have a separate case file that contains all documentation related to that specific case. Each file should have a unique case identification number for easy identification and retrieval as needed. Some states have legislated requirements to maintain death case files, as well as specify the documents and records they must contain. The laws also grant government inspectors the authority to review these files to verify regulatory compliance or conduct an investigation into any consumer complaints.

At a minimum and when available, a death case file should include copies of these records:

➢ record of transfer (removal) of human remains, including staff assignments;

➢ embalming reports, including the signature of an authorized embalmer;

➢ arrangement conference checklist or worksheet to document FTC required lists were distributed for retention or review as required;

➢ written statement of the person asserting the priority right to control a final disposition;

➢ FTC Statement of Funeral Goods and Services Selected;

- ➤ final funeral bill with any estimates or other adjustments reconciled;

- ➤ military service discharge papers, as well as all records relative to military service benefits and programs for which the funeral establishment assisted the consumer in obtaining, such as the VA Before You Call Checklist or an Application for Presidential Memorial Certificates;

- ➤ documentation to support cash advance payments and reconciliations in the amounts specified on the itemized statement;

- ➤ a designation of intentions with respect to cremated remains, signed by both the person making such designation and a funeral service professional;

- ➤ receipts for the transfer of remains to another entity or individual for safeguarding;

- ➤ death reports, certificates, and transcripts, as well as burial or cremation authorizations and permits;

- ➤ death notices, short notices, and obituaries;

- ➤ insurance policies and records related to any assignment of proceeds;

- ➤ the SSA Statement of Death by Funeral Director form; and

- ➤ preneed agreement documentation, including reconciliation of the account.

Professional Liability
Any failure to perform a professional service with the ability and care generally exercised by others in the profession is the definition of **malpractice**. It may also be known as professional negligence.

Malpractice claims typically are founded on allegations of negligence or incompetence on the part of professionals in the medical, legal, and financial communities, although other professions may also be subject to this level of scrutiny depending on the requirements of the employment position they hold. As there is no standard definition of a professional or a professional occupation, the question of who may be the subject of a malpractice claim is open to interpretation by the courts.

West's Encyclopedia of American Law provides the following definition and description of malpractice:

> [Malpractice is] *the breach by the member of a profession of either a standard of care or a standard of conduct. The failure to meet a standard of care or standard of conduct that reaches a level of malpractice when a client or patient is injured or damaged because of error.*

There are civil court cases in which a funeral service practitioner has been sued for malpractice and the court recognized the professional nature of the occupation. To defend against these claims requires the same level of adherence to exercising and documenting due diligence as has been described in this chapter.

<u>Archives</u>

The FTC requires records related to the Funeral Rule must be maintained for one year. These maintenance time frames are called record retentions, and state governments have developed record retention schedules for every conceivable document or other recording medium subject to government oversight. Some of these records, such as an original death certificate, may be classified as permanent, meaning they can never be destroyed. Others specify a time period after which they may be destroyed.

Funeral directors and establishment owners must first determine what state or local retention schedules exist for the communities they serve. A written policy should then be developed and distributed to all staff members to provide guidance and direction on which records must be maintained and for how long. The intention is to ensure none are destroyed prematurely in violation of federal, state, or local law.

With a few notable exceptions, such as fetal death case records in certain states, there is nothing to prohibit a funeral establishment from maintaining case records and documentation beyond the government mandated retention periods. Many funeral establishments retain records for decades, as they provide valuable information for future generations in:

➢ writing death notices and newspaper obituaries;

➢ identifying family burial plots and grave site locations;

➢ describing previous goods and services selected; and

➢ notations on any special events or activities a family historically requests.

Note: The one-year *federal* retention period for Funeral Rule price lists is an unusually short period of time, with the majority of *state* rules and regulations requiring records of funeral service transactions, including copies of FTC price lists and other documentation, be retained for much longer periods.

Chapter 9: Prefunded Preneeds

Overview
Previous chapters focused on elements of funeral service as they relate to **at-need cases**, those in which a death has already occurred. This chapter and the one that follows review **preneed cases**, those in which funeral plans are made for a death that has not yet occurred.

Chapter Definitions
At-need cases - when a death has occurred.

Beneficiary - means the named individual for whom a preneed agreement is purchased. The beneficiary may also be the purchaser [by Author].

Contract - a legally enforceable agreement.

Guaranteed contract - an agreement where the funeral establishment promises that the services and merchandise will be provided at the time of need for a sum not exceeding the original amount of the contract plus any accruals, regardless of the current prices associated with providing the services and merchandise at the time of the funeral.

Irrevocable contract - an agreement for future funeral services which cannot be terminated or canceled prior to the death of the beneficiary.

Non-guaranteed contract - agreement in which the funeral establishment promises to apply the amount pre-paid plus any accruals to the balance due. However, the cost of the funeral will be based upon the current price for services and merchandise at the time death occurs.

Prefunded funeral arrangements - funeral arrangements made in advance of need that include provisions for funding or prepayment.

Preneed cases - cases where funeral arrangements are made prior to a death occurring, in preparation for use in the future [by Author].

Preplanned funeral arrangements - funeral arrangements made in advance of need that do not include provisions for funding or prepayment.

Purchaser - means the named individual paying for and purchasing a preneed account. The purchaser may also be the beneficiary [by Author].

Revocable contract - agreement which may be terminated by the purchaser at any time prior to the death of the beneficiary with a refund of monies paid on the contract as prescribed by state law.

Consumer Awareness
In 2017, the National Funeral Directors Association (NFDA) issued a press release relative to the NFDA 2017 Consumer Awareness and Preferences Study. In the study, they found:

... consumers acknowledge the importance of preplanning their own funeral, but fail to do so in practice. This year's findings reveal that 62.5 percent of consumers felt it was very important to communicate their funeral plans and wishes to family members prior to their own death, yet only 21.4 percent had done so.

This is a puzzling statistic, as the benefits and advantages to having a preneed have been the source of numerous positive articles, reviews, and endorsements in national media outlets. In addition, consumers that have chosen to preplan a funeral have almost universally expressed satisfaction and gratitude.

In addressing this anomaly, the NFDA went on to report:

Even though nearly two-thirds of Americans acknowledge the importance of prearrangements, respondents cited several factors as preventing them from planning, namely that preplanning is not a priority, that they have not thought about it, or that prepaying is too costly.

Types of Preneeds
Funeral arrangements made in advance of need are called preneeds. A true preneed is one in which a consumer has met with a funeral service professional and made funeral arrangements, including selection of the goods and services they wish to have provided at the time of their passing. Preneeds should not be confused with other pre-death care options, such as final expense insurance policies, savings accounts for funerals, or life insurance policies. These options plan for having the funds available to cover the costs of a funeral service but do not specify or provide details about exactly what goods and services are going to be included.

There are two types of preneeds and both include: meeting with a funeral director, making arrangements, planning funeral events, selecting goods and services, and gathering pertinent information and documentation. The singular difference between the two types is whether or not the preneed is simply a **pre-planned funeral arrangement**, or **pre-planned *and prefunded* funeral arrangement**.

Note: The terminology used to describe and define types of preneeds (such as preplanned, prepaid, advance need, and prefunded) are not universally recognized by all of the allied professionals in the funeral service industry. They are also not consistent in the various state laws, rules, and regulations found in the 50 states. For these reasons, readers should familiarize themselves with terms used in the states and communities they serve; however, official definitions for the purpose of taking the national board examination may be found in chapter definitions or the glossary.

Reasons for Preneeds
Financial considerations - By having a funeral preplan, an individual also has the opportunity to take responsibility for paying the associated expenses in advance of need. This gives them time to make financial arrangements and thereby relieve the burden on survivors to do so at the time of death. Other financial benefits may include prepaid discounts and guaranteed pricing, as well as reducing assets for any future Medicaid eligibility applications or awards.

Consumer control - A preneed allows the consumer to provide detailed instructions on various aspects of a funeral service, as well as stipulate the purchase of specific goods and services, including:

- ➢ the method of final disposition, e.g., burial, cremation, natural, etc.;

- ➢ a preferred burial location, cemetery plot, or grave;

- ➢ the choice of a burial container, e.g., casket, urn, e-coffin, etc.;

- ➢ whether or not to have certain events, such as calling hours and/or a funeral;

- ➢ the preference for an open or closed casket at any funeral service event;

- ➢ if, when, and where to hold a funeral or memorial service; and

- ➢ information to include in a death notice or obituary.

Decision making - By documenting and memorializing death care decisions in advance of need, the family of a decedent is relieved of making difficult and emotional decisions at a time when grief and loss are a burden on their ability to cope and reason. These decisions may also eliminate or resolve conflicts between family members attempting to reconcile service-related issues at the time of arrangements.

End of life affairs - Putting end of life affairs in order before death is a thoughtful, considerate, and caring decision, and making arrangements in advance of need offers individuals the opportunity to take the time they require to make thoughtful and informed decisions. In contrast, making plans at the time of death is hindered by time constraints and the burden of making decisions while subject to emotional stress and anxiety. In addition, the individual making preneed arrangements for their own funeral is comforted by knowing they took the initiative to ease the grief and sorrow of their family by eliminating the need to make difficult decisions under trying circumstances. This is especially true for prefunded preneed arrangements.

Types of Preneed Contracts

Contracts - Preneed funeral arrangements conclude with an agreement between the parties involved. The funeral director agrees to provide certain goods and services to the consumer and, in return, will receive a financial payment from the consumer. A **contract** is a legally enforceable agreement and the generally accepted means to establish a legally binding and express promise to pay for a preneed. In some states, funeral establishments include contractual language on the FTC Statement of Funeral Goods and Services Selected; in other states the agreement is a stand-alone document. Regardless of the form the agreement takes, they are contracts – a term that has legal connotations and implications that bind the parties to the terms.

Express contracts - Express contracts are those in which the parties have clearly and plainly set out and agreed to the terms of the agreement. Each service or item of the contract is specifically described and stated, and the purchaser offers an express promise to pay when they sign the agreement. Both at-need contracts and prefunded funeral agreements are express contracts that itemize the intangible services and tangible goods funeral directors agree to provide in exchange for compensation (payment).

Types - There are four basic types of preneed contracts: revocable, irrevocable, guaranteed, and non-guaranteed. However, there may be hybrid contracts made up of more than one of these four basic types, such as a *revocable non-guaranteed contract* or an *irrevocable guaranteed contract*. Our discussion here will review the four types as pairs: revocable or irrevocable; and guaranteed or non-guaranteed.

Revocable or irrevocable contracts - A **revocable contract** agreement may be terminated by the **purchaser** at any time prior to the death of the **beneficiary**, with a refund of monies paid on the contract as prescribed by state law. The majority of states require the refund to also include the interest earned on any trust or other preneed account type.

An **irrevocable contract** is an agreement for future funeral services which cannot be terminated or canceled prior to the death of the beneficiary. When the beneficiary of a prefunded preneed is seeking government benefits, such as Medicaid or Supplemental Security Income (SSI), states usually mandate a preneed contract be irrevocable.

Guaranteed or non-guaranteed contracts - A **guaranteed contract** is an agreement where the funeral establishment promises the services and merchandise will be provided at the time of need for a sum not exceeding the original amount paid on the contract, plus any accruals, and regardless of the current prices associated with providing the services and merchandise at the time of need. These contracts may be guaranteed for a specified length of time and, in some states, may be extended for five- or ten-year increments for an additional fee.

A **non-guaranteed contract** is an agreement in which the funeral establishment promises to apply the amount pre-paid plus any accruals to the balance due. However, the cost of the funeral will be based on the current price for services and merchandise at the time of need.

Note: If a funeral establishment decides to offer guaranteed pricing for a prefunded preneed, the common practice is to guarantee the funeral establishment charges but not the cash advance charges. The reason for this is a funeral establishment has no control over what cash advance expenses from a third-party vendor will be in the future, as it does for their own funeral establishment charges in the future.

The laws applicable to preneed contracts are enacted by state governments – not the federal government. Funeral directors must therefore be familiar with the laws in the state or states where they engage in funeral directing activities when dealing with prefunded preneeds.

Chapter 10: Preneed Arrangement Conferences

Overview
This chapter will conclude the discussion on preneeds by reviewing the preneed arrangement conference; identifying types of changes and alterations that may influence a preneed agreement; highlighting legal considerations; and exploring the various types of funding available for prefunded preneeds.

Chapter Definitions
Beneficiary - means the named individual for whom a preneed agreement is purchased. The beneficiary may also be the purchaser [by Author].

Prefunded funeral arrangements - funeral arrangements made in advance of need that include provisions for funding or prepayment.

Purchaser - means the named individual paying for and purchasing a preneed account. The purchaser may also be the beneficiary [by Author].

Third party contracts - agreements which involve the funeral practitioner/funeral establishment because the family being served has contracted with someone else (a third party) for services or merchandise also available from the funeral establishment i.e. caskets, vaults, urns, preneed insurance, etc.

Trust account - account established by one individual to be held for the benefit of another (as a method of payment of funeral expenses); creates a fiduciary responsibility. Money paid to a funeral establishment for future services is placed in an account with the funeral establishment as trustee for the benefit of another.

Preneed Arrangement Conferences
The majority of consumers meeting to discuss preneeds with a funeral service professional want to both preplan and prefund funeral arrangements. In these cases, the funeral director agrees to provide certain goods and services, and the **purchaser** agrees to pay for those goods and services in advance for the **beneficiary**. The agreement is then documented in a legally binding contract and signed by both parties.

On occasion, there are consumers that wish to discuss or make funeral plans but not pay in advance for those goods and services. In these cases, the funeral director provides the consumer a written summary with estimated prices but does not prepare a contract or other legally binding agreement requiring either party to commit to the contents of the summary. A copy is provided to the consumer and another copy maintained in the funeral establishment files to be used as a guide during any future at-need conference.

The FTC and Preneeds
Generally - FTC Funeral Rule requirements apply to all preneeds (prepaid or not) and at-need funeral arrangements. The FTC guide states:

In preneed situations, you must comply with all Rule requirements at the time funeral arrangements are pre-planned. You also need to comply with the Rule after the death of the individual who made preneed arrangements. If the survivors inquire about goods or services, alter the pre-planned arrangements, or are required to pay additional sums of money, you must give them all relevant disclosures and price lists.

For example, survivors may be asked to pay additional amounts if the pre-paid plan does not guarantee prices at the time of death. In other cases, survivors may change arrangements specified in the preneed plan, adding or subtracting certain goods or services. In both situations, the requirements of the Rule apply. You must give the survivors relevant price lists, as well as an itemized Statement of Funeral Goods and Services Selected.

The Funeral Rule does not apply to any preneed agreements or contracts that were executed before the rule went into effect in 1984. However, if a pre-1984 preneed is amended or changed for any reason, the changes automatically trigger and require full compliance with all of the rule requirements as they exist at the time.

Conference location - A conference to purchase **prefunded funeral arrangements** may be held in a funeral establishment, private residence, or any other suitable location. However, if the preneed arrangement conference is going to take place at any location other than the funeral establishment, funeral directors should ensure compliance with the federal Cooling-off Rule that regulates door-to-door and other similar sales This rule provides a seller must give written notice to a consumer of the right to cancel a contract for goods and services within a set number of days. The rule is triggered when the seller (funeral director) personally solicits and makes the sale at a place other than their place of business, such as the purchaser's home.

There are various exceptions, waivers, and conditions that may require or, in some cases, negate the need to provide such written notice, but funeral directors should determine what action they must take to comply with the rule on a case-by-case basis. In addition, several states have enacted similar rules to protect consumers when funeral arrangements are made in a location other than the business location of the seller.

General Price List - A copy of the current funeral establishment General Price List (GPL) must be given to a consumer when discussing the type of funerals or dispositions the establishment can provide; the specific goods and services they offer; or the prices of their goods and services. All three of these items will be part of the conversation during a preneed arrangement conference, and the funeral director must ensure the consumer promptly receives a copy of the GPL. It must contain all of the FTC mandatory disclosures, as well as any state or local statements. Certain states may also require additional disclosures or statements related specifically to a contract for preneed arrangements.

The Funeral Rule allows for a funeral establishment to have a different GPL for preneed arrangements if they sell different goods and services on a preneed basis. However, a preneed

GPL must include all of the same required disclosures and offer all goods and services on an itemized basis. It is not permissible to offer only package funerals to preneed customers.

Other price lists - In addition to the GPL, a funeral director should be prepared to provide a Casket Price List and/or Outer Burial Container Price List, if these items are going to be purchased. These must be given to the consumer *before* they enter a selection room and see prices on individual products or are orally given any pricing information by the funeral director.

Embalming - Consumers must be given written notice the law does not usually require embalming. Written notice is accomplished when the consumer receives a copy of the GPL which, by FTC mandate, must have the disclosure in immediate conjunction with the price for embalming. The FTC requirement to have prior permission for embalming applies equally to preneed cases.

Required statement - The requirement to give the consumer a Statement of Funeral Goods and Services Selected (Statement) at the close of the arrangement conference applies equally to both at-need and preneed cases. The Statement must contain the Funeral Rule mandated disclosures relating to legal requirements, embalming, and cash advance items.

*Non-declinable fee*s - Consumers making preneed arrangements should be made aware of the one non-declinable fee on a GPL. This charge, to pay for basic services and overhead, is added to the total cost of the funeral arrangements the family selects. The Basic Services section on a GPL also has an FTC mandatory disclosure.

Cash advances - The FTC Funeral Rule does not require any specific prefunded goods or services be listed as a cash advance, nor does it prohibit a funeral establishment from making a profit on a cash advance purchase. However, individual states have passed a plethora of legislative initiatives to regulate how cash advances are handled. Some have requirements mandating certain named items be offered *only* as cash advances, such as a crematory fee and purchasing certified copies of death certificates. Other states totally prohibit funeral establishments from making any profit whatsoever on cash advances. Practitioners are therefore advised to research all state and local laws with respect to cash advance funeral charges before developing and distributing a GPL or offering guaranteed prefunded preneeds.

Note: The author has not reviewed the FTC Funeral Rule here in great detail as it goes beyond the scope of this book. The topic is explored extensively in college textbooks adopted for use in funeral service law courses all across the nation. One such textbook is *Funeral Service Law in the United States: A Guide for Funeral Service Students*. Additional information on this book may be found in the Sources Consulted listing in the back of this book.

Changes to Prefunded Preneeds

As noted earlier, a prefunded preneed is a legally binding contract between the parties. As such, it must adhere to contemporary standards and practices in business law and may be subject to judicial review if any component of the contract calls into question its validity. This also applies to any changes or alterations made to a preneed contract after its execution by the parties involved.

Void or voidable - Contracts, including those for a prefunded preneed, may be void or voidable. Kristy DeSmith, in a June 2015 online posting, explains these two contract terms as follows:

> *When a contract is void, it is not valid. It can never be enforced under state or federal laws. A void contract is null from the moment it was created and neither party is bound by the terms. Think of it as one that a court would never recognize or enforce because there are missing elements.*
>
> *A contract can be void for the following reasons:*
> - *The terms of the agreement are illegal or against public policy (unlawful consideration or object).*
> - *A party was not of sound mind while signing the agreement.*
> - *A party was under the age of consent.*
> - *The terms are impossible.*
> - *The contract restricts the rights of a party.*
>
> *Alternatively, a voidable contract is valid and may be enforceable in certain situations if both parties agree to move forward. One party is bound to the terms of the contract, whereas the other party can oppose the contract for legal reasons if they so choose. Therefore, if the unbound party rejects the contract, it becomes voidable.*
>
> *A contract can become voidable under the following circumstances:*
> - *A party was coerced or threatened into signing the agreement.*
> - *A party was under undue influence (one party is able to dominate the will of another).*
> - *A party is not of sound mind or mentally competent (minor or mentally ill).*
> - *The terms of the contract were breached.*
> - *Mutual mistakes on behalf of both parties.*
> - *The contract is fraudulent (omitting or falsifying facts or information, or the intention to not carry out the promise in the contract).*
> - *Misrepresentation occurs (a false statement of fact).*

Changes - One change that could affect a contract is the unavailability of certain goods and services at the time of need. For this issue, most states require language be included in a prefunded preneed contract that require a funeral establishment substitute items of 'equal or greater value' for those originally selected and no longer available – at no additional cost to the consumer.

Reconciliation - State laws usually specify how to reconcile the account at the time of need when the cost of the goods and services exceeds the amount of the monies paid or, conversely, when the amount of monies paid exceeds the cost of the goods and services. As these statements are a part of the contract, changes will not generally render a contract invalid.

Non-guaranteed - In the case of non-guaranteed preneeds, changes in the goods and services selected may result in a change to the total price. Both the purchaser and the funeral director would need to formalize the changes, but the contract would not necessarily be void or voidable simply because of the alterations.

Guaranteed - In the case of a guaranteed preneed, changes in the goods and services the purchaser wishes to have for a funeral will not affect the contract if the parties are in agreement. A funeral director must however be diligent in minimizing any additional financial risk as a result of the change. For example, if a purchaser wanted to change from a basic wooden casket to a more expensive bronze casket, the funeral director could accept the change and new price, but refuse to guarantee the price if they thought the risk of a substantial change in future metal prices was unacceptable. The contract would then have to be re-negotiated, including whether or not it is will be guaranteed.

The duration of any guaranteed pricing may or may not be limited. If limited, extensions may be available for an additional fee. Any changes to the terms of the guarantee would again require the mutual agreement of the parties involved.

Other Legal Considerations

Third-party contracts - By the very nature of a preneed contract, one party agrees to provide certain goods and services, while the second party provides some form of consideration (usually financial) for providing those goods and services. If the purchaser and beneficiary in a preneed contract are *not* the same person, the agreement may be called a **third-party beneficiary contract**, with the three parties being: 1) the purchaser, 2) the funeral establishment; and 3) the beneficiary However, in most contractual relationships, only the parties signing the contract can mutually make changes and alterations.

Other - In addition to the preneed contract itself, there may be laws or other documentation that could impose legal obligations on the parties at the time of death, especially when the purchaser of a preneed is not the beneficiary. These include:

> ➤ Last will and testament records. These may contain specific instructions from the decedent on what they want for funeral goods and services following their death. In some states, these instructions may be deemed reflective of the decedent's intent, while in others absolute.

> ➤ State or local laws. Statutes may include a listing of persons legally holding a priority right to control the final disposition of human remains. These laws may then grant the person holding the priority right to control the disposition the authority to change the terms of a preneed contract, even when such person is not a party to the preneed.

> ➤ Designated agents. Some states provide a mechanism for an individual to designate an agent to have control over the final disposition of their remains. These are usually in the

form of a legally binding designation or declaration and, in most cases, a person so designated will hold the highest priority position in those states with priority right laws.

There are clearly a number of variables that may impact a preneed contract at the time of need, all of which are usually specific to a state or geographic location. Funeral directors must therefore be diligent in maintaining a current understanding of the laws and regulations related to preneeds in the communities they serve.

Preneed Funding Mechanisms
State laws usually require funds paid to a funeral establishment to purchase a prefunded preneed be deposited in a recognized financial institution. Generally speaking, the funds may only be withdrawn as a consumer refund or to pay for the pre-arranged funeral following death. Once again, state laws concerning these accounts vary significantly, and the control they exercise over the account types and handling of preneed funds are often detailed and complex.

Trust accounts - A funeral director receiving funds for a prefunded preneed account may be legally required to deposit them into an interest-bearing **trust account**, defined as an account established by one individual to be held for the benefit of another. The funds are held in the trust to pay for future funeral goods and services. Some states require each preneed have their own trust account, while others may allow for the funds to be commingled in one master trust account.

Insurance policies - Another option to fund a preneed is the purchase of insurance specifically to provide for the payment of funeral expenses at the time of death. These policies may list a funeral establishment or funeral director as the beneficiary to receive the proceeds and require they be used to pay for funerals – preplanned or otherwise. However, some states prohibit funeral directors or funeral establishments from being named as a beneficiary on an insurance policy to pay for either a prefunded or at-need funeral.

Financial institutions - Individuals may open a savings or passbook account, purchase a certificate of deposit, or open other similar bank accounts with a financial institution for the deposit of funds to pay for a preneed. Depending on individual state regulations, these could be joint accounts naming the funeral establishment or funeral director as one of the account holders, thereby allowing access to the funds under 'right of survivorship' rules at the time of death.

Preneed entrepreneurs - There are private businesses whose sole focus is on the administration of preneed funds for funeral establishments. They may be operated as a subsidiary to an existing company or operate as an independent service organization. State funeral director associations are one of the groups that has begun to take advantage of this concept and many have formed subsidiary organizations that offer to administer preneed funds.

Chapter 11: Preparing for Funeral Events

Overview

This chapter is the first of three that review the organization, preparation, and execution of funeral events chosen by a family for inclusion in a funeral service. These three activities are collectively known as funeral directing, with the emphasis on directing. Funeral directors do not participate in a funeral service, they direct the funeral service and provide leadership to others, often at a time when people need considerable guidance and support.

Chapter Definitions

Calling hours - (visitation, visiting hours) - time set aside for friends and relatives to pay respect for the deceased prior to the funeral service.

Celebrant funeral - a funeral service not focused on any specific religion, belief, faith, or rite; officiant by a trained and qualified, non-clergy official [by Author].

Cemetery - an area of ground set aside and dedicated for the final disposition of dead human remains.

Cemetery tent - a portable shelter employed to cover the grave area during the committal.

Church truck - a wheeled collapsible support for the casket used in the funeral home, church, or home.

Crematory - a furnace or retort for cremating dead human bodies; a building that houses a retort.

Fraternal - relating to a social organization.

Gratuity - gift or small sum of money tendered (tip) for a service provided.

Kneeler - (prayer rail, prie dieu) - a small bench placed in front of the casket or urn to allow a person to kneel for prayer.

Memorial book (register book) - a book signed by those attending a visitation or service.

Prayer card - a card with the name of the decedent and a prayer or verse, which may or may not include the dates of birth and death.

Lead Director Concept

Most funeral establishments subscribe to the concept of having one funeral service professional designated to serve as the lead director for each death case. This individual is then tasked with directing and coordinating all other staff assigned to participate or contribute to the events that make up the funeral service. For this concept to be effective, funeral establishment owners must delegate the proper authority to the designated funeral director, and thereafter support the decisions and actions they make in directing other staff members.

The advantages and benefits to having a lead director include:

➢ providing a single named source to whom all subordinate staff and assisting directors may turn for direction and clarification;

➢ providing a single named source to whom the immediate family may address any inquires or concerns;

➢ ensuring a clear understanding of who makes the final decision when individuals of equal or higher standing are organizing, preparing, and executing funeral events;

➢ ensuring accountability by having written guidelines in place that outline the duties and responsibilities of a lead director;

➢ identifying the person who will be responsible for ensuring all parts of the funeral service are fulfilled according to the terms of the funeral contract; and

➢ eliminating duplicity, confusion, and errors that occur when subordinates answer to more than one supervisor, often with conflicting instructions and orders.

Lead director primary duty - While the lead director oversees all aspects related to a death case, most funeral establishments make it clear they expect them to focus their attention on caring for, responding to, and communicating with the immediate family. Many survivors are not familiar with funeral service protocols and procedures, and the presence of the same familiar face is reassuring, comforting, and respectful.

It must be remembered, the funeral establishment is working for and being paid by the family, not the decedent; and it is the family that needs support, guidance,

Left - *Two* funeral directors and 10 assistants working a funeral.
Right - *One* funeral director and 10 assistants working a funeral.

and direction, not the decedent. As an example, the lead director should be escorting the *family* into church; subordinate staff should be escorting the *casket* into church.

Additional directors - If a second funeral director is going to work a funeral event, most establishments have a policy that identifies their primary duty as the safe movement and transport of the remains from one event location to the next, such as from the funeral home to the church to the cemetery. If more than one director is going to work a funeral, it is highly recommended the lead director concept be in place to avoid any confusion, conflict, or unintentional error.

<u>Worksheets and Checklists</u>
Case worksheet - Every death case should have a master worksheet enumerating the actions and activities that need to take place to prepare for a funeral, as well as record when they have been completed. These provide a single-source location for staff members to review assigned tasks and a quick-reference snapshot of the progress being made as work proceeds. There should be only one master list, kept in a specific central location or available online where all staff members regularly update the list on their progress.

Note: See Form 11 to view a Case Checklist and Worksheet.

Staff assignments - The lead director should prepare staff assignments with respect to carrying out the visitation and **calling hours**; funeral or memorial service; interment or other disposition; and any other planned events, such as an after-service gathering.

Note: See Form 12 to view a Staff Assignments form.

<u>Coordination with Staff, Allied Professionals, and Others</u>
Staff - Once the family of a decedent has selected the events they wish to include in a funeral service, the lead funeral director determines the tasks that must be completed to carry out the events individually and the funeral service as a whole. They also delegate staff members to carry out those tasks and coordinate activities while providing general supervision.

The average number of tasks to be completed for a traditional burial funeral is estimated to be between 55 and 60. This may include such assignments as: embalming, cosmetics, dressing and casketing, filing a death certificate, obtaining a burial permit, ordering merchandise, setting up a chapel or reposing room, submitting newspaper notices, printing prayer cards, and contacting allied professionals to coordinate their participation.

Allied professionals - The individuals, organizations, and entities that interact with funeral directors are collectively referred to as allied professionals, i.e., those associated in some way with providing either funeral goods or funeral services. All individuals and locations hosting or taking part in one or more of the events for a funeral service must be contacted to coordinate activities.

These allied professionals may include:

➢ A clergy or officiant - The funeral director will need to work closely with clergy and officiants when events are being held in a place of worship. In these cases, the clergy exercises significant control over the activities that take place, and funeral directors must be prepared to perform tasks in harmony with clergy requirements.

➢ Venue officials - When venues other than a funeral establishment are being used to host a funeral event, the funeral director needs to coordinate with the appropriate officials. This may include such locations as: an auditorium, government building, high school, outdoor theater, convention center, state park, or other suitable location.

- Final disposition officials - **Cemetery** superintendents, **crematory** operators, mausoleum managers, and other similar officials are another group of allied professionals a funeral director must coordinate with when planning an interment, inurnment, or other disposition of human remains. Coordinating with them ensures compliance with legal mandates related to the final disposition of human remains, as well as any facility rules and regulations.

- Military officials - If the family wishes to have an armed forces honor guard or other military type ceremony for a deceased veteran, the funeral director must reach out to the officials of the appropriate branch of the armed services and make a formal request.

- Fraternal leaders - The word **fraternal** comes from the Latin word 'frater,' meaning brother. Fraternal organizations are social brotherhoods or clubs where individual members associate together for the mutual benefit of all the members. They most often have social, professional, or academic principles and goals. When a decedent was a member of a fraternal organization, the group may wish to play a role in a funeral event, such as offering a brief service or ceremony during calling hours. These groups include such well-known organizations as the Benevolent Order of Elks, Freemasons, Independent Order of Odd Fellows, Lions Club International, Knights of Columbus, and Veterans of Foreign Wars – to name just a few.

- Speakers - As discussed in previous chapters, the increased number of home, natural, and **celebrant funerals** has brought a new dimension to funeral ceremonies and a frequent call for non-clergy speakers. These may include friends or relatives of the decedent, or trained and qualified celebrants whose presentations do not focus on any specific religion, belief, faith, or rite. Regardless of who speaks, the funeral director will need to coordinate with them before the service.

- Musicians - Singers and musicians not directly affiliated with or employed by a venue may be asked to participate in a funeral service. The funeral director must coordinate with these groups on such matters as where they will be seated or located; when they will be expected to participate; and what support they may need, such as a power source or PA system.

- Hairstylists - Grooming and hairstyling are essential components to the preparation of human remains for viewing, especially when it comes to styles, cuts, and hairdos for female decedents. A family may request a personal hairstylist or barber provide these services rather than funeral establishment staff. Any use of outside services to supplement the work being performed in-house must be coordinated to ensure sufficient time is allotted for embalming, cosmetics, dressing, casketing, and setup for funeral events.

Others - Funeral directors must also be in contact with family members, close friends, and associates when they are going to actively participant in a funeral service event in such roles as speakers, pallbearers, drivers, ushers, etc. Coordinating, organizing, and choreographing the activities of all the participants in a funeral is the only way to ensure a smooth, dignified, and respectful service.

Providing Goods and Preparing Service Items

Steps must be taken to provide the tangible goods a consumer selects at the time of arrangements. Items that are not in-stock or require customization or personalization should be the first priority to ensure there is no delay that would necessitate changing dates and times for services already published online and in newspaper obituaries. Many funeral establishments list merchandise purchases on the case checklist and worksheet to reduce the potential for mistakes and errors and establish a level of accountability.

Ordering items - Recent trends and consumer demands in the funeral service industry have increased the number of requests for goods that include personalization and customization. In addition, the escalating number of routine options available, such as casket colors and interior fabric styles, has further complicated the ordering process. Therefore, when ordering from funeral service suppliers, the best practice in the industry is to follow these five steps:

Step 1: Prepare the order in writing. The order should include a full description of the item being ordered; detailed instructions for any personalization or customization; name and address of the funeral establishment; funeral director contact information; and the deadline requirements for delivery.

Step 2: Submit the order electronically through the supplier. Most suppliers now have online programs that provide for the electronic submission of orders. For those that do not, the most expeditious ways to submit an order are by facsimile or scanned attachments to an email.

Step 3: Confirm the order was received. Call the supplier to confirm the order was received, and the instructions were clear and workable in the time frame specified. Be sure to get the name, title, and phone number of the company representative who provided the confirmation, and enter this information on the written order for future reference.

Step 4: Complete case worksheet entry. Make a notation on the case checklist and worksheet that the item has been ordered to let others know the task has been completed, and place the order documentation in the case file.

Step 5: Set a reminder. Record the deadline for delivery and set a reminder to verify the item has been received by the deadline previously recorded on the written order.

The steps above may not always be carried out in the exact order shown, but the concept of having the transaction in writing and independently confirmed by the supplier will ensure the merchandise the consumer ordered will be available when needed.

In addition, if a mistake is discovered at the time of delivery, the step-by-step process will quickly and positively identify where the error occurred. As an example, if there is a spelling error on an urn plaque, the documentation will enable all parties to determine if the mistake was on the part of the funeral establishment or the merchandise supplier.

Personalized or customized items - These may include such items as: monograming on a casket overthrow, engraving on an urn, **prayer cards** with a personal message, or video presentations with family photos. Careful attention to detail must be given to these items when submitting orders, as most companies will not refund or replace items when an error, such as a spelling or date mistake made by the funeral establishment, is discovered at the time of delivery. In those cases where they will provide a replacement item, it may be too late to get it delivered in time for the funeral event.

In-house items - Merchandise in-stock at a funeral establishment facility should be pulled from the inventory and thoroughly inspected to ensure there is no evident damage or other reason it cannot be used. In addition, any personalization of an item, such as engraving a plaque, should be completed well in advance of when needed to allow for any unforeseen delays.

Themed funerals - Themed funeral events have become very popular with millennials, offering the means to style a funeral service to represent the individual. Having ready-to-go alternative themes also affords greater flexibility in ensuring each funeral service experience is special and unique. Preparing a themed funeral event is a service that requires attention to details unique to the case being handled at the time. In addition, time must be allotted to allow for the setup of the various matching components and personalized items.

Food and beverage services - When food and beverage services are selected for a funeral service event, the funeral establishment must be thorough in making plans. There are many facets to this service item, including: the purchase and preparation of the food and beverage items; storage and refrigeration; venue selection, delivery, and setup; staffing and supervision; cleanup; and compliance with public health laws.

Floral arrangements - The inclusion of flowers and floral arrangements are an integral part of most funeral services and usually delivered to a funeral event location by a florist. With respect to floral arrangements, these are the most common tasks to complete:

> Create a written record for each floral arrangement delivery, including the name of the party that sent it and a brief description of the floral piece, such as 'red roses with baby's breath in a glass vase.' **Memorial books (register books)** have designated pages for recording this information. If a register book is not being used, the floral information should be recorded on a separate list so it may be given to the family after the funeral events have concluded.

> Determine if the piece has been sent by an immediate family member, extended family member, close friend, acquaintance, or organization. A floral piece from a family member often has a colored ribbon with lettering to identify the relationship of the sender to the decedent, such as mother, son, or brother.

> Display the floral arrangements near the casket or urn, giving those from immediate family members the highest priority and therefore closest proximal location to the decedent. These are then followed by extended family members, close friends, and others. The priority of placement is not absolute and adjustments may be needed to accommodate special circumstances, such as the display of an odd-shaped or over-sized arrangement.

➤ Verify message cards with the name of the sender are visible on each floral piece as it is set in place for visitation and funeral services. Individuals who send flowers will be looking to see if they are among those being displayed, and visitors will be reading the message cards to see who they are from.

➤ At the conclusion of all service events, remove the message cards and put them into an envelope. Give the family the list of floral arrangements received, including the name of the sender and the brief description, as well as the envelope with all the message cards.

Identify and Provide Equipment

Nearly all funeral services include at least one event that will require the use of equipment. Funeral establishments may own the equipment themselves or arrange for those items they do not own to be provided by others. In either case, preparing for funeral events includes identifying and making the necessary arrangements to have all equipment available when and where needed, regardless of the source.

Transportation needs - By far, the most prevalent equipment need for a funeral service will be livery vehicles for the transportation of the decedent, family members, funeral establishment staff, flowers, clergy, pallbearers, and related equipment. When motorized vehicles belonging to the funeral establishment are being utilized, funeral establishments should have a written driver policy enumerating duties and responsibilities as they relate to having vehicles fueled, cleaned, and ready to go at the designated times and places.

Special requests for unique modes of transportation, such as horse-drawn carriages, farm wagons, executive coaches, buses, motorcycle escorts, fire trucks, and military vehicles should be promptly addressed. Arrangements to hire or obtain these vehicles and drivers must be completed well before scheduled events to ensure enough time to accommodate any special needs, such as finding an alternate route, regulatory compliance issues, requesting law enforcement traffic support and assistance, and developing contingency plans for unforeseen events, such as a detour or accident.

Graveside services - Portable equipment for limited seating is a common occurrence for funeral and committal services on cemetery grounds. **Cemetery tents** may also be erected to provide protection from the elements. For funeral establishments that own this type of equipment, staff members must be assigned to deliver and set it up before the arrival of the funeral procession and then removed after the service has concluded and the guests have departed. For establishments that do not have this type of equipment, arrangements must be made with a private vendor to schedule and provide the services and equipment needed.

For gravesite services with cremated remains, a small table or stand will almost always be needed. The size will be dependent on the dimensions of the urn and any other items that may need to be placed in close proximity to it, such as a photo of the decedent, a bouquet of flowers, a cross or crucifix, or other special remembrance item.

Casket and vault handling - Lowering a vault into a grave and the subsequent placement of the casket into the vault often requires special heavy-duty equipment. This is especially true for concrete vaults and grave linings due to excessive weight. Few funeral establishments have the necessary equipment to perform these tasks and almost always hire the company supplying the vault or grave liners to handle these tasks. The most common agreements include the provision of a lowering device, imitation grass, and a limited number of seats. Tents are usually an added item when specifically requested. The funeral director is responsible for ordering the equipment and coordinating with the supplier on scheduling.

Equipment for alternate locations - For calling hours and funeral services in locations other than a funeral establishment, consideration must be given to equipment needs at the alternate site. Such equipment might include:

➤ Podium - A lectern, podium, or other similar platform may be needed for speakers at an offsite location.

➤ Audio - Larger locations may require audio equipment to amplify the voices of those speaking to the assembled visitors.

➤ Video - Power-point presentations and recorded videos may require computers, amplifiers, and screens sufficient to handle spaces much larger than a typical funeral establishment.

➤ Casket display - In addition to having the necessary equipment to move the casket into the venue, such as a **church truck**, many of the traditional equipment items found in a funeral establishment may need to be provided. These may include a casket stand, light torchiers, a **kneeler**, a stand or basket for mass cards, and a religious cross or crucifix.

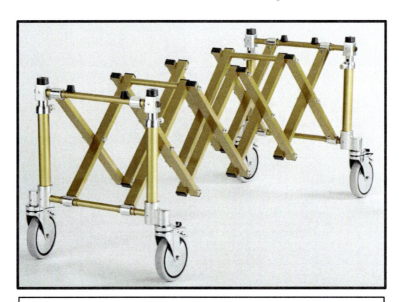

A typical church truck.

➤ Tables and stands - Consideration should be given to having a sufficient number of tables and stands available to accommodate a register book, framed photos, collages, event programs, prayer cards, and other remembrance items provided by the family. Plans must also be made to provide for the equipment needed to display larger items, such as a set of golf clubs.

➢ Flower stands and racks - An adequate number of stands and racks to facilitate the display of floral baskets, sprays, and potted plants should be onsite and readily available, as needed.

Once a list of equipment needs has been compiled, the funeral director can determine if they are already available at the location or need to be provided by the funeral establishment. Certain locations, such as meeting rooms, schools, and churches, often have some equipment available onsite that will meet the needs of the funeral director. Other locations, such as a home residence or outdoor shelter, may not have any of the equipment needed.

Finalizing Preparations

There are a number of activities related to finalizing preparations before the funeral events actually take place. Once these final measures are taken, everything should be in place to move forward with the events. These final steps often include:

Public notifications - Giving adequate notice of the events to the public must be considered at the time of the arrangements. There are currently three common methods to providing these notices: newspapers (both in print and online), funeral establishment websites, and social media outlets. Online mediums must be kept current and updated as event information becomes available or changes.

In-house paperwork - All paperwork should be checked for accuracy and completeness. Paperwork that must be distributed to other organizations or government agencies, such as the mandatory notification of death to the Social Security Administration, should be confirmed and recorded as completed on the Case Checklist and Worksheet.

Financial considerations - Checks needed to pay for services and expenses, such as an honorarium fee for the clergy; and cash for **gratuities**, such as tips for cemetery and vault staff members, should be prepared in advance and given to the staff members responsible for their distribution.

Regulatory compliance - The receipt of government regulatory documents needed to carry out the various funeral events must be confirmed. Such documents might include a certified copy of the death certificate, a burial or disposition permit, a cremation permit or certificate, or a designation of intentions with respect to the disposition of cremated remains.

Positioning the deceased - A final check of the decedent's position, arrangement, and features in the casket should be performed to ensure proper cosmetics, hairstyle, clothing, and appearance are all in order. The placement of any personal items inside the casket or on the person of the deceased should also be verified.

Merchandise items - A final check of all merchandise items for accuracy should be performed. This includes reviewing printed materials, such as prayer cards, a register book, and service programs to check for such things as errors in spelling or dates. Any personalization of merchandise, such as monogramming on the overlay or engraving on an urn nameplate, should be checked for accuracy.

Travel routes - All funeral procession routes to be taken to and from the various funeral events should be confirmed and checked to verify there are no temporary or scheduled detours or other obstacles, such as a parade or street event taking place on the date of the procession. In those cases where the family has requested a special route – such as passing by a particular home, business, or other landmark – special care should be taken to alert all procession drivers of the planned deviation from the most direct route.

Inspecting and Approving Funeral Event Sites

Visitation (calling hours) and/or funeral service events may take place in a funeral establishment, a church facility, or any other structure suitable for the purpose. Regardless of the venue, there are certain steps that should be followed at each event location to verify suitability. In following these steps, the funeral director will be in a position to identify any problems well in advance and, when possible, correct them. In other cases, these inspections may bring issues to light that would preclude using the site. The five steps are:

Step 1: Conduct a safety inspection. This includes an inspection of the site to ensure safety equipment and systems are in order. This may include tasks such as verifying fire extinguishers and first-aid kits are in place and functional, and emergency exit signs are properly posted and visible.

Step 2: Check for suitability. The suitability of the facility for any particular funeral event must be verified, as each event is unique. This would include such items as confirmation of adequate space for the casket for viewing purposes; sufficient seating to accommodate the expected number of guests; space requirements for displays; the ability to move the casket in and out of the facility easily; audio/visual systems and capabilities; and a speaker podium or other suitable alternative.

Step 3: Check for cleanliness. A thorough inspection of the facility should be made to ensure all public areas are neat, clean, and hygienic. Special attention should be given to restroom facilities, areas used for the preparation of food and beverages, and any associated dining accommodations for the event.

Step 4: Verify compliance with Americans with Disabilities Act (ADA). Public facilities must be in compliance with the ADA as it relates to providing certain accommodations. For funeral events, it is especially important to confirm systems are in place to accommodate the entry and exit of disabled individuals to and from the facility, as well as having ADA compliant restrooms.

Step 5: Check the environmental conditions. This may include verifying heating and cooling systems are operational; lighting needs are acceptable; power requirements are adequate; parking availability (including handicapped), is satisfactory; and sound systems are in place and functional.

Preparing Funeral Event Sites

After a funeral director has carefully inspected and approved a funeral event site, the location must be prepared and set-up for the event. There are any number of tasks required to prepare for calling hours, funeral ceremonies, and committal services, with many of these tasks common to all three events.

Placement of casket or urn for viewing - In funeral establishments, the casket placement for calling hours has already been pre-determined by past practice. In locations other than a funeral establishment, there are factors that must be considered, including:

➢ the accommodation of any items needed to emphasize any particular theme or personalization;

➢ lighting, both natural and artificial;

➢ available seating for family members and mourners;

➢ visitor ease of access and flow of pedestrian traffic;

➢ space needs for floral arrangements, a kneeler, and other items that may be placed adjacent to the casket or urn;

➢ church protocols and policy with regard to the orientation of a casket in a place of worship; and

➢ entry to and exit from the event venue.

A typical kneeler (prayer rail, prie dieu).

Other preparations - In addition to the placement of the casket or urn, there are other preparation needs when setting up for a funeral event, including:

➢ Placement of appropriate religious, fraternal, or military symbols, logos, emblems, sacred objects, or insignias, as well as any other special items being displayed as a tribute or remembrance mechanism. Placement may include inside, on, and in close proximity to the casket or urn.

➢ Arrangement of floral pieces, taking into consideration the priority of placement as described earlier, as well as any restrictions or limitations on the number or placement of floral pieces in a particular venue;

➢ Arrangement of photos and photo collections throughout the facility, taking into account the need to place them in locations where visitors will have adequate time to view them; while at the same time not hindering the movement of others waiting to greet the family or trying to be seated for a service or ceremony. One method often used to mitigate this problem is placing photo collections at both entry and exit points of the venue.

➢ Placement and set-up of audio-visual presentations to provide the greatest exposure to those attending.

➢ Placement of a register book in a location where all visitors will have an opportunity to record their attendance. For a large number of visitors, more than one register book may be used. The location of the register book(s) is also the most desirable place to display prayer cards and donation envelopes, if any.

Chapter 12: Supervising Funeral Events

Overview
The previous chapter concluded with a review of the tasks involved in preparing for funeral events. Executing, supervising, and managing those funeral events is the topic of this chapter and will review the dynamics and activities necessary to ensure the wishes of the family are carried out in a dignified and respectful manner.

Chapter Definitions
Acolyte - an altar attendant.

Altar - an elevated place or structure on which sacrifices are offered or at which religious rites are performed; in the Christian faith, a table on which the Eucharist or Holy Communion is offered.

Calling hours - (visitation, visiting hours) - time set aside for friends and relatives to pay respect for the deceased prior to the funeral service.

Casketbearer (pallbearer) - one who actively bears or carries the casket during the funeral service and at the committal service.

Chapel - a building or designated area of a building in which services are conducted.

Committal service - that portion of the funeral conducted at the place of disposition of dead human bodies.

Crucifer or crossbearer - one who carries the crucifix/cross during an ecclesiastical procession.

Dismissal - procedures or invitation intended to facilitate an organized departure.

First viewing (preview) - a private time for the family to view the deceased before public visitation begins.

Foyer (narthex, vestibule) - the entry way into a church, funeral establishment, or other public building; entrance hall.

Funeral coach (hearse) - specialty vehicle designed to transfer casketed remains.

Funeral procession - the movement of vehicles from the place of the funeral to the place of disposition.

Funeral service - the rites held at the time of disposition of human remains, with the deceased present.

Honorarium - compensation or recognition for services performed.

Honorary casketbearers (honorary pallbearers) - friends of the family or members of an organization or group who act as an escort or honor guard for the deceased. They do not carry the casket.

Pall - a symbolic cloth placed over the casket.

Procession/processional - the movement, in an orderly fashion, at the beginning of a service.

Recession/recessional - the movement, in an orderly fashion, at the end of a service.

Vestments - ritual garments worn by the clergy.

Calling Hours (Visitation) Event

Calling hours (visitation, visiting hours) are defined as time set aside for friends and relatives to pay respect to the deceased prior to the funeral service. They are usually the first funeral event to take place and offer a period of time for extended family members and friends to gather together to pay respects and mourn the deceased. They may also be called a viewing or wake.

The norm for many years was to have two sessions of two or three hours each in one day, with the funeral service event to take place on the next following day. More recently, in many regions of the United States it is not unusual to have one session of calling hours immediately followed by the service event in the funeral establishment on the same day. It is also not unusual, in some cases, for the committal to take place immediately following the service, thereby allowing all three events to occur on the same day.

Many factors have influenced this evolving shift, including

  ➢ fewer funeral service events being held in churches;

  ➢ a family desire to not prolong events;

  ➢ prohibitive expenses for those travelling and attending events over a period of several days;

  ➢ additional facility and supervision charges for events on multiple days; and

  ➢ a trend to celebrate a life lived rather than a life lost, resulting in fewer formal events and more semi-formal social gatherings, memorials, and celebrations.

First viewing - A **first viewing** is a private time for the family to view the deceased before public visitation begins. This is an important time for the funeral director, as it provides an opportunity to make any last-minute adjustments before the general public arrives. First viewings are usually scheduled to take place one hour before the public calling hours commence, but the time may be adjusted to accommodate the wishes of the family for a longer or shorter period. The casket is most often open for the first viewing but may be closed before the public viewing begins dependent on the wishes of the family.

The first viewing of the decedent is an emotionally charged moment for the immediate family and must be handled with considerable care and compassion. The lead funeral director should begin by escorting them into the reposing room or **chapel**. Some directors prefer to then step back and allow them to approach the casket alone, while others walk up to the casket with them. In either case, these options place the funeral director in a position to actively support the family during this difficult time and answer any questions. This also affords an opportunity for the family to request any changes, adjustments, or corrections, and for the funeral director to verify the presentation is acceptable, including:

➤ the correct placement and order of floral pieces from family members or close friends;

➤ acceptable positioning of remembrance items in or around the casket or other container;

➤ any need to adjust the cosmetics, hairstyling, or clothing on the decedent;

➤ verifying the visibility and location of jewelry and personal effects, such as a watch or glasses; and

➤ confirming location and placement of photo collages, video presentations, and static displays.

Many funeral directors also take a moment during the first viewing to familiarize the family with the plan to greet guests in a receiving line, including where they will be standing or seated and the flow of traffic being directed to them. Before leaving the family, the astute funeral director will inquire one last time if everything is acceptable and in order. After all questions have been answered and any issues or concerns resolved, the funeral director should remind the family to reach out to staff members if they need anything during the calling hours.

Staff considerations - Funeral establishments should have policies detailing duties, responsibilities, and expectations of staff members working funeral events, including visitation, funeral services, and committals. Items that should be included in a policy regarding visitation include:

➤ expected standards for dress, appearance, and grooming;

➤ duty to greet all guests at public viewing events and assist them in securing personal articles of clothing or accessories in a designated safe place;

➤ the need to be in position near entryways and visible to guests at all times;

➤ reminders to be courteous, friendly, and readily available to assist family and guests;

➤ requesting guests to sign the register book and directing them to the receiving line;

➤ opening and closing doors for guests entering or exiting facilities;

➢ responsibility to be familiar with facility amenities, such as the location of receptacles for depositing condolence, donation, and mass cards;

➢ responsibility to check on the family for a restroom break, drink of water, or brief rest period when the receiving line has been non-stop for an extended period of time;

➢ maintaining a working knowledge of the location of emergency exits, first-aid kits, and fire extinguishers, as well as procedures to follow in the event of an emergency; and

➢ responsibility to familiarize themselves with the current case, including:

✓ names of the decedent and immediate family members;

✓ dates, times, and locations of future funeral events;

✓ routes and directions to additional event venues;

✓ family preferred donations and availability of donation envelopes;

✓ details of any post-event activities, such as a home gathering of friends; and

✓ any special instructions or requests from the family for a particular event.

Public visitation - The public visitation period immediately follows the first viewing, and staff must be diligent to ensure the private viewing is not interrupted by early guests for the public calling hours. Certain individuals intentionally arrive early for a public visitation in an attempt to avoid a long receiving line and thereby 'get in and get out' quickly. This is not an acceptable practice and unfair to the family, and it is the responsibility of the staff to restrict public access until the time published in the death announcement, understanding the family may make exceptions for certain close friends.

About ten minutes before the start of the public viewing period, the family should be alerted to the imminent start of calling hours. This gives them the opportunity to use a restroom, possibly sit for a moments rest, and mentally prepare themselves before receiving guests. It also gives the staff time to make any last-minute adjustments, such as: closing the casket, checking the cosmetics and appearance of the decedent, and positioning the family in a workable receiving line.

Maintaining the facilities - Staff members should conduct periodic checks of: exterior entryways during times of inclement weather; restrooms for cleanliness and supplies; food and beverage service locations; seating capacity needs; heating and air-conditioning considerations; and provisions for handicap accessibility.

If a funeral service is going to be held in the funeral establishment immediately following the viewing, staff should verify the readiness and availability of the amenities needed for the service, such as a microphone, podium, music, service programs, and accommodations for clergy or speakers.

Concluding calling hours - If funeral services are going to be held at a location other than the funeral establishment, formally conclude the calling hours by **dismissal**, defined as the procedures or invitation intended to facilitate an organized departure. The measures for concluding calling hours are dependent on individual funeral establishments. Some may prefer to let calling hours run as long as the family wants to stay, while others may make an announcement that calling hours will end in 'x' minutes.

Calling hours should never be concluded when there are guests still standing in line to greet the family, unless a delay would result in a significant negative impact on other scheduled events. One such example would be the need to arrive promptly for a scheduled committal in a national cemetery and, in not doing so, risk being placed at the end of the schedule for the day. National cemeteries will not inconvenience families with scheduled committals because a family scheduled before them arrives late.

The funeral director is responsible for the orderly dismissal of the gathered guests and family at the conclusion of calling hours. It is important the family be the last to leave, as this may be their final occasion to see their loved one. Guests who linger or appear to be waiting until the family leaves should be politely asked to give the family privacy and, if necessary, asked to step out of the chapel or visitation room. When in doubt, it is advisable to ask the family if there are any close friends or guests they would like to stay after hours have officially concluded.

After Calling Hours
Following the formal conclusion of calling hours, there are several items of importance the funeral director will need to address.

Closing the casket - The director will need to communicate with the family to determine if any items in the casket – such as pictures, jewelry, notes, letters, cards, or mementos – are to be removed before the casket is closed. And, on occasion, a family may also have something they want to put in the casket before it is closed.

If family members wish to observe the closing of the casket, they should be allowed to do so, as well as any other person the family may invite. There are two equally good reasons for this. First, some families need to actually see the casket closed and secured with the remains inside to achieve full closure and acceptance of the death. Secondly, it provides independent witnesses to the presence of any valuables being secured with the remains in the casket for burial, such as an expensive watch or ring.

Floral arrangements - The family must consult with the funeral director to identify which, if any, floral arrangements are going to be taken with a casket or urn to the funeral service and/or committal event. The remaining pieces may then be taken home with the family; given to extended family members and close friends; or donated to a nursing home, hospital, senior center, or other similar type facility.

Cards and gifts - During calling hours, guests may drop off condolence, mass, or donation cards. In addition, it is not unheard of for some guests to bring gifts for the family to the funeral establishment. Most funeral directors prefer to have the family take cards and gifts home with them at the conclusion of calling hours, while others favor waiting until all of the funeral events have concluded, then personally delivering them to the family home.

The next event - Before the family leaves at the conclusion of calling hours, the funeral director will want to briefly review the next service event with them. This may be a funeral service, if one was not held immediately following visitation; or a committal event, if the funeral service ceremony was already performed subsequent to calling hours. In either case, the family will need guidance on when and where to arrive for the next event or the formation of a procession to go to the next event. They should also be provided with a summary of the activities that will be taking place, with special attention given to any element in which family members are going to actively participate, such as reading a prayer or entering the name of a decedent in a church registry.

Family first - All attention at the conclusion of calling hours should be focused on the family. Hours are a stressful and exhausting undertaking, and most families need a moment to gather their thoughts and reflect on the magnitude of what has taken place. Funeral directors should be overly patient and supporting at this time. Busy work in the presence of the family should be avoided, including activities such as turning off lights, rearranging furniture, and removing picture boards. These activities can wait.

When the family is ready to leave, they should be assisted in retrieving any personal items – such as a coat, handbag, or cellphone – then escorted from the funeral establishment to their vehicles. Opening and closing vehicle doors is a personal courtesy and gives the director an opportunity to have one last word of encouragement with the family before closing the vehicle door.

Funeral Service Event

The most important goal for a funeral director supervising a **funeral service** event is to fulfill the express wishes of the family, and to do so by orchestrating a respectful and dignified ceremony. With the venue prepared in advance, the funeral director will simply need to direct and assist others in the proper execution of the funeral plan. Minor adjustments, such as additional seating to accommodate a large number of guests, may be needed, but if there is a structured plan in place very few changes will be required.

Churches - The protocols and procedures in a house of worship for a funeral service are dependent on the funeral rites and customs of the religion, as well as the clergy member supervising the ceremony. Rites vary widely, not only by religion but often within religions in different regions of the United States. Funeral directors must comply with the wishes and directions of the clergy officiating at a funeral service. They control all activities in the house of worship, which may include such minor issues as the placement of flowers; or more significant actions, such as granting permission for others to speak at the service.

Clergy/speaker - The funeral director should endeavor to accommodate the needs of clergy members or speakers participating in the service. This may include providing them with a place to review their remarks; change into **vestments** or other attire; and meet briefly with the family, if requested by either party. Consideration should also be given to offering transportation to and from event venues and ensuring they receive any **honorarium**.

Casketbearers - Both **casketbearers** and **honorary casketbearers** need instruction and guidance on what to expect and how to carry out their duties under the direction of a funeral staff member. Casketbearers are generally going to be used four times during a traditional funeral service to move the casket:

1. From the funeral establishment to the **funeral coach (hearse)**.

2. From the funeral coach into the funeral service venue.

3. From the funeral service venue into the funeral coach again.

4. To the gravesite on arrival at the cemetery or other place of final disposition.

A typical funeral coach (hearse).

The staff member supervising the movement of the casket should meet with the casketbearers in advance to discuss the proper means to load, unload, and carry the casket, as well as advise them of any special seating arrangements for bearers. They should be reminded of the times and locations when they will be needed and where the staff member working with them will be located.

The funeral director or staff member must also be prepared to provide real-time progressive instructions to casketbearers during casket movements. In the experience of the author, casketbearers are often tense and nervous about performing their duties but reluctant to speak up or ask questions. A good dose of reassurance will go a long way in easing the tension and make for a smooth operation. Assuring them in advance they will be receiving step-by-step instructions is a good practice to follow.

Honorary casketbearers will also need direction on where to position themselves at each funeral event, as well as their proper lineup for any formal procession into a building or facility.

Processional - A formal **processional** is another common practice over which church doctrine or an individual clergy member may exercise some level of control. Recognizing every religion and clergy member in the country has some level of influence over a funeral service, and no single practice or component is absolute, a processional in a church may include these elements in this order:

➢ The funeral staff member in charge of all casket movements assists the bearers in bringing the casket into the **narthex (foyer)** of the church about five minutes before the scheduled service. At this time and in some religions, they may drape a **pall** over the casket, a symbol of all persons being equal in the eyes of God.

➢ As the casket is moved into the church narthex, the lead funeral director escorts the immediate family members in walking behind the casket.

➢ If a clergy member is going to join the procession going down the aisle, they will be positioned in front of the casket. They may have one or more altar attendants (**acolytes**) in front of them and a **crucifer or crossbearer** positioned in front of the attendants to lead the procession. If there are honorary casketbearers, they are placed directly behind the clergy and in front of the casket. In some religions, the clergy will bless the casket before the processional begins.

➢ The crucifer (if there is one) or clergy and attendants lead the procession down the aisle, followed by the casket and casketbearers, with the funeral staff member supervising the casket movement positioned at the end of the casket and facing the **altar**. This places them in a position where they can easily and quietly communicate with the bearers.

➢ The lead director escorts the family and any guests with them down the aisle behind the staff member supervising the casket movement.

➢ The staff member positions the casket in accordance with the applicable religious custom and directs the casketbearers to their seats, usually located on the left side of the church as you face the altar; while the lead director escorts the family to their reserved seats, located on the right side of the church.

Note: Those in attendance are standing while the casket is brought into the church, and care must be taken to ensure the family and casketbearers remain standing when they go to their seats, waiting until the clergy begins the service and asks everyone to be seated.

➢ Before returning to the entrance of the church, the funeral establishment staff show respect by facing the altar and bowing in unison.

Note: See Guide 2 to view a Typical Christian Church Interior Design.

Religious practices that embrace the processional concept almost always conclude services with a similar **recessional**. With some potential variants, the recessional follows the same order and alignment of the participants that took part in the processional. Upon reaching the exit of the church, the recessional will stop to provide for a short prayer or blessing; removal of the pall; draping of the American Flag (if there is one); and possibly a brief announcement.

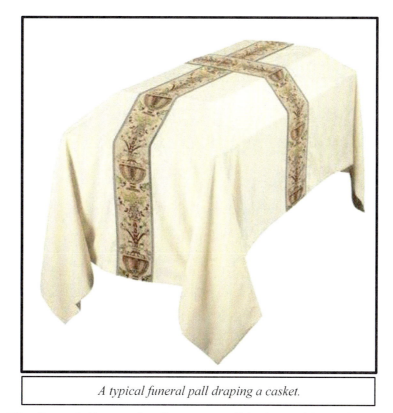

A typical funeral pall draping a casket.

Announcements - The funeral director is often responsible for making a few brief announcements to coordinate and direct planned activities as they progress. The nature of these announcements will be dependent on whether the service is being held in a place of worship, the funeral establishment, or some other location. Announcements may include:

➢ the introduction of a clergy member or speaker;

➢ opening and concluding the funeral service ceremony when held in the funeral establishment;

➢ the orderly dismissal of gathered guests and family; and

➢ information the family may want conveyed to the guests, such as a bereavement luncheon or invitation to a family home to continue the celebration of a life.

Feet first? - Although not formally adopted or practiced in all religions, the notion of whether a casket should be carried and moved feet-first or head-first is grounded in ancient religious customs and ceremonial rites. The basic premise is the decedent being moved in a casket should be facing in the same direction as they would in life. Taking casketed remains into a church feet first has the decedent facing the front of the church as they approach the altar, the same as they would face the front of the church if they were walking down the aisle. This convention for the movement of casketed remains plays through all of the different scenarios one might encounter during funeral events, such as loading a casket into a funeral coach and carrying the casket in a cemetery.

After being carried into a church, the casket may be placed perpendicular to or parallel with the altar, depending on religious custom. When set perpendicular, the feet are placed closer to the altar, which has the decedent facing the altar as they would if seated in a pew. When set parallel, the side where the casket caps open faces the altar, which again has the decedent in a position to face the altar if the head cap were open. As might be expected, when moving a casket out of a facility, the orientation of the casket is reversed with the decedent facing the exit, as they would if walking out of the church.

One exception to this unofficial feet first rule centers around the casketed remains of an ordained clergy member, in which case the positioning of the casket in a church is reversed, so the head of the casket is closer to the altar. This positions the deceased clergy member facing the parishioners or congregation, as they would when preaching from the altar.

Note: See Guide 3 to view the Proper Way to Turn a Casket Around in a Church.

Funeral Processions
A **funeral procession**, the movement of vehicles from the place of the funeral to the place of disposition, is an integral component of a funeral service. Also known as a funeral cortege, their use has seen a significant decline in certain regions over the years, with many families electing to have a private committal service on a later date. This trend has been accelerated with the increasing number of direct cremations, as well as requests for the cremation process to take place *after* a traditional viewing and ceremony with the body present.

From the funeral establishment - A formal funeral procession may or may not be used to transport the casket (or other container) from the funeral establishment to a funeral service event location, such as a church, synagogue, or other place of worship. When chosen, they generally only include family members, casketbearers, and funeral establishment staff. When not chosen, family and friends meet at the church and await the arrival of the funeral coach and funeral establishment staff.

Parking considerations - To ensure the orderly departure of a procession, funeral establishment staff must be assigned to parking lots to meet guests as they arrive, and direct them to the proper parking location dependent on whether or not they are going to be in the procession. Vehicles that are going in the procession must be parked and arranged to facilitate the smooth formation of the procession, such as being backed into parking spaces or kept in a reserved parking location to allow for a prompt and orderly exit.

When more than one funeral event is going to take place in succession, consideration must be given to the proper parking and position of the vehicles at each location, to again ensure ease in reforming the procession line and getting underway without confusion and delay.

Car lists - Many funeral establishments use a car list to prioritize and arrange the procession order for the family vehicles. Other establishments include all vehicles on the car list, but this requires gathering vehicle and occupant information on a potentially significant number of people during calling hours. It also mandates considerable attention be paid to the arrival and proper parking of every vehicle that appears at the establishment for the funeral service. The use of car lists for all vehicles in a procession is on the decline, with many funeral establishments now maintaining a priority list for family member vehicles only.

Escorts - Escorts may include official government vehicles, such a law enforcement vehicle to assist with traffic or fire apparatus to honor the decedent. There are also an infinite number of fraternal organizations, private groups, clubs, and non-profit entities who may wish to provide an escort in an honorary capacity.

Funeral directors must be cognizant of potentially significant civil liability exposure whenever they elect to use or support the use of a private escort. This is especially true when private entities and untrained individuals may be deployed to direct or control traffic on public highways. Various state traffic laws regulate funeral processions, escorts, and traffic direction activities, and funeral directors should fully familiarize themselves with applicable state and local laws for those jurisdictions where they desire to provide a private escort.

Identification - There are a number of ways to help identify and draw attention to automobiles in a funeral procession and thereby alert other vehicle operators to the presence of a funeral cortege. These include window placards, magnetic signs, fender flags, flashing yellow lights, and the use of headlights. Some funeral directors urge vehicle operators to use four-way flashers, but this practice is illegal in many states when flashers are being operated on a moving vehicle, as it often creates an even greater hazard and causes more confusion to the motoring public.

Traffic rules - Broadly speaking, drivers in a funeral procession do not have the right to disobey traffic laws or regulations of the road. They may not pass through red signals, ignore stop signs, speed, pass stopped school buses, or disregard any other traffic law unless directed to do so by an authorized public official, such as a police officer, flag person, or traffic aide. However, there are exceptions, as some states have statutory laws and administrative rules specific to regulating funeral processions on public highways. These exceptions may exempt procession vehicles from compliance with certain provisions of traffic laws; while others may impose additional requirements on non-procession vehicles when they encounter a funeral procession.

For example, a state may exempt the operators of funeral procession vehicles from being ticketed for 'following too close' or 'operating hazard lights (four-way flashers) when in motion.' Another state may prohibit vehicles from crossing between cars when a funeral procession is passing through an intersection; passing or cutting into a procession on a two-lane highway; or failing to yield to a procession turning into a cemetery.

Routes, bridges, and tolls - The routes to be followed by a funeral procession should be checked for any potential hazards or conditions that might be cause for concern on the day of the funeral events. These include such situations as scheduled paving or road construction, unforeseen road closures, and known heavy traffic periods. Alternate routes may be required, and longer routes may necessitate handing out written directions to vehicle operators in the event they are separated from the group or unable to maintain position in the line.

If toll roads are a part of the route, funeral directors must predetermine the safest and easiest means to enter and exit these roadways as a procession. This may require consultation with public highway administrators and traffic enforcement officials to ensure the plan to navigate these roads provides an adequate level of safety to all vehicle operators, toll booth staff, road work crews, and procession participants.

Toll bridges are another obstacle and concern for a funeral procession, especially in heavy metropolitan areas like New York City (with 11 toll bridges) and San Francisco (with toll bridges to enter the city, but not exit the city). Similar to toll roads, the funeral director should predetermine the safest and easiest means to cross these bridges as a procession. In many states and municipalities, bridge tolls may be prepaid based on the number of vehicles making a special crossing in a procession. In addition, bridge authorities in these states often provide an escort to help ensure a safe and smooth crossing.

Interstate highways - Funeral processions on interstate highways and other roadways with higher speed limits are of special concern, as the potential for multi-vehicle mishaps at higher speeds is greatly increased. *Funeral processions should not operate on these roads at low speeds.* The best practice for a procession on an interstate or controlled access highway is to stay in the far right-hand lane and maintain a speed equal to the posted limit. Speeds should be reduced only when off the main travelled portion of the highway and on exit ramps. This alleviates the potential for a serious, chain-reaction, read-end collision when multiple vehicles reduce speed while still on the main highway surrounded by high-speed traffic.

Order - The traditional order of vehicles in a funeral procession is as follows, subject of course to the wishes of the family:

1. Escort(s), if any.

2. Funeral establishment lead vehicle.

3. Clergy, if not in funeral establishment lead vehicle.

4. Honorary casketbearer vehicles, if any.

5. Casketbearer vehicles.

6. Funeral coach (hearse).

7. Immediate family.

8. Extended family.

9. Close friends.

10. Others.

Note: Although the order of vehicles in a funeral procession is not absolute, it is a commonly accepted practice no vehicle should ever be placed between the immediate family and the funeral coach carrying the casket or other container.

Committal Event

A **committal service** is defined as that portion of the funeral conducted at the place of disposition of dead human bodies.

Legal considerations - Note the definition clearly states 'dead human bodies.' This would, by definition, exclude cremated remains and the remnants of human remains after being subjected to the alkaline hydrolysis process. Most states legally consider cremation to be one of several methods for the final disposition of human remains, as they also consider a burial or interment to be another method. The same applies to entombment in a mausoleum, burial at sea, and the alkaline hydrolysis process.

The importance of these distinctions is that certain states mandate the presence of a licensed and/or registered funeral service professional to provide for and supervise a final disposition. Therefore, funeral directors must familiarize themselves with the legal definitions of the final disposition methods in the communities they serve and remain cognizant of any legal duties imposed on them in supervising a final disposition.

While there is a clear difference, and in some states a significant legal distinction, between the various methods of final disposition, for the general public a committal service could apply to any method. Families request a committal service for a cremation case just as often as they do for a burial case, and the need for them to understand the subtle difference is of no consequence. The need for the funeral director to know the difference is however of significant importance to ensure regulatory compliance.

Planning considerations - A committal service is usually a brief service but requires a funeral director to coordinate with several key players, including: cemetery staff, vault suppliers, honor guards, clergy members, family, and casketbearers. While the event is often the shortest of the three common funeral events (visitation, funeral, and committal), it requires considerable pre-planning to ensure successful execution.

Director duties - The funeral director is generally responsible for ensuring the following activities are handled by funeral establishment staff:

➢ Movement of the casketed remains and flowers to the gravesite.

➢ Escorting and seating the family at the grave.

➢ Gathering participants in front of the clergy/speaker.

➢ Opening the service by introducing the clergy/speaker.

➢ Making any announcements, such as a gathering of friends after the service.

➢ Concluding the service by thanking those in attendance (dismissal).

➢ Remaining at the gravesite until all guests have departed.

➢ As required by state or local law, observe and/or witness the lowering of the casket; placement of the vault cover (if a vault is used); and/or filling in the grave with earth.

Chapter 13: Post-Funeral Follow-up and Aftercare

<u>Overview</u>
Post-funeral follow-up and aftercare are two separate, yet related funeral service topics. They have been placed together in this chapter for the convenience of the reader. The first discussion will explore the proper procedures for closing and archiving a death case file. The second discussion will briefly review the activities funeral establishments may provide on a continuing basis to the communities and families they serve after the funeral events.

<u>Chapter Definitions</u>
Aftercare - those appropriate and helpful acts of counseling, personal and/or written contact that come after the funeral.

Ecumenical - representing a number of different Christian churches [by Author].

<u>Post-Funeral Follow-up</u>
When the funeral goods and services selected by a family have been furnished and the various funeral events have been concluded, the funeral establishment must review the funeral contract and follow-up on any open items before closing the case. There may be any number of open items to be resolved before a case file may be fully closed. The first step to managing these tasks is to identify them by conducting a complete review of the paperwork, including the required FTC written statement, funeral establishment checklists, orders for goods, and staff notes.

Paperwork - The paperwork review includes:

> verifying government required documentation and applications have been completed and submitted, including such items as the SSA Statement of Death by a Funeral Director and a Claim for a Government Medallion;

> reconciling the final funeral bill by updating previously estimated charges and applying any payments, additional purchases, insurance proceeds, late fees, discounts, or other adjustments;

> obtaining certified copies of death certificates or transcripts and providing them to the family as requested during the arrangement conference;

> ensuring any funeral-related paperwork or records required to be retained for a set period of time by law are in the file, such as: cremation authorizations, burial permits, body receipts, transit permits, cash disbursement records, and cancelled checks; and

> reviewing funeral establishment checklists to verify all documentation and records created for the case are in the file.

Funeral goods and services - A review of the funeral goods and services purchased includes:

➢ verification the family received the funeral *goods* they ordered during the arrangement conference – such as a registration book, prayer cards, and keepsake items – with special attention given to the delivery of the urn or other container safeguarding cremated remains if it is not already in the possession of the family;

➢ verification the family received any funeral *services* they ordered or requested, such as the marking or lettering of a headstone; placement of a temporary marker at the gravesite; delivery of floral arrangements; or the separation of cremated remains into keepsake urns, portion urns, or other customer-supplied containers; and

➢ verification the family received any goods they ordered subsequent to the arrangements, such as audio/video recordings of the funeral service, personalized memory candles, a flag case, cremation jewelry, cemetery monument, and fingerprint-based knick-knacks or remembrances.

Benefits - a review of family benefits includes:

➢ applications for benefits associated with veteran cases, such as presidential memorial certificates, monuments and markers, and government issued medallions;

➢ applications for benefits under insurance policies and other private sources of income for payment of the funeral bill;

➢ applications for government assistance from social service agencies to pay for allowable funeral expenses; and

➢ applications to receive any available retirement death benefits or other employment-based death benefits.

Spring burials - When current climate conditions prohibit an immediate interment, burial may need to take place in the spring. Most funeral establishments have a written policy on how to properly record the future need for a spring burial after the arrangement conference. These records are maintained in a master folder or binder pending the start of dispositions in the spring and used to schedule interments. The files for these cases will not be closed until after the spring burial or other disposition has taken place.

Note: See Form 13 to view a typical Spring Burial Worksheet.

Direct Aftercare
Direct **aftercare** activities represent the personal communication and interactions with a specific family designed to build upon the trust established when serving the family at the time of need. The relationships fostered by these aftercare activities become more closely related to friendships, rather than business transactions.

Follow-up phone calls. These provide an opportunity for the funeral director to maintain open lines of communication, inquire if they can do anything to assist the family further, and reaffirm the commitment of the staff to be available at any time in the future. Funeral directors often maintain a written schedule for the purposes of reminding them when to place follow-up phone calls to families they recently served.

Sending cards, brief notes, or letters. These simple yet thoughtful gestures reinforce the personal connection and bond that develops between a family, the lead director, and other staff members. Mailing a card or note to let someone know they are in your thoughts and prayers during a particularly difficult time, such as on major holidays or the anniversary of a death, sends a powerful message of support to the family.

Attend after-events and gatherings. The dynamics of funerals in the 21st century continues to shift from a somber, subdued affair to mourn the loss of a loved one to a more joyful and uplifting gathering to celebrate the success, work, achievements, and accomplishments of a loved one. With this shift has come a significant increase in the number of events taking place several days, weeks, or months after the formal funeral events. Funeral directors should be alert to the potential for these events and, when possible, attend them to demonstrate commitment to the family and a desire to be supportive.

Emails. Five years ago, the thought of sending someone an email as a means to communicate with a family and express continued support would have been unthinkable. Today, emailing a family has become an accepted practice and very commonplace. Still, funeral directors must be selective in using this method, as older generations may not be as receptive to this approach as younger generations.

Personal visits. Taking the time to stop at a residence and personally call on someone is probably the most powerful and expressive means to convey genuine concern and caring for a family.

Service of remembrance - One final aftercare method commonly used in the funeral service industry today is the annual sponsorship of a remembrance service. Many establishments choose the time period around Christmas and Hanukah to schedule a gathering to honor those who died in the previous year. Often held in church meeting halls or other similar venues, light refreshments may be served after a remembrance service is celebrated by local clergy members and other speakers.

The author is familiar with one such service held every year in a local community around Christmas time. The names of the deceased are listed in the service program and engraved on individual Christmas ornaments hung on a tree, with the family members given the ornaments to take home at the conclusion of an **ecumenical** service.

Indirect Aftercare
Indirect aftercare activities represent an opportunity to meet with members of the general public, as well as previous clients, to build personal relationships over an extended period of time.

Sponsoring community educational programs. Lectures and presentations on such topics as life insurance, prefunded preneeds, estate taxes, social security benefits, and health care lend themselves well to drawing elder members from the community. This demographic develops a keen interest in these topics as they grow older and welcome an opportunity to educate themselves and speak with knowledgeable professionals.

Hosting support groups. These regularly scheduled meetings are directed toward those individuals who have experienced the death of a close relative. They provide an inviting, friendly forum to meet, talk, and share experiences in an open environment with other similarly situated individuals in a social setting.

Hosting social events for seniors. Hosting events for senior citizens and their families is an excellent method to develop new relationships as well as reinforce those already established. These events pay a high dividend when a family needs the services of a funeral director, and the parties are already acquainted with each other after having met at a social event.

Professional referrals. Funeral directors are uniquely situated to refer family members to professionals in areas such as financial counseling, legal advice, grief counseling, health concerns, and psychological needs. When asked for assistance, they should be prepared to make appropriate recommendations and referrals.

Informational literature and media. National and state funeral director associations usually have a wealth of handout materials and information resources for families seeking direction and guidance on death care issues.

For example, in addition to other print media and resources, the National Funeral Directors Association lists the availability of these materials on their website:

Understanding Grief	Loss of a Parent	Sudden or Tragic Death	Burial Options
Suicide	Honoring a Life	Grief and the Holidays	Preneed Contracts
Funeral Etiquette	Loss of a Child	Making Arrangements	Losing a Sibling
Why Preplan?	Cremation	Friends and Family	Unique Tributes

Chapter 14: Shipping Cremated Remains

<u>Overview</u>

Whether shipping cremated remains by common carrier or transporting them by **private carrier**, funeral directors will always need to ensure compliance with all applicable federal, state, and local regulations. The complexity for doing so is far less cumbersome than for the shipment of human remains, but there is a heightened risk associated with the relatively small size of these shipments, exposing them to mishandling, damage, or loss. This chapter reviews domestic and international requirements and recommendations as they relate to shipping and transporting cremated remains.

Note: For the purpose of this chapter, *shipping* refers to the <u>unsupervised</u> movement of cremated remains by the post office or a common carrier; while *transportation* refers to the <u>supervised</u> transportation of cremated remains by individuals, such as the carry-on bag of an airline passenger.

<u>Chapter Definitions</u>

Apostille - certification/legalization of a document for international use (under terms of the 1961 Hague Convention).

Common carrier - any carrier required by law to convey passengers or freight without refusal if the approved fare or charge is paid (airline, train, etc.).

Private carrier - those who transport only in particular instances and only for those they chose to contract with (e.g. funeral establishment vehicles and livery).

<u>Domestic Shipping</u>

The United States Postal Service (USPS) offers a convenient method for shipping cremated remains using Priority Mail Express Service. United Parcel Service (UPS), Federal Express (FedEx), and DHL do not accept *human remains* or *cremated remains* for shipment. Each of these companies specifically list them as prohibited items on their respective websites.

Shipping labels - The use of special USPS Labels (Label 139) are *mandatory* on all shipments to provide increased visual awareness and give notice of the importance of the package contents. They must be placed on all four sides, the top, and the bottom of the shipping container. These labels are available from USPS at no charge from the online Postal Store or any USPS retail counter.

USPS Label 139

Shipping boxes - Preferably, cremated remains should be packaged and shipped in the USPS boxes they provide specifically for this purpose when using Priority Mail Express Service; however, other boxes or containers may be used. Regardless of the container chosen, the USPS requirements for packing, protecting, addressing, and labeling must be strictly followed.

Tracking - Priority Mail Express Service includes standard tracking. In addition, if requested at the time of shipment, a proof of delivery signature record is available. It is highly recommended this 'signature required' option be chosen to provide a signed, written record of the cremated remains having been received.

Shipping kits - USPS offers two different kits for the packaging and shipping of cremated remains. Both of these kits include a box that has the required labels imprinted on all six sides.

Kit #1 includes a sturdy box and
a roll of Priority Mail Express tape.

Kit #2 includes a sturdy box; bubble cushioning; a self-sealing bag; a roll of Priority Mail tape; and a copy of Publication 139, 'How to Package and Ship Cremated Remains.'

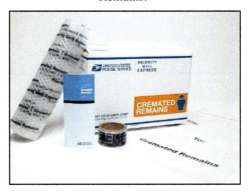

These kits can be ordered free of charge from the Postal Store on the USPS website and may also be available in some local post office locations. When packed and ready for shipment, these boxes may be sent through any local post office, at which time the shipping fee is paid.

Extra services - In addition to the signature required service noted earlier, other optional USPS services include return receipt, insurance, and signature waived.

Online assistance - USPS Publication No. 139 contains detailed and explicit instructions for the selection and preparation of containers, packing materials, and labels; as well as information on special requirements, such as the need for two containers consisting of one inner primary container and an outer shipping package.

Note: See Guide 4 to read all the USPS Guidelines for Shipping Cremated Remains.

Domestic Transportation
The Transportation Security Administration (TSA) is the agency of the U.S. Department of Homeland Security that has authority over the security of the traveling public in the United States. The stated mission of the TSA is to protect the nation's transportation systems to ensure freedom of movement for people and commerce. Relevant to our review here, the TSA sets the requirements for the transportation of cremated remains on domestic **common carriers**.

Checked baggage - The TSA does not prohibit the transportation of cremated remains in checked baggage; however, they highly recommend transporting them in carry-on bags, "*to help protect the contents from the risks associated with checked baggage.*" They further amplify this recommendation by explaining, *"checked bags are subjected to rapid and sometimes rough movement along a series of conveyor belts as they make the trek to and from the aircraft."*

Although the TSA does not prohibit using checked baggage to transport cremated remains, some individual airlines do have such prohibitions. It is therefore important to check with the airline of choice, well in advance of travel, to determine if there are any such restrictions.

Carry-on bags - The TSA recommends cremated remains be transported in carry-on bags and suggest the container be made of a light weight material, such as wood or plastic. The container must also be scannable by an x-ray machine.

Cremated remains in carry-on bags *must* pass through an x-ray machine to be screened. The rationale behind this requirement is that a container purportedly carrying cremated remains could be exploited by someone wanting to conceal a dangerous item or weapon. If the container is made of a material that prohibits an x-ray examination of the contents, the TSA operator will receive an alarm. If they cannot clear the alarm at the x-ray machine, they may apply other non-intrusive means in an attempt to resolve the issue. If the officer is still unable to determine the container does not contain a prohibited item, it will not be allowed on the carrier.

Note: TSA officers will not open a cremation container for inspection, even if requested or authorized to do so by a passenger.

Paperwork - The TSA does not require any support documentation or paperwork for shipping or transporting cremated remains, but the best practice is to always carry a copy of both the death certificate and certification of cremation in case they are needed for presentation to an airline or government official at either the departure location or arrival destination.

International Shipping
USPS shipping option - Cremated remains may be shipped to an international address by USPS as long as the country and destination where they are being sent:

> ➢ does not prohibit mailing cremated remains; and

> ➢ USPS Priority Mail Express *International* service is available.

Prior to using this service, funeral directors should always verify the country where the cremated remains are being sent does in fact accept USPS Priority Mail Express International deliveries. The USPS online International Mail Manual (IMM) lists all of the countries where these services are allowed. When unable to ship by USPS, a funeral director will need to contact the appropriate government embassy for direction and guidance.

Government embassies - The U.S. Department of State has government representatives working in almost 400 embassies, consulate offices, and diplomatic missions all over the world. Embassy buildings serve as the headquarters and place of work for U.S. government employees and are usually located in the capital city of the foreign country.

An ambassador, also known as the chief of mission, is the highest-ranking diplomat to the host country and a personal representative of the President. Branches of an embassy within the same country are known as consulates and often located in larger cities of the foreign country. One of the primary purposes of a U.S. embassy (or consulate) is to assist American citizens who travel to or live in the host country. This includes assisting families when a U.S. citizen dies in a foreign country.

Foreign countries have similar facilities and personnel stationed all over the world for the same reasons the United States does. As of this writing, 178 foreign countries have an embassy office in Washington, D.C., with many maintaining additional consulate offices in large metropolitan areas of the United States. When human or cremated remains must be shipped internationally, these world-wide embassy and consulate offices play a major role in facilitating the process.

Shipping to another country - When cremated remains must be shipped from the United States to a foreign country, the funeral director should contact the embassy or consulate office located in the United States that represents the foreign country destination for assistance. The requirements and documentation vary from one country to the next but may include any or all of the following:

➢ certified copy of the death certificate;

➢ government issued burial, transit, cremation, or disposition permit;

➢ foreign passport or visa of the decedent (if they had one);

➢ copy of the flight or other mode of transportation itinerary;

➢ letter from the funeral establishment attesting to the contents of the transportation container(s);

➢ letter from the funeral establishment or a shipping company acting on behalf of the funeral establishment that international shipping container requirements in the destination country have been complied with fully;

➢ translation of U.S. documents to the language of the destination country; and

➢ compliance with customs requirements of the destination country.

Documentation may need to be endorsed by **apostille**, defined as the certification or legalization of a document for international use in accordance with the 1961 Hague Convention. An apostille endorsement is affixed to a document by designated authorities, such as embassies, ministries, courts, and state or local governments. In the United States, each of the Departments of State in the 50 states are designated authorities.

When shipping cremated remains internationally, some countries may require the participation, approval, or assistance of legal or funeral service professionals. They will also undoubtedly have additional document and handling requirements specific to their country. As an example, the

Foreign Missions of the Federal Republic of Germany embassy located in the United States issues certificates for shipping cremated remains to their homeland. They require they be shipped from a funeral establishment in the United States to a funeral home or undertaker in Germany, as German law prohibits the handling of human remains or cremated remains by private individuals.

The German missions require the following documents and fees to issue a certificate for shipping cremated remains:

- a certificate of death;

- a certificate of cremation, with a confirmation from the funeral establishment the urn contains the cremated remains of the deceased person (urns should be sealed and numbered);

- if available, a copy of the passport of the deceased person;

- a fee of 25.00 euros for the issuance of the certificate, payable in U.S. dollars by money order; and

- a self-addressed and prepaid USPS certified mail envelope.

Funeral directors must ensure strict compliance with all foreign country requirements and related fees. If cremated remains arrive without the required documentation or fees, or the documents are not authenticated as required, cremated remains may be refused and returned to the United States.

Note: A comprehensive listing of all the embassy offices located in the United States, including contact information, may be found on the embassy.org website.

International Transportation
Many of the requirements and recommendations listed in the previous Domestic Transportation section about checked baggage and carry-on bags are equally applicable to international transportation of cremated remains; however, additional consideration must be given to complying with requirements and protocols in the country where the cremated remains are being taken.

Passengers carrying or flying with cremated remains in checked baggage or carry-on bags will be subject to the laws, regulations, and policies of:

- the country where the flight originates;

- any countries where the itinerary calls for a stop and change of planes; and

- the country where the flight will terminate.

These considerations apply to all international flights but are especially important when the flight departing the United States is that of a foreign airline.

Funeral director role - Generally speaking, funeral directors will not be transporting cremated remains anywhere internationally; however, they should be prepared to assist and offer guidance to family members planning to do so. This may include reaching out to foreign embassy offices on their behalf for guidance and then assisting in gathering documentation.

Preparation recommendations - When planning to travel with cremated remains on an international flight or other mode of transportation, passengers should allow themselves sufficient time to contact airlines or other common carriers, as well as government authorities to inquire about rules and regulations specific to these transports. Similar to shipping cremated remains, the requirements and documentation for transportation will vary from one country to next, but the complexity is often far less difficult. Regardless, many of the items listed in the previous bulleted paragraph titled *shipping to another country* may apply.

Every airline company, government agency, and funeral service entity that deals with the shipping and transportation of human remains or cremated remains has written recommendations for consumers, and always provide additional support services to funeral service practitioners seeking assistance.

When transporting cremated remains, these groups may recommend the following:

- ➢ use a container that is light-weight and capable of being examined by an x-ray machine;

- ➢ transport the cremation container in a carry-on bag, rather than in checked baggage;

- ➢ place cremated remains in a heavy-duty and sealed plastic bag to protect against sifting before placing them in the container for transportation;

- ➢ carry a certified copy of the death certificate;

- ➢ carry the original or a certified copy of the certificate of cremation;

- ➢ do not leave the cremated remains unattended while on route to the destination; and

- ➢ always obtain information by calling the applicable foreign embassy and speaking directly to an official representative, as information found online may not always be current.

UNITED STATES POSTAL SERVICE ®

Chapter 15: Shipping Human Remains

Overview

This chapter will review the requirements, procedures, and protocols for shipping human remains, both domestically and internationally. The following chapter will review the different containers available for shipping human remains.

Chapter Definitions

Apostille - certification/legalization of a document for international use (under terms of the 1961 Hague Convention).

Common carrier - any carrier required by law to convey passengers or freight without refusal if the approved fare or charge is paid (airline, train, etc.).

Forwarding remains - one of the categories required to be itemized on the GPL (if the funeral provider offers the service). This involves services of the funeral provider in the locale where death occurs and preparation for transfer to another funeral provider as selected by the family (consumer). Funeral Rule requires package pricing of this service with a description of the components included.

Private carrier - those who transport only in particular instances and only for those they chose to contract with (e.g. funeral establishment vehicles and livery).

Receiving remains - one of the categories required to be itemized on the GPL (if the funeral provider offers the service). This involves services of the funeral provider after initial services have been provided by another establishment at the locale of death. Funeral Rule requires package pricing of this service with a description of the components included.

Domestic Shipping

Types of carriers - The requirements for shipping human remains will vary depending on whether they are being transported by a **common carrier**, defined as any carrier required by law to convey passengers or freight without refusal, if the approved fare or charge is paid (airline, train, etc.); or transported by **private carrier**, defined as those who transport only in particular instances and only for those they chose to contract with (e.g. funeral establishment vehicles and livery).

Common carriers include any mode of public transportation, with the two most common carriers for the transportation of human remains being airlines and trains. For international transports, cargo ships are another alternative. Each of these common carriers are regulated by one or more federal government agencies, such as the Federal Aviation Administration, United States Coast Guard, and Surface Transportation Board.

State transportation boards and authorities may also have regulations specific to a particular mode of transportation, especially when it comes to surface fleets (trucks and trains) on state and local highways and railroads. For the purposes of transporting human remains, states almost always exercise some degree of regulation and oversight, including when the transportation is being provided by a private carrier, such as a funeral establishment.

Common carrier oversight - Any or all of the following elements may be included in state rules and regulations as they relate to transporting human remains domestically by *common* carrier:

➢ bodies must be encased in a rigid container, constructed to withstand hazards associated with the method of transportation;

➢ bodies must be in a leak-proof pouch or container to prevent the leakage of any body fluids;

➢ bodies must be clothed or covered by a shroud or other similar covering;

➢ body orifices must be closed with absorbent cotton or other like material;

➢ a government issued transit, disposition, or similar type permit must accompany the remains and available for inspection upon demand; and

➢ a name tag must be affixed to the body, with the name as it appears on the transit or similar type permit, along with other pertinent information.

Private carrier oversight - Any or all of the following elements may be included in state rules and regulations as they relate to transporting human remains by *private* carrier:

➢ bodies must be encased in a casket or container, or in a leakproof pouch, and steps must be taken to prevent the leakage of any body fluids from the container;

➢ bodies must be secured to a rigid stretcher, litter, or cot, and obscured from public view;

➢ the interior of the vehicle and all associated equipment must be maintained in a clean and sanitary manner; and

➢ the remains must be accompanied by, and/or received by, a licensed funeral director or other similar licensed professional.

Note: The geographical area, distance of travel, and crossing of state lines may trigger additional limits or requirements, such as the need for a government issued transit, disposition, or other similar type permit to accompany the remains.

FTC Funeral Rule - There are two provisions in the FTC Funeral Rule that apply to the domestic shipping of human remains: **forwarding remains** to another funeral home and **receiving remains** from another funeral home. These two items must be listed on a General Price List if they are services offered by the funeral establishment.

The Rule requires package pricing for each of these services. The package price must include a description of all components in the package, including any basic services fees, facility charges, and equipment fees. Some states have passed legislation that requires any common carrier charges being passed on to the consumer be the actual cost, with no mark-up or profit for the funeral establishment allowed.

International Shipping

Government embassies - The U.S. Department of State has government representatives working in almost 400 embassies, consulate offices, and diplomatic missions all over the world. Embassy buildings serve as the headquarters and work place for U.S. government employees and are usually located in the capital city of the foreign country.

An ambassador, also known as the chief of mission, is the highest-ranking diplomat to the host country and a personal representative of the President. Branches of an embassy within the same country are known as consulates and often located in larger cities of the foreign country. One of the primary purposes of a U.S. embassy (or consulate) is to assist American citizens who travel to or live in the host country. This includes assisting families when a U.S. citizen dies in a foreign country.

Foreign countries also have facilities and personnel stationed all over the world for the same reasons the United States does. As of this writing, 178 foreign countries have an embassy office in Washington, D.C., with many maintaining additional consulate offices in large metropolitan areas of the United States. When human remains must be shipped internationally, these world-wide embassy and consulate offices play a major role in facilitating the process.

Time considerations - Time delays when shipping internationally are very common. These may be due to a number of factors, including:

> legal mandates;

> conflicting time zones;

> the number of parties involved;

> documentation authentication requirements;

> flight schedules and availability; and

> language barriers.

Care should therefore be taken by a funeral establishment to inform families to expect the process to take up to a week or more.

On the same token, many countries have strict parameters limiting the length of time that may pass before a final disposition must, by law, take place. It is therefore very important when handling international cases that decisions be made as soon as possible to avoid any delay that might result in failure to comply with the laws or customs of foreign countries.

Shipments to another country - When human remains must be shipped from the United States to a foreign country, the funeral director should contact the embassy or consulate office located in the United States that represents the foreign country. They are familiar with regulatory compliance issues that must be met for their country to receive an international shipment of human remains from the United States. The requirements and documentation vary from one country to the next but may include any or all of the following:

➢ certified copy of a death certificate;

➢ government issued burial, transit, or disposition permit;

➢ a 'Letter of Non-Contagious Disease,' stating the decedent did not have a contagious disease or illness at the time of death;

➢ an affidavit, sworn statement, letter, or other written documentation from a licensed or certified embalmer, or other authorized funeral service practitioner, that the body has been embalmed;

➢ the decedent's foreign passport or visa (if they had one);

➢ copy of the flight or other mode of transportation itinerary;

➢ letter from the funeral establishment attesting to the contents of the transportation container(s);

➢ letter from the funeral establishment or a shipping company acting on behalf of the funeral establishment that international shipping container requirements in the destination country have been complied with fully;

➢ translation of U.S. documents to the language of the destination country; and

➢ compliance with customs requirements of the destination country.

Documentation may need to be endorsed by **apostille**, defined as the certification or legalization of a document for international use in accordance with the 1961 Hague Convention. An apostille endorsement is affixed to a document by designated authorities, such as embassies, ministries, courts, and state or local governments. In the United States, each of the Departments of State in the 50 states are designated authorities.

Funeral directors must ensure strict compliance with the foreign country requirements and any related fees. If human remains arrive without the required documentation or fees, or the documents are not authenticated as required, human remains may be refused and returned to the United States.

Shipments from another country - When a United States citizen dies abroad, notification of the death is usually received by the family via cable from the U.S. embassy (or consulate office) located in the foreign country where the person died. This same office will coordinate with a funeral establishment in the United States to assist in getting the remains returned as soon as possible. They also provide assistance and guidance for any family members in the host country at the time.

When working with a foreign country, funeral directors should be aware of the following:

➢ The U.S. Embassy located in the foreign country will provide information on the available disposition options in the country of death and the associated costs.

➢ The preparation, handling, and disposition of human remains must comply with the laws and customs of the host country, not the United States.

➢ Many foreign countries do not offer or include embalming as an option in caring for the dead and, in those countries that do, embalming and cosmetics may not meet standards commonly accepted in the United States. Families should be made aware the remains may not be suitable for viewing.

➢ International air freight charges are very expensive.

➢ All of the expenses related to a death in a foreign country are the responsibility of the immediate family. The United States government does not provide any financial support to pay for funeral expenses or to repatriate (return) human remains to the United States.

➢ The U.S. Embassy in the foreign country will assist with transmitting funds; disbursing those funds on behalf of the family; providing an account of the disbursements; and refunding any surplus funds.

➢ If no one assumes financial responsibility for a final disposition, the U.S. consulate office is required to request local authorities to provide for the disposition, in accordance with the laws of the host country.

➢ Cremation is an option in most countries, but there are locations where local laws or customs may forbid the cremation of human remains. In addition, cremation facilities may not be located in close proximity to where the death occurred, and the cost for transportation may be excessive when compared to standards in the United States.

➢ Burial in the foreign country where the death took place may also be an option for final disposition and potentially far less expensive than transporting the remains back to the United States. There are however some countries that do not allow for the burial of foreign nationals on their soil.

Shipping by Airline
While different modes of transportation are available, airline service is the predominate means to move human remains long distances, both domestically and internationally. Funeral establishments must comply with the shipping requirements for the airline they have chosen.

These requirements vary from one carrier to the next; however, all of the major carriers usually have the requirements for shipping human remains posted on their websites.

In addition to the airline requirements, funeral establishments must apply to each airline they wish to use to be registered as a *known shipper*. The known shipper program, administered by the federal Transportation Security Administration (TSA), is designed to:

> ...*impose significant barriers to terrorists seeking to use the air cargo transportation system for malicious purposes*.

By accepting shipments only from known shippers, the TSA has significantly reduced this potential threat.

As an alternative, funeral establishments may contract with a private entity that specializes in shipping human remains and already registered as a known shipper with all the major airlines. These companies schedule the flights; coordinate with the sending and receiving funeral establishments; pay cash advance expenses; and ensure compliance with airline regulations.

Note: See Guide 5 to view Typical Airline Shipping Requirements.

Chapter 16: Shipping Containers

Overview
There will always be times when human remains must be transported from one distant location to another, even in some cases from one continent to another. The situation may require the transport of human remains only, or human remains and the container in which they are being held, such as a casket. In either case, there are transportation containers designed to handle any potential scenario in the funeral service industry. This chapter reviews the containers available for the transfer and/or transportation of human remains all over the world.

Chapter Definitions
Air tray - a transfer container consisting of a wooden tray with a cardboard covering for the casket.

Combination case (AKA combo case) - a transfer container for uncasketed remains consisting of a particle board tray with a cardboard cover.

Metal case (Ziegler case) - a gasketed container, which can be used as an insert in a casket or as a separate shipping container.

Pouch - a leak resistant, zippered bag designed to contain human remains and any body fluids; used primarily for the removal of human remains from the place of death.

Transfer container - an enclosure used for the protection of human remains during transportation.

Ziegler case - see metal case (represents a specific brand of metal case, but in use have become synonymous terms).

Transfer Containers
With the increased ease of mobility in the United States, more and more extended families are living considerable distances apart from each other. This results in more instances where decedent remains need to be transported, if not for a funeral service, than for return to a hometown family plot already safeguarding the remains of previous generations.

A **transfer container** is the general term used to define an outer enclosure utilized for the protection of casketed or uncasketed remains during transportation beyond local destinations.

There are four types of transfer containers:

1. Air trays (casketed remains).

2. Combination cases (remains only, no casket).

3. Wood boxes, or shipping crates (casketed remains).

4. Metal (or Ziegler) shipping cases (remains only, no casket).

1. *Air tray* - This transfer container consists of a wooden tray with a cardboard covering for the casket. They are commonly used for the transfer of casketed human remains. Air trays have a solid wooden tray bottom with a cardboard cover, lifting straps, and cinching straps to secure the top. Most also have corner protectors to prevent damage during shipping and add strength to the base of the unit.

When prepared for shipping, the remains should be lowered as far down as possible in the casket, and the face and hands should be covered to prevent any cosmetics from being transferred to the interior of the casket during transport. Padding may be placed around the body as needed to minimize any unnecessary shifting of the remains in the container.

Air tray containers may be advertised in the United States as being certified to carry certain weights by Airlines for America (A4A), formerly the Air Transport Association (ATA).

This is an AMA Containers, fully-assembled, wood base air tray, certified to carry up to 1000 pounds by the A4A. It has a solid plywood bottom with a wood frame, corner edge protectors, lifting handles, and cover cinching straps.[4]

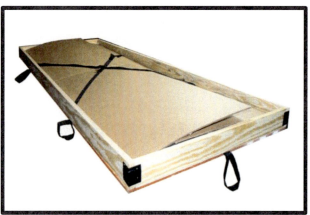

This is the same wood base air tray shown above, configured for delivery to a funeral home, and thereafter, preparation for receiving casketed human remains.[4]

2. *Combination case (AKA combo case)* - This transfer container for uncasketed remains consists of a particle board tray with a cardboard cover. They are for one-time use only.

Combination cases usually have a plastic bag or liner to contain any body fluids that may leak; however, the use of plastic undergarments is a common and good practice to follow. The body should never be wrapped in plastic, as this may capture moisture and create mold. Remains should always be clothed, either with a shroud, hospital gown, or similar covering, and a name tag should be affixed to the body for identification. The body itself should be safely secured to the base of the combo case by using the cinching straps provided. For the purposes of removing remains at the receiving funeral establishment, a sheet should be placed under the body. Other items being shipped in the container, such as clothing and shoes, should be placed in plastic bags and secured so they cannot move about in the container during transit.

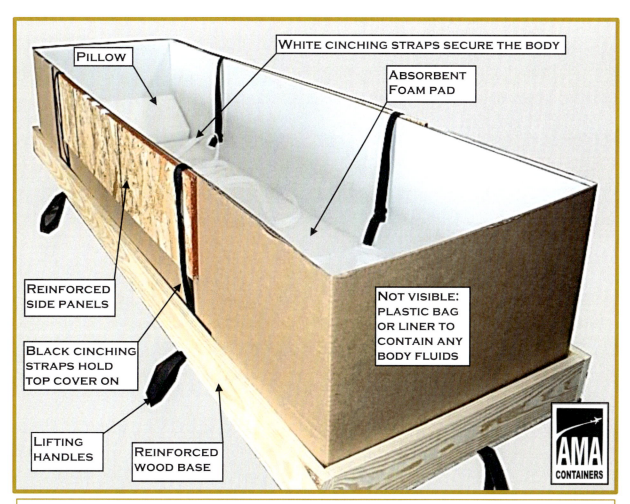

PILLOW

WHITE CINCHING STRAPS SECURE THE BODY

ABSORBENT FOAM PAD

REINFORCED SIDE PANELS

NOT VISIBLE: PLASTIC BAG OR LINER TO CONTAIN ANY BODY FLUIDS

BLACK CINCHING STRAPS HOLD TOP COVER ON

LIFTING HANDLES

REINFORCED WOOD BASE

AMA CONTAINERS

The images on this page are of the AMA Containers combination case (tray). They are designed to hold and protect a human body for transport. The lower left image is the "combo" case configured for delivery to a funeral home; and, on the lower right, fully assembled with the top secured in place for transportation.[4]

Note: The definitions for air tray and combination case are not universally recognized as precise definitions by all of the allied professionals in the funeral service industry. The definitions provided at the beginning of this chapter are those used by the American Board of Funeral Service Education and may therefore appear in the form of test questions on national board examinations.

3. *Wooden boxes* - These containers may be used to transfer human remains internationally. Commonly called shipping crates, these boxes are rugged containers designed specifically to carry casketed remains or metal Ziegler cases.

Shipping crates made of wood and being transported internationally must comply with the International Plant Protection Convention (IPPC), the purpose of which is to prevent and control the introduction and spread of pests from plants and plant products. The wood is either heat treated (HT) or fumigated with methyl bromide (MB), then stamped or branded with a mark of compliance. Containers in compliance must display the certification symbol on the wood. The symbols are commonly referred to as a bug or wheat stamp.

The image below has a certification stamp showing the wood was heat treated (HT) to comply with IPPC requirements.

This is an AMA Containers cleated wood International Shipping Crate. These wooden boxes are built specifically to hold and protect a casket or metal case containing human remains for transportation, especially those being sent internationally.[4]

4. *Metal shipping case* - Also known as a **Ziegler case**, this gasketed container is used as an insert inside a casket or as an independent shipping container. They may also be placed inside a wooden international shipping box.

These containers are usually constructed using 20-gauge steel and have a gasket that seals the contents inside when the lid is closed and compressed against the body of the case. The compression of the two pieces is achieved with threaded fasteners, a method that mates metal screws with pre-formed internal threads, or metal screws that form their own thread as they are inserted.

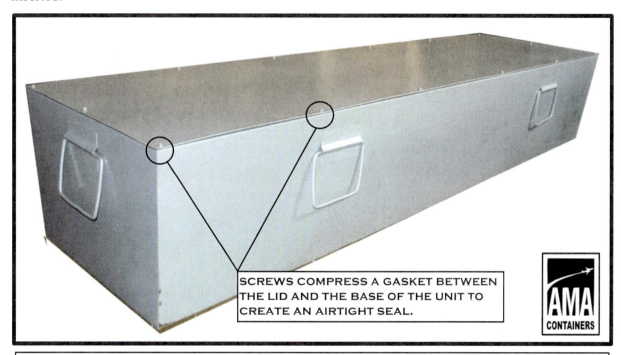

SCREWS COMPRESS A GASKET BETWEEN THE LID AND THE BASE OF THE UNIT TO CREATE AN AIRTIGHT SEAL.

This is an AMA Containers Ziegler metal shipping case. The screws compress the lid against a rubber gasket in the base piece of the case to create a seal and protect the contents.[4]

Note: While passenger cabins on airplanes are pressurized, the cargo bins where human remains are loaded are pressurized. Therefore, care must be taken when shipping remains in metal sealer caskets or Ziegler metal shipping cases, to ensure they are properly vented to allow for changes in air pressure. Failure to do so could result in the collapse of the container due to extreme pressure at higher altitudes.

When using a metal sealer casket, the sealed cap covering the casket key hole should be removed, secured in an envelope, and placed inside the casket before it is locked for transport. Ziegler cases usually have a built-in vent that can be opened whenever they are being carried on a flight.

Miscellaneous Containers
There are three additional miscellaneous containers used in funeral service, including: 1) casket liners, 2) pouches, and 3) combination units.

Casket liners - These liners are made of metal and placed inside a casket shell to provide additional protection for human remains. They are most often used with wooden caskets. These liners are rarely seen today in modern caskets, having been largely replaced by metal caskets, metal burial vaults and the option to have metal liners in concrete burial vaults.

Pouches - defined as leak resistant, zippered bags used to hold human remains and any body fluids. They provide important sanitary protections to those individuals tasked with handling human remains and ensure containment of any body fluids that may be present. They are made of a plastic-based material and available in a range of weight thicknesses, with heavy-duty pouches often used at the scene of a violent death, such as an automobile accident or suicide by firearm.

Sometimes crudely referred to as body bags, pouches are commonly used for the removal of human remains from the place of death to ensure a level of privacy and respect for the deceased. As a general rule, medical care institutions will place human remains in pouches at the time of death to await release to an authorized funeral service provider. In addition, most states require human remains delivered to a crematory be in a leak-proof container, with the standard, light-duty pouch the container of choice for cremations.

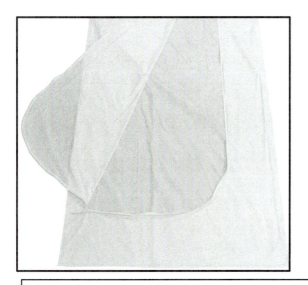 

Left - Typical light-duty pouch; usually white in color with no carrying handles.

Right - Typical heavy-duty pouch; usually black in color with eight carrying handles.
They may be referred to as a disaster or mortuary pouch.

Combination units - These containers are designed and intended to be used as an all-in-one casket and permanent burial receptacle. They are usually manufactured using a plastic or polymer-based material and produced specifically for infant and child cases.

Form 1: New Case Intake Sheet

The New Case Intake Sheet is used at the time of receiving an initial notification of death. It provides a record of the primary and supplementary information provided to the funeral establishment, as discussed in the chapter titled, *Notification of Death*.

Funeral establishment owners may customize this form to reflect the communities they serve and the unique aspects of their business. For instance, they may add a section about the arrangement conference date, time, and location; and then take the form with them to the transfer location to fill-in this information after speaking with the family.

It is important to note the supplementary information section of the form concerning embalming, disposition, and related issues does not need to be completed at the time of the initial notification. Families are struggling to cope with the death of their loved one at the time of the first call, and questions of this nature can be overwhelming and counter-productive. These inquiries are usually better left until a funeral director can personally meet face-to-face with the individual having the legal right to control the final disposition. This affords the opportunity to answer any immediate questions and be supportive during the time of greatest need.

A New Case Intake Sheet form is shown on the next page.

XYZ Funeral Home - New Case Intake Sheet

Notification Date/Time: _____ **By Staff Member:** _____

DECEASED and NOK CONTACT INFORMATION

Deceased: _____ Gender: ❑ Male ❑ Female

DOB: _____ DOD: _____ TOD: _____ ❑ am ❑ pm

NOK 1: _____ ❑ Spouse ❑ Other _____

Phone 1 _____ ____Phone 2 _____ Right to control final disposition? ❑ Yes ❑ No

Address _____ Email _____

NOK 2: _____ ❑ Spouse ❑ Other _____

Phone 1 _____ ____Phone 2 _____ Right to control final disposition? ❑ Yes ❑ No

Address _____ Email _____

LOCATION OF TRANSFER (FROM)

Institution or address: _____

Instructions, notes: _____

CERTIFIER OF DEATH

Certifier: _____ **Title:** _____ **License/Reg. No.** _____

Certifier has authorized release of remains to funeral home: ❑ Yes ❑ No ❑ Pending (explain in notes)

Medical examiner/coroner case? ❑ Yes ❑ No If yes, name/title _____

Notes: _____

NOTIFICATIONS FROM INSTITUTIONS

Name: _____ **Title:** _____ **Phone:** _____

Remains released and ready for removal: ❑ Yes ❑ No

Refrigeration/holding available, if needed: ❑ Yes ❑ No

Family member present (or may be) when funeral service arrives? ❑ Yes ❑ No ❑ Unknown

For institution cases, request NOK contact information and enter in first section above.

FUNERAL HOME STAFF ASSIGNMENT(S)

Assigned to: _____ Date/Time: _____

Assignment notes:

SUPPLEMENTARY INFORMATION (*Use Discretion! - NOT Required Immediately*)

Disposition: ❑ Interment ❑ Cremation ❑ Green burial ❑ Alkaline hydrolysis ❑ Other _____

Embalming: ❑ Yes ❑ No ❑ Unknown If yes, authorized by: _____

Notes: _____

_____

_____

Instructions: Complete as much information as possible at time of receiving death notification and take to transfer location to obtain any missing information. When discussing embalming, disposition, or related matters, always speak in-person with the individual(s) holding the legal right to control the final disposition.

Form 2: Arrangement Conference Handout

As provided in the chapter titled, *Transfer (Removal) of Remains*, many families are not familiar with the complexities involved in the planning, preparation, and directing of a funeral service. It is therefore highly recommended funeral directors provide them with a written guide or list of questions and topics to be discussed during the arrangement conference. This gives them the opportunity to gather the documentation and information they need for the meeting, as well as get them thinking about the decisions they are going to be making at the conference.

Those establishments that have chosen to adopt an arrangement conference guide or similar system to aid consumers in preparing for the meeting, have found them to be a valuable resource, both in time and effort spent and in developing a strong, trustful relationship with the families they serve.

An Arrangement Conference Guide is shown on the next page

𝕳𝖚𝖉𝖘𝖔𝖓 𝖁𝖆𝖑𝖑𝖊𝖞 𝕱𝖚𝖓𝖊𝖗𝖆𝖑 𝕳𝖔𝖒𝖊

123 Baker Street
Anytown, NK 12345

ARRANGEMENT CONFERENCE GUIDE FOR OUR VALUED FRIENDS

The Hudson Valley Funeral Home and staff would like to express their deepest appreciation for your decision to entrust us with guiding and assisting you and your family during this difficult time. We will strive to meet and exceed your every expectation, as we work to provide a personal and meaningful experience to honor, remember, and memorialize your loved one.

We will be meeting soon for an arrangement conference – an opportunity to sit down with your family to discuss your thoughts and wishes. In preparation for this meeting, we are providing you with this conference guide. It includes a list of things you may want to think about; things to bring with you; a vital statistics worksheet; and a newspaper notice worksheet.

If you come across any issues or problems as your review this guide or fill out the forms, be assured we will resolve them with you at the time of the arrangement conference.

Things to Think About Doing or Including	Things to Bring with You
Calling hours and visitation?	Clothing and clothing accessories (shoes optional)
A funeral service? When and where?	Military discharge papers and documents
A memorial service? When and where?	Cemetery information and records; deed, lot, etc.
A preferred clergy or other officiant? Who?	Life insurance information; policy, etc.
Disposition options: burial, cremation, natural, etc.	Social security number and related documents
Preferred hairdresser?	Photo for newspaper, online obituary, etc.
Pallbearers available, if needed?	Birth records, including parents birth names

Your arrangement conference has been scheduled and confirmed for _____ ❑ am ❑ pm on _____ with _____ at our 123 Baker Street, Anytown, NK, location.

If you need to speak with us for any reason before the conference, please do not hesitate to call us at 555-555-5555.

VITAL STATISTICS WORKSHEET

We need the information listed here to meet our legal obligations to file a certificate of death. We will resolve any issues or questions about this information with you at the conference meeting.

Legal Name: _____ **Sex:** ❏ M ❏ F
           (first)   (middle)   (last)   (suffix)

DOB: _____ **Age:** _____ **City and State of Birth:** _____

Military Service: ❏ Yes ❏ No If yes, years of service, or conflict: _____
      If yes, be sure to bring military discharge papers to the arrangement meeting.

Highest Level of *Completed* Education:
❏ Less than or equal to 8th grade ❏ Some college, no degree ❏ Master's degree
❏ 9th-12th grade, no diploma ❏ Associates degree ❏ Doctorate/professional degree
❏ High School grad, or GED ❏ Bachelor's degree

Social Security No.: _____ - _____ - _____

Marital Status: ❏ Never married ❏ Married ❏ Widowed ❏ Separated ❏ Divorced
Surviving Spouse: _____
      If married or separated, enter birth name of spouse.

Occupation - For the section below, the information relates to the work this person performed for the <u>longest period in their lifetime</u>. It may not necessarily be the occupation they performed last, liked the most, or held at time of death. The required criteria is the *length* of work service.

Usual occupation: _____

Kind of business/industry: _____

Employer name/location: _____

Residence: _____

Parents (use maiden/birth names)

Father: _____

Mother: _____

Person Providing this information:

Name _____

Address _____

Phone 1: _____ _____ Phone 2: _____
     ❏ Home ❏ Work ❏ Cell   ❏ Home ❏ Work ❏ Cell

NEWSPAPER NOTICE WORKSHEET

Education: Schools and colleges, graduation dates, sports participation, awards, club memberships or other school related activities, etc.

Notes for education: _____

Church Affiliations: Names, locations, length of membership, positions held, participation in activities, any special recollections, etc.

Notes for church affiliations: _____

Employment: Employers, length of service, retirement dates, job titles, duties, and responsibilities, etc.

Notes for employment: _____

Marriage: Where, when, clergy, length, ages at the time, etc.

Notes for marriage: _____

Enjoyment. Activities enjoyed - cooking, gardening, family, friends, bingo, camping, boating, sports, casinos, animals, etc.

Notes for enjoyment: _____

Military Service: Branch of, when, where, decorations, ranks, etc.

Notes for military service: _____

Memberships: Memberships, such as bowling leagues, senior citizens, fire departments, EMS agencies, volunteer groups, boy scouts, hunting clubs, and fraternal organizations (i.e. Elks, Lions, Veteran's etc.).

Notes for memberships: _____

Donations: If you are going to suggest donations, name the organizations.

Notes for donations: _____

Predeceased By:

1. _____   4. _____
2. _____   5. _____
3. _____   6. _____

Survived By: (include relationship)

1. _____   6. _____
2. _____   7. _____
3. _____   8. _____
4. _____   9. _____
5. _____   10. _____

Other Items for a Newspaper Notice:

_____
_____
_____

Form 3: Disposition Permits

As described in the chapter titled, *Death Reporting and Registration*, disposition permits are issued by registrars to authorize the final disposition of human remains or the transportation of those remains to another jurisdiction. Each state develops their own form and, while they are all slightly different, the information and signatures they require are very similar from one state to the next. These permits are used to track the final disposition of human remains.

Sample disposition permits issued by the states of Tennessee, California, New York, and Michigan are provided below.

TENNESSEE DEPARTMENT OF HEALTH
OFFICE OF VITAL RECORDS
PERMIT FOR FINAL DISPOSITION OF HUMAN REMAINS

Name of Decedent	Sex	Date of Birth	Date of Death

Place of Death-City or Town, County — Name of Informant

Name of Funeral Director (or Person Acting as Such) — Name of Physician Who Will Certify Death

State of Tennessee

Address of Funeral Director (or Person Acting as Such)

Application for Permit

I hereby apply for a permit for the disposition of the remains of the above named decedent. I agree to abide by all laws and rules of the Tennessee Department of Health and all other laws pertaining to the preparation, container, transportation, and burial of human remains. If I have not been able to submit a certificate of death for this person at the time of this application, I agree to file, within five days of the date of death, the properly completed certificate with the local registrar in the county where the death occurred.

Signature _____ Date Signed _____

Address _____

TYPE OF PERMIT REQUESTED - Check all that are applicable

☐ Burial   ☐ Transit   ☐ Scientific Use

Note: This form may NOT be used as a permit for cremation.

BURIAL — Name and Address of Cemetery where Remains are to be Interred

TRANSIT — From: _____ To: _____

SCIENTIFIC USE — Name and Address of Facility Receiving Remains

PERMIT OF LOCAL OR DEPUTY REGISTRAR

This permit for the final disposition of the remains of the person named above is granted for the purpose(s) checked above.

Signature of Local or Deputy Registrar _____ Date Signed _____

Address _____

CERTIFICATION OF PERSON IN CHARGE OF THE DISPOSITION

I certify that the disposition of the remains of the above named was made in accordance with this permit on

Date _____ at _____ Place _____

Signature _____

Address _____

When the disposition is complete, mail this form to the local or deputy registrar who issued this permit.

PH-3774   RDA 1468

APPLICATION AND PERMIT FOR DISPOSITION OF HUMAN REMAINS

USE BLACK INK ONLY — MAKE NO ERASURES, WHITEOUTS, PHOTOCOPIES, OR OTHER ALTERATIONS

1A. NAME OF DECEDENT—FIRST	1B. MIDDLE	1C. LAST

2. SEX	3. DATE OF BIRTH (MONTH, DAY, YEAR)	4. DATE OF DEATH (MONTH, DAY, YEAR)	5. (FETAL DEATH ONLY) DATE OF EVENT (MONTH, DAY, YEAR)

6A. CITY OF DEATH	6B. COUNTY OF DEATH—IF OUTSIDE OF CALIFORNIA, ENTER STATE

7A. NAME OF INFORMANT	7B. RELATIONSHIP TO DECEDENT	8A. TYPED NAME AND ADDRESS OF CALIFORNIA-LICENSED FUNERAL DIRECTOR OR PERSON ACTING AS SUCH—STREET NUMBER AND NAME, CITY, STATE, ZIP CODE	8B. CALIFORNIA LICENSE NUMBER—IF APPLICABLE
7C. INFORMANT'S FULL MAILING ADDRESS—STREET NUMBER AND NAME, CITY, STATE			

State of California

ACKNOWLEDGEMENT OF APPLICANT—I hereby acknowledge as applicant that I have the right to control disposition pursuant to Health & Safety Code Section 7100, and that the disposition stated herein is one of the dispositions authorized by Health & Safety Code Section 103055.	9A. APPLICANT SIGNATURE ▶	9B. DATE SIGNED

PERMIT AND AUTHORIZATION OF LOCAL REGISTRAR—ANY CHANGE IN DISPOSITION REQUIRES A NEW PERMIT TO SHOW FINAL DISPOSITION

This permit is issued in accordance with provisions of the California Health and Safety Code and is the authority for the disposition specified in this permit. **NOTE: This permit gives no right of disposal outside of California.**

10A. AMOUNT OF FEE PAID $	10B. DATE PERMIT ISSUED	10C. SIGNATURE OF LOCAL REGISTRAR ISSUING PERMIT ▶

10D. ADDRESS OF REGISTRAR OF DISTRICT OF DEATH—IF DEATH OCCURRED IN CALIFORNIA	10E. ADDRESS OF REGISTRAR OF DISTRICT OF DISPOSITION—IF DIFFERENT FROM 10D

11. AUTHORIZED DISPOSITION(S)—CHECK APPLICABLE ITEMS

☐ A. BURIAL OR SCATTERING IN A CEMETERY (INCLUDES ENTOMBMENT)
☐ B. CREMATION
☐ C. DISPOSITION OF CREMATED REMAINS OTHER THAN IN A CEMETERY

☐ D. SCIENTIFIC USE
☐ E. TEMPORARY ENVAULTMENT
☐ F. DISINTERMENT
☐ G. SHIP IN TO CALIFORNIA
☐ H. TRANSIT OUTSIDE OF CALIFORNIA

FOR CORONER'S USE ONLY
☐ I. DISPOSITION PENDING—LOCATION OF REMAINS—NAME AND ADDRESS

BURIAL OR SCATTERING IN A CEMETERY (INCLUDES ENTOMBMENT)	12A. NAME AND ADDRESS OF CALIFORNIA CEMETERY	12B. DATE BURIED	12C. INTERMENT NUMBER—IF APPLICABLE
		12D. SIGNATURE OF PERSON IN CHARGE OF BURIAL OR SCATTERING ▶	

CREMATION	13A. NAME AND ADDRESS OF CALIFORNIA CREMATORY	13B. DATE CREMATED	13C. CREMATION NUMBER—IF APPLICABLE
		13D. SIGNATURE OF PERSON IN CHARGE OF CREMATION ▶	

SCIENTIFIC USE	14A. NAME AND ADDRESS OF CALIFORNIA FACILITY RECEIVING REMAINS	14B. DATE RECEIVED
		14C. SIGNATURE OF PERSON IN CHARGE OF FACILITY ▶

TRANSIT	15A. NAME AND ADDRESS IN RECEIVING STATE OR COUNTRY WHERE REMAINS OR CREMATED REMAINS ARE TO BE SHIPPED	15B. NAME AND ADDRESS OF PERSON IN CHARGE OF PLACING WITH THE CARRIER
		15C. SIGNATURE OF PERSON IN CHARGE OF PLACING WITH THE CARRIER ▶ / 15D. DATE SHIPPED

SCATTERING/ BURIAL AT SEA OR DISPOSITION OTHER THAN IN A CEMETERY	16A. ADDRESS, NEAREST POINT ON SHORELINE, OR OTHER DESCRIPTION SUFFICIENT TO IDENTIFY FINAL PLACE AND CALIFORNIA DISTRICT OF DISPOSITION; IF BURIAL AT SEA, ONLY ENTER LATITUDE AND LONGITUDE	16B. DATE OF DISPOSITION	16C. LICENSE NUMBER OF CREMATED REMAINS DISPOSER—IF APPLICABLE
		16D. SIGNATURE OF PERSON IN CHARGE OF SCATTERING OR BURIAL ▶	

UPON AUTHORIZATION OF PERMIT, DISTRIBUTE COPIES AS FOLLOWS:

COPY 1 – ACCOMPANIES REMAINS TO THE STATED PLACE OF DISPOSITION. PERSON IN CHARGE OF DISPOSITION IS RESPONSIBLE FOR COMPLETING AND FORWARDING THE PERMIT WITHIN 10 DAYS OF DISPOSITION TO THE REGISTRAR OF THE DISTRICT IN WHICH DISPOSITION OCCURRED OR THE DISTRICT NEAREST THE POINT WHERE THE CREMATED REMAINS WERE SCATTERED AT SEA.*
COPY 2 – RETAINED BY PERSON IN CHARGE OF THE CEMETERY, CREMATORY, FACILITY FOR SCIENTIFIC USE, OR BY THE PERSON IN CHARGE OF DISPOSING OF THE CREMATED REMAINS.
COPY 3 – RETURN TO COUNTY OF DEATH WHEN THE REMAINS ARE DISPOSED OF IN ANOTHER DISTRICT. IF NOT APPLICABLE, COPY 3 MAY BE DISCARDED.*
COPY 4 – RETAINED BY REGISTRAR ISSUING THE PERMIT.*

* THE LOCAL REGISTRAR MAY DESTROY ANY ORIGINAL OR DUPLICATE PERMIT AFTER ONE YEAR FROM ISSUE DATE.

STATE OF CALIFORNIA, DEPARTMENT OF PUBLIC HEALTH, OFFICE OF VITAL RECORDS

VS 9 Rev. 01/01/2008

NEW YORK STATE DEPARTMENT OF HEALTH
Vital Records Section

Burial - Transit Permit

DECEDENT

Name	First	Middle	Last	Sex

Date of Death	Age	If Veteran of U.S. Armed Forces, War or Dates

Place of Death City, Town or Village	Hospital, Institution or Street Address

Manner of Death ☐ Natural Cause ☐ Accident ☐ Homicide ☐ Suicide ☐ Undetermined Circumstances ☐ Pending Investigation

Medical Certifier	Name	Title
	Address	

State of New York

Death Certificate Filed City, Town or Village	District Number	Register Number

DISPOSITION

☐ Burial ☐ Entombment ☐ Cremation	Date	Cemetery or Crematory
	Address	

☐ Removal and/or Hold	Date	Place Removed and/or Held
	Address	

☐ Transportation by Common Carrier	Date	Point of Shipment
	Destination	

☐ Disinterment	Date	Cemetery Address

☐ Reinterment	Date	Cemetery Address

PERMIT

Permit Issued to Name of Funeral Home	Registration Number
Address	

Name of Funeral Firm Making Disposition or to Whom Remains are Shipped, If Other than Above

Address

Permission is hereby granted to dispose of the human remains described above as indicated.

Date Issued _____ Registrar of Vital Statistics _____

(signature)

District Number _____ Place _____

ENDORSEMENT

I certify that the remains of the decedent identified above were disposed of in accordance with this permit on:

Date of Disposition _____ Place of Disposition _____

(address)

_____ _____ _____

(section) *(lot number)* *(grave number)*

Name of Sexton or Person in Charge of Premises _____

(please print)

Signature _____ Title _____

(over)

DOH-1555 (02/2004)

BURIAL–TRANSIT PERMIT   No. _____

MICHIGAN DEPARTMENT OF COMMUNITY HEALTH

Full name of deceased _____ Date of death_____ 20____

Place of death _____ Sex _____ Date of birth _____ _____
(County)   (Township or village or city)

Cause of death _____

Method of disposal _____ Veteran? _____
(Whether burial, cremation, storage, etc)   (Cemetery or crematory)   (Yes or No)

State _____

APPROVED FOR CREMATION

Signature of Medical Examiner_____ Date _____ 20____

State of Michigan

A certificate of death having been filed as required by the laws or regulations of this state, permission is hereby given

to _____ Address_____

to dispose of body of said deceased.

Signature_____ Date _____ 20____
(Check one: ☐ Registrar   ☐ Funeral Director   ☐ Mortuary Science Licensee)

CEMETERY OR CREMATORY AUTHORITY SHALL FILL OUT SPACE BELOW

Body was _____ on _____ 20____ in _____
(State whether cremated, buried, stored, etc.)   (Cemetery or crematory)

Place_____ Signature _____
(Sexton or person in charge)

This permit must be endorsed by the sexton (*or by the funeral director or Mortuary Science licensee where there is no sexton*).

(OVER)

DCH-0490A (5/02) Authority: Act 368 of 1978 and Act 299 of 1980

Form 4: Statement of Death by Funeral Director

Funeral directors are responsible for notifying the United States Social Security Administration (SSA) whenever they are going file a Certificate of Death with a state vital records office. The one-page form for this purpose, *Statement of Death by Funeral Director*, may be mailed or faxed to a local or district SSA office. This notification meets one of the criteria requirements for a family when they are applying for survivor benefits and assists the SSA in making a determination on the awarding of benefits.

Many states that have adopted electronic filing methods for death certificates allow funeral directors to submit the social security number for verification and filing with SSA at the same time as they file the death with the state. If the number is verified by SSA at the same time the certificate if filed, there is no need to send the paper statement of death.

An SSA Statement of Death form is shown on the next page.

SOCIAL SECURITY ADMINISTRATION

Form Approved
OMB No. 0960-0142

STATEMENT OF DEATH BY FUNERAL DIRECTOR

| NAME OF DECEASED | SOCIAL SECURITY NUMBER |
| | __ __ |

FOR SSA USE ONLY

Please complete the items below, and return the form in the enclosed addressed, postage paid envelope. Your assistance and cooperation are appreciated.

PRIVACY ACT/PAPERWORK ACT NOTICE: The information on this form is authorized by Section 404.715 and 404.720 of the Federal Regulations (20 CFR 404.715 and 404.720). While your response is voluntary, we need your assistance to make an accurate and timely determination concerning the death of the individual named above, and to determine if there are survivors who may be eligible for Social Security benefits.

We may also use the information you give us when we match records by computer. Matching programs compare our records with those of other Federal, State or local government agencies. Many agencies may use matching programs to find or prove that a person qualifies for benefits paid by the Federal government. The law allows us to do this even if you do not agree to it.

Explanations about these and other reasons why information you provide us may be used or given out are available in Social Security Offices. If you want to learn more about this, contact any Social Security Office.

Paperwork Reduction Act Statement - This information collection meets the requirements of 44 U.S.C. § 3507, as amended by Section 2 of the Paperwork Reduction Act of 1995. You do not need to answer these questions unless we display a valid Office of Management and Budget control number. We estimate that it will take about 3.5 minutes to read the instructions, gather the facts, and answer the questions. **SEND THE COMPLETED FORM TO YOUR LOCAL SOCIAL SECURITY OFFICE.** The office is listed under U.S. Government agencies in your **telephone directory or you may call Social Security at 1-800-772-1213 (TTY 1-800-325-0778).** *You may send comments on our time estimate above to: SSA, 6401 Security Blvd., Baltimore, MD 21235-6401.* **Send only** *comments relating to our time estimate to this address, not the completed form.*

| 1. NAME OF DECEASED | 2. SOCIAL SECURITY NUMBER __ __ |
| 3. DATE OF DEATH | 4. DATE OF BIRTH *(if known)* | 5. Check (x) whether the deceased was ☐ Male ☐ Female |

6. NAME OF WIDOW OR WIDOWER *(if known)*

7. ADDRESS (No. and Street, P.O. Box) OF WIDOW OR WIDOWER*(if known)*

| CITY | STATE | ZIP CODE | TELEPHONE NUMBER (if Available) (____) area code |

I hereby certify that I am an authorized funeral director and prepared for final disposition the body of the person named above. I understand this statement may be used in connection with an application for Social Security benefits. I declare under penalty of perjury that I have examined all the information on this form, and on any accompanying statements or forms, and it is true and correct to the best of my knowledge. I understand that anyone who knowingly gives a false or misleading statement about a material fact in this information, or causes someone else to do so, commits a crime and may be sent to prison, or may face other penalties, or both.

| NAME AND ADDRESS OF FUNERAL DIRECTOR OR FIRM | SIGNATURE OF FUNERAL DIRECTOR OR AUTHORIZED REPRESENTATIVE |
| | TELEPHONE NUMBER (____) area code | DATE |

FOR SOCIAL SECURITY USE ONLY - DO NOT WRITE IN THIS SPACE

DO Processed (Date)

Form **SSA-721** (5-2005) EF (8-2008) Use 1-2004 edition until supply exhausted

Form 5: Claim for Standard Headstone or Marker

GENERAL INFORMATION SHEET
CLAIM FOR STANDARD GOVERNMENT HEADSTONE OR MARKER

RESPONDENT BURDEN - Public reporting burden for this collection of information is estimated to average 15 minutes per response, including the time for reviewing instructions, searching existing data sources, gathering and maintaining the data needed, and completing and reviewing the collection of information. VA cannot conduct or sponsor a collection of information unless it has a valid OMB number. Your obligation to respond is voluntary, however, your response is required to obtain benefits. Send comments regarding this burden estimate or any other aspect of this collection of information, including suggestions for reducing this burden to the VA Clearance Officer (005R1B), 810 Vermont Avenue, NW, Washington, DC 20420. Please DO NOT send claims for benefits to this address.

PRIVACY ACT - VA considers the responses you submit confidential (38 U.S.C. 5701). VA may only disclose this information outside the VA if the disclosure is authorized under the Privacy Act, including the routine uses identified in the VA system of records, 48VA40B, published in the Federal Register. VA considers the requested information relevant and necessary to determine maximum benefits under the law.

BENEFIT PROVIDED

    a. BURIAL HEADSTONE OR MARKER

      Only for Veterans who died on or after November 1, 1990 - Furnished for the grave of any eligible deceased Veteran and provided for placement in private and local government cemeteries regardless of whether or not the grave is marked with a privately-purchased headstone or marker.

      Only for Veterans who died before November 1, 1990 - Furnished for the **UNMARKED GRAVE** of any eligible deceased Veteran. The applicant must certify that a privately-purchased headstone or marker or Government-furnished headstone or marker is not present on the grave.

    b. MEMORIAL HEADSTONE OR MARKER - Furnished to commemorate an eligible deceased Veteran whose remains have not been recovered or identified, were buried at sea, donated to science, or cremated and the remains scattered. VA will only furnish a memorial headstone or marker after the disposition of the Veteran's remains. A memorial headstone or marker **must be placed in an established cemetery**, and will not be used as a memento. For a memorial headstone or marker please check box in block 34 and explain the disposition of the remains in block 33.

    c. MEDALLION - Eligible deceased Veterans may receive a Government-furnished headstone or marker, or a medallion, but not both. *If requesting a medallion, please use VA Form 40-1330M, Claim for Government Medallion for Placement in a Private Cemetery.*

    d. PRESIDENTIAL MEMORIAL CERTIFICATE - A Presidential Memorial Certificate (PMC) is an engraved paper certificate, signed by the current president, to honor the memory of Veterans discharged under other than dishonorable conditions. If the Veteran is eligible for a headstone, marker, or medallion, one PMC will automatically be provided unless otherwise specified. Additional PMCs may be requested by indicating how many in block 22 of this form.

WHO IS ELIGIBLE - Any deceased Veteran who was discharged under conditions other than dishonorable or any Servicemember of the Armed Forces of the United States who dies on active duty may be eligible. Please attach a copy of the deceased Veteran's discharge certificate (DD Form 214 or equivalent) or a copy of other official document(s) establishing qualifying military service. If you are unable to locate copies of military records, apply anyway, as VA will attempt to obtain records necessary to make an eligibility determination. **Do not send original documents**; they will not be returned. **Service after September 7, 1980, must be for a minimum of 24 months continuous active duty or be completed under special circumstances, e.g., death on active duty.** Persons who have only limited active duty service for training while in the National Guard or Reserves are not eligible unless there are special circumstances, e.g., death while on active duty, or as a result of training. Reservists and National Guard members who, at time of death, were entitled to retired pay, or would have been entitled, but for being under the age of 60, are eligible; please submit a copy of the Reserve Retirement Eligibility Benefits Letter with the claim. Reservists called to active duty other than training and National Guard members who are Federalized and who serve for the period called are eligible. Service prior to World War I requires detailed documentation, e.g., muster rolls, extracts from State files, military or State organization where served, pension or land warrant, etc.

WHO CAN APPLY - Federal regulation defines "applicant" for a **Burial Headstone or Marker** that will mark the gravesite or burial site of an eligible deceased individual as:

    (i) A decedent's family member, which includes the decedent's spouse or individual who was in a legal union as defined in 38 CFR 3.1702(b)(1)(ii) with the decedent; a child, parent, or sibling of the decedent, whether biological, adopted, or step relation; and any lineal or collateral descendant of the decedent;

    (ii) A personal representative, defined as a family member or other individual who has identified himself or herself as the person responsible for making decisions concerning the interment of the remains of or memorialization of a deceased individual;

    (iii) A representative of a Congressionally-chartered Veterans Service Organization;

    (iv) An individual employed by the relevant state, tribal organization, or local government whose official responsibilities include serving veterans and families of veterans, such as a state or county veterans service officer;

    (v) Any individual who is responsible, under the laws of the relevant state or locality, for the disposition of the unclaimed remains of the decedent or for other matters relating to the interment or memorialization of the decedent; or

    (vi) Any individual, if the dates of service of the veteran to be memorialized, or on whose service the eligibility of another individual for memorialization is based, ended prior to April 6, 1917.

Federal regulation defines "applicant" for a **Memorial Headstone or Marker** to commemorate an eligible individual as a member of the decedent's family, which includes the decedent's spouse or individual who was in a legal union as defined in 38 CFR 3.1702(b)(1)(ii) with the decedent; a child, parent, or sibling of the decedent, whether biological, adopted, or step relation; and any lineal or collateral descendant of the decedent.

HOW TO SUBMIT A CLAIM

FAX VA Form 40-1330 claims and supporting documents to **1-800-455-7143**.
IMPORTANT: If faxing more than one claim - fax each claim package (claim plus supporting documents) individually, i.e., disconnect the call and redial for each submission.

        MAIL claims to: **Memorial Products Service (41B)**
                     Department of Veterans Affairs
                     5109 Russell Road
                     Quantico, VA 22134-3903

SIGNATURES REQUIRED - The applicant signs in block 23; the person agreeing to accept delivery (consignee) in block 28, and the cemetery or other responsible official in block 30. If there is no official on duty at the cemetery, the signature of the person responsible for the property listed in block 27 is required. Entries of "None," "Not Applicable," or "NA" will not be accepted. State Veterans' Cemeteries are not required to complete blocks 25, 26, 27, 28 or 29.

ASSISTANCE NEEDED - Should you have questions when filling out this form, you may contact our Applicant Assistance Unit toll free at: 1-800-697-6947, or via e-mail at mps.headstones@va.gov. If additional assistance is needed to complete this claim, contact the nearest VA Regional Office, national cemetery, or a local veterans' organization. No fee should be paid in connection with the preparation of this claim. Use block 33 for any clarification or other information you wish to provide.

TRANSPORTATION AND DELIVERY OF MARKER - The headstone or marker is shipped without charge to the consignee designated in block 25 of the claim. The truck driver is required to bring the pallet or monument to the end of the trailer. The consignee must utilize their equipment to unload the pallet or monument from the truck. **Deliveries will not be made to a Post Office (PO) box unless the delivery address is outside the continental US (CONUS).** You must provide the full delivery address (PO Box is acceptable if outside the CONUS) and telephone number of the consignee. Please explain in block 33 if the consignee is not a business. For delivery to a Rural Route address, you must include a daytime telephone number including area code in block 26. If you fail to include the required address and telephone number, we will not deliver the marker. The Government is not responsible for costs to install or remove the headstone or marker in private cemeteries.

CAUTION - To avoid delays in the production and delivery of the headstone or marker, please check carefully to be sure you have accurately furnished all required information before faxing or mailing the claim. If inaccurate information is furnished, it may result in an incorrectly inscribed headstone or marker. Headstones and markers furnished remain the property of the United States Government and may not be used for any purpose other than to be placed at an eligible individual's grave or in a memorial section within a cemetery.

DETACH AND RETAIN THIS GENERAL INFORMATION SHEET FOR YOUR RECORDS.

VA FORM
DEC 2017 **40-1330**   ALL PREVIOUS VERSIONS OF THIS FORM ARE OBSOLETE.

ILLUSTRATIONS OF STANDARD GOVERNMENT HEADSTONES AND MARKERS

FLAT MARKERS

UPRIGHT HEADSTONE
WHITE MARBLE (U) OR
LIGHT GRAY GRANITE (V)

BRONZE NICHE (Z)

BRONZE (B)

This headstone is 42 inches long, 13 inches wide and 4 inches thick. Weight is approximately 230 pounds. Variations may occur in stone color, and the marble may contain light to moderate veining.

This niche marker is 8-1/2 inches long, 5-1/2 inches wide, with 7/16 inch rise. Weight is approximately 3 pounds; mounting bolts and washers are furnished with the marker. Used for columbarium or mausoleum interment. Also provided to supplement a privately-purchased headstone or marker for eligible Veterans who died on or after November 1, 1990 and are buried in a private cemetery.

This grave marker is 24 inches long, 12 inches wide, with 3/4 inch rise. Weight is approximately 18 pounds. Anchor bolts, nuts and washers for fastening to a base are furnished with the marker. The base is not furnished by the Government.

LIGHT GRAY GRANITE (G) OR WHITE MARBLE (F)

This grave marker is 24 inches long, 12 inches wide, and 4 inches thick. Weight is approximately 130 pounds. Variations may occur in stone color; the marble may contain light to moderate veining.

SMALL FLAT GRANITE (L)

This grave marker is 18 inches long, 12 inches wide, and 3 inches thick. Weight is approximately 70 pounds. Variations may occur in stone color.

NOTE: Historic headstones (Prior to World War I) - In addition to the headstone and markers pictured, two special styles of upright headstones are available for those who served with Union Forces during the Civil War or for those who served in the Spanish-American War. Another style headstone is available for those who served with the Confederate States of America during the Civil War. Requests for these special styles should be made in block 33 of the claim. It is necessary to submit detailed documentation that supports eligibility. Inscriptions on these headstone types are intentionally limited to assure historic accuracy. For example, only rank above 'Private' was historically authorized; emblems of belief and the words 'Civil War' are not authorized.

INSCRIPTION INFORMATION

MANDATORY ITEMS - Information in English about the decedent (provided by an authorized applicant). Such items are: Legal Name, Branch of Service, Year of Birth, Year of Death, and for State Veterans and National Cemeteries only, the section and grave number. Branches of Service are: U.S. Army (USA), U.S. Navy (USN), U.S. Air Force (USAF), U.S. Marine Corps (USMC), U.S. Coast Guard (USCG), U.S. Army Air Forces (USAAF), and other parent organizations authorized for certain periods of time; and special units such as Women's Army Auxiliary Corps (WAAC), Women's Air Force Service Pilots (WASP), U.S. Public Health Service (USPHS), and National Oceanic & Atmospheric Administration (NOAA). Different examples of inscription formats are illustrated above. More than one branch of service is permitted, subject to space availability. The phrase "IN MEMORY OF" is a mandatory inscription on all memorial headstones and markers, as required under 38 CFR 38.630(c).

OPTIONAL ITEMS - Information in English about the decedent (provided by an authorized applicant). Optional items are in bold outlines, which includes month and day of birth in block 10A, month and day of death in block 10B, highest rank attained in block 12, awards in block 14, war service in block 16, and emblem of belief in block 17. War service includes active duty service during a recognized period of war and the individual does not have to serve in the actual place of war, e.g., Vietnam may be inscribed if the Veteran served during the Vietnam War period, even though the individual never served in the country. Supporting documentation must be included with the claim if you wish to include the highest rank and/or awards.

ADDITIONAL ITEMS - Information in English or non-English text about the decedent (provided by an authorized applicant), consisting only of characters of the Latin alphabet and/or numbers. Examples of additional items include appropriate terms of endearment, nicknames (in expressions such as "OUR BELOVED POPPY"), military or civilian credentials or accomplishments such as DOCTOR, REVEREND, etc., and special unit designations such as WOMEN'S ARMY CORPS, ARMY AIR CORPS, ARMY NURSE CORPS or SEABEES. All requests for additional inscription items must be stated in block 18, and are subject to VA approval. No graphics, emblems or pictures are permitted except authorized emblems of belief, the Medal of Honor, and the Southern Cross of Honor for Civil War Confederates.

INCOMPLETE OR INACCURATE INFORMATION ON THE CLAIM MAY RESULT IN ITS RETURN TO THE CLAIMANT, A DELAY IN RECEIPT OF THE HEADSTONE OR MARKER, OR AN INCORRECT INSCRIPTION.

Form approved, OMB No. 2900-0222
Expiration Date: Dec. 31, 2020
Respondent Burden: 15 minutes

CLAIM FOR STANDARD GOVERNMENT HEADSTONE OR MARKER

IMPORTANT: Please read the General Information Sheet before completing this form. Type or print clearly all information except for signatures. Illegible printing could result in an incorrect headstone or marker or delivery. Failure to complete each block may result in delayed processing. *Blocks outlined in bold are optional inscription items.* **PLEASE INCLUDE MILITARY DISCHARGE DOCUMENTS.**

1. DID VA PREVIOUSLY DETERMINE ELIGIBILITY FOR BURIAL AT A VA NATIONAL CEMETERY?
☐ YES ☐ NO ☐ UNSURE

2. TYPE OF REQUEST
☐ INITIAL REQUEST *(First time)*
☐ REPLACEMENT *(Specify reason in Block 33, Remarks)*

3. NAME OF DECEASED TO BE INSCRIBED ON HEADSTONE OR MARKER *(No Nicknames or titles permitted)*

FIRST *(Or Initial)*	MIDDLE *(Or Initial)*	LAST		SUFFIX *(Sr., Jr., II, III, etc.)*

4. GRAVE IS:
☐ CURRENTLY MARKED *(with privately purchased marker)*
☐ NOT MARKED

5. RACE OR ETHNICITY *(You may select more than one. Information will be used for statistical purposes only.)*
☐ AMERICAN INDIAN OR ALASKA NATIVE ☐ NATIVE HAWAIIAN OR OTHER PACIFIC ISLANDER
☐ BLACK OR AFRICAN AMERICAN ☐ WHITE
☐ HISPANIC OR LATINO ☐ OTHER *(Specify)* _____

6. GENDER *(Information will be used for statistical purposes only.)*
☐ MALE
☐ FEMALE

7. AGE AT TIME OF DEATH

VETERAN'S SERVICE AND IDENTIFYING INFORMATION *(Use numbers only, e.g., 05-15-1941)*

8. VETERAN'S SOCIAL SECURITY NO. AND/OR SERVICE NO.
SSN: _____ AND/OR SVC. NO.: _____

9. PLACE OF BIRTH *(City and State or Country)*

10A. DATE OF BIRTH			10B. DATE OF DEATH		
MONTH	DAY	YEAR	MONTH	DAY	YEAR

PERIODS OF ACTIVE MILITARY DUTY *(For additional space use Block 33)*

11A. DATE(S) ENTERED			11B. DATE(S) SEPARATED		
MONTH	DAY	YEAR	MONTH	DAY	YEAR

12. HIGHEST RANK ATTAINED *(No pay grades)*

13. BRANCH OF SERVICE *(Check applicable box(es) - must be consistent with rank in Box 12)*

ARMY	NAVY	MARINE CORPS	COAST GUARD	AIR FORCE	ARMY AIR FORCES	MERCHANT MARINE	OTHER *(Specify)*
☐	☐	☐	☐	☐	☐	☐	☐

14. VALOR OR PURPLE HEART AWARD(S) *(Documentation must be provided)*

MEDAL OF HONOR	DST SVC CROSS	SILVER STAR	DST FLYING CROSS	PURPLE HEART	AIR MEDAL	OTHER *(Specify)*
☐	☐	☐	☐	☐	☐	☐

15. TYPE OF HEADSTONE OR MARKER REQUESTED *(Check one)*

FLAT BRONZE	FLAT GRANITE	UPRIGHT MARBLE	FLAT MARBLE	BRONZE NICHE	UPRIGHT GRANITE	SMALL FLAT GRANITE
☐ B	☐ G	☐ U	☐ F	☐ Z	☐ V	☐ L

16. WAR SERVICE *(Check applicable box(es)*
☐ WORLD WAR II ☐ PERSIAN GULF
☐ KOREA ☐ AFGHANISTAN
☐ VIETNAM ☐ IRAQ
☐ OTHER *(Specify)*

17. EMBLEM OF BELIEF *(Optional)*
EMBLEM NUMBER *(Specify)*
(See page 5 for available emblems)
☐ _____
☐ NONE

18. ADDITIONAL INSCRIPTION/TERM OF ENDEARMENT *(Optional)* *(Space will vary according to type of marker)*

19a. NAME AND MAILING ADDRESS OF APPLICANT *(No., Street, City, State, and ZIP Code)*

19b. DAYTIME OR CELL PHONE NO. OF APPLICANT *(Include Area Code)*

19c. E-MAIL ADDRESS *(Optional)*

19d. FAX NO. *(Optional)*

20. ARE YOU:
☐ FAMILY MEMBER *(Specify relationship)* _____
☐ PERSONAL REPRESENTATIVE *(Person responsible for decisions concerning burial of decedent; include written authorization)*
☐ VETERANS SERVICE OFFICER
☐ FUNERAL HOME MANAGEMENT *(that received the unclaimed remains)*
☐ CEMETERY MANAGEMENT *(where the unclaimed remains are buried)*
☐ OTHER *(Specify)* _____

21. I WOULD LIKE A PRESIDENTIAL MEMORIAL CERTIFICATE
☐ YES ☐ NO

22. IF "YES" HOW MANY?

CERTIFICATION: By signing below I certify the headstone or marker will be installed in the cemetery listed in block 27 at no expense to the Government and all information entered on this form is true and correct to the best of my knowledge. I also certify, to the best of my knowledge, that the decedent has never committed a serious crime, such as murder or other offense that could have resulted in imprisonment for life, has never been convicted of a serious crime, and has never been convicted of a sexual offense for which he or she was sentenced to a minimum of life imprisonment.

PENALTY: The law provides severe penalties, which include fine or imprisonment, or both, for the willful submission of any statement or evidence of a material fact, knowing it to be false or for the fraudulent acceptance of any benefit to which you are not entitled.

23. SIGNATURE OF APPLICANT

24. DATE *(MM/DD/YYYY)*

25. NAME AND DELIVERY ADDRESS OF BUSINESS (CONSIGNEE) THAT WILL ACCEPT PREPAID DELIVERY *(No., Street, City, State, and ZIP Code; P.O. BOX for non-CONUS address)* **MUST SIGN IN BLOCK 28**

26. DAYTIME OR CELL PHONE NO. OF CONSIGNEE *(Include Area Code)*

27. NAME AND ADDRESS OF CEMETERY OR FAMILY PLOT WHERE GRAVE IS LOCATED *(No., Street, City, State, and ZIP Code)* **MUST SIGN IN BLOCK 30**

CERTIFICATION: By signing below I agree to accept prepaid delivery of the headstone or marker.

28. PRINTED NAME AND SIGNATURE OF PERSON REPRESENTING BUSINESS (CONSIGNEE) NAMED IN BLOCK 25

29. DATE *(MM/DD/YYYY)*

CERTIFICATION: By signing below I certify the type of headstone or marker checked in block 15 is permitted in the cemetery named in block 27.

30. PRINTED NAME AND SIGNATURE OF CEMETERY OR OTHER RESPONSIBLE OFFICIAL

31. DAYTIME PHONE NO OF CEMETERY *(Include Area Code)*

32. DATE *(MM/DD/YYYY)*

33. REMARKS

34. CHECK BOX BELOW IF REMAINS ARE NOT BURIED AND EXPLAIN BELOW *(e.g., buried at sea, remains scattered, etc.)*
☐ REMAINS NOT BURIED

35. SECTION/GRAVE NO. *(State Cemetery Only)*

VA FORM DEC 2017 **40-1330** ALL PREVIOUS VERSIONS OF THIS FORM ARE OBSOLETE

AVAILABLE EMBLEMS OF BELIEF FOR PLACEMENT ON GOVERNMENT HEADSTONES AND MARKERS *(See block 17)*

(01) LATIN CROSS (Christian)

(02) BUDDHIST (Wheel of Righteousness)

(03) JEWISH (Star of David)

(04) PRESBYTERIAN CROSS

(05) RUSSIAN ORTHODOX CROSS

(06) LUTHERAN CROSS

(07) EPISCOPAL CROSS

(08) UNITARIAN CHURCH (Flaming Chalice)

(09) UNITED METHODIST CHURCH

(10) AARONIC ORDER CHURCH

(11) MORMON (Angel Moroni)

(12) NATIVE AMERICAN CHURCH OF NORTH AMERICA

...

(13) SERBIAN ORTHODOX

(14) GREEK CROSS

(15) BAHAI (9 Pointed Star)

(16) ATHEIST

(17) MUSLIM (Crescent and Star)

(18) HINDU

(19) KONKO-KYO FAITH

(20) COMMUNITY OF CHRIST

(21) SUFISM REORIENTED

(22) TENRIKYO CHURCH

(23) SEICHO-NO-IE

(24) CHURCH OF WORLD MESSIANITY

(25) UNITED CHURCH OF RELIGIOUS SCIENCE

(26) CHRISTIAN REFORMED CHURCH

(27) UNITED MORAVIAN CHURCH

(28) ECKANKAR

(29) CHRISTIAN CHURCH

(30) CHRISTIAN & MISSIONARY ALLIANCE

(31) UNITED CHURCH OF CHRIST

(32) HUMANIST

(33) PRESBYTERIAN CHURCH (USA)

(34) IZUMO TAISHAKYO MISSION OF HAWAII

(35) SOKA GAKKAI INTERNATIONAL (USA)

(36) SIKH (KHANDA)

(37) WICCAN (Pentacle)

(38) LUTHERAN CHURCH MISSOURI SYNOD

(39) NEW APOSTOLIC CHURCH

(40) SEVENTH DAY ADVENTIST CHURCH

(41) CELTIC CROSS

(42) ARMENIAN CROSS

(43) FAROHAR

(44) MESSIANIC JEWISH

(45) KOHEN HANDS

(46) CATHOLIC CELTIC CROSS

(47) CHRISTIAN SCIENTIST (Cross & Crown)

(48) MEDICINE WHEEL

(49) INFINITY

(51) LUTHER ROSE

(52) LANDING EAGLE

(53) FOUR DIRECTIONS

(54) CHURCH OF NAZARENE

(55) HAMMER OF THOR

(56) UNIFICATION CHURCH

(57) SANDHILL CRANE

(58) CHURCH OF GOD

(59) POMEGRANATE

(60) MESSIANIC

(61) SHINTO

(62) SACRED HEART

(63) AFRICAN ANCESTRAL TRADITIONALIST (Nyame Ye Ohene)

(64) MALTESE CROSS

(65) DRUID (AWEN)

(66) WISCONSIN EVANGICAL LUTHERAN SYNOD

(67) POLISH NATIONAL CATHOLIC CHURCH

(98) ISLAMIC 5-POINTED STAR (not shown due to copyright)

Form 6: Claim for Government Medallion

GENERAL INFORMATION SHEET
CLAIM FOR GOVERNMENT MEDALLION FOR PLACEMENT
IN A PRIVATE CEMETERY

RESPONDENT BURDEN - Public reporting burden for this collection of information is estimated to average 15 minutes per response, including the time for reviewing instructions, searching existing data sources, gathering and maintaining the data needed, and completing and reviewing the collection of information. VA cannot conduct or sponsor a collection of information unless it has a valid OMB number. Your obligation to respond is voluntary, however, your response is required to obtain benefits. Send comments regarding this burden estimate or any other aspect of this collection of information, including suggestions for reducing this burden to the VA Clearance Officer (005R1B), 810 Vermont Avenue, NW, Washington, DC 20420. Please DO NOT send applications for benefits to this address.

PRIVACY ACT - VA considers the responses you submit confidential (38 U.S.C. 5701). VA may only disclose this information outside the VA if the disclosure is authorized under the Privacy Act, including the routine uses identified in the VA system of records, 48VA40B, published in the Federal Register. VA considers the requested information relevant and necessary to determine maximum benefits under the law.

BENEFIT PROVIDED - MEDALLION (Only for eligible deceased Veterans who served in the Armed Forces on or after April 6, 1917, regardless of their date of death)

Furnished upon receipt of claim for affixing to an existing privately-purchased headstone or marker placed at the gravesite of an eligible deceased Veteran who is buried in a private or local Government cemetery. The medallion is made of bronze and available in three sizes: Large, Medium, Small. Each medallion is inscribed with the word VETERAN across the top and the Branch of Service at the bottom *(see Note in Block 11 of the claim for further information)*. An eligible deceased Veteran may receive a Government furnished headstone or marker, or a medallion, but not both. *If requesting a headstone or marker, please use the VA Form 40-1330, Claim for Standard Government Headstone or Marker.*

Shown below are the three medallions with the actual dimensions (+/- 1/32") for width and height.

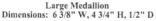

| **Large Medallion** | **Medium Medallion** | **Small Medallion** |
| Dimensions: 6 3/8" W, 4 3/4" H, 1/2" D | Dimensions: 3 3/4" W, 2 7/8" H, 1/4" D | Dimensions: 2" W, 1 1/2" H, 1/3" D |

WHO IS ELIGIBLE - Any deceased Veteran discharged under honorable conditions, who served in the Armed Forces on or after April 6, 1917, and is buried in a private cemetery in a grave marked with a privately purchased headstone or marker. Any Servicemember of the Armed Forces of the United States who served on or after April 6, 1917, and died on active duty and is buried in a private cemetery in a grave marked with a privately purchased headstone or marker. Please attach a copy of the deceased Veteran's discharge certificate (DD Form 214 or equivalent) or a copy of other official document(s) establishing qualifying service. If you are unable to locate copies of military records, apply anyway, as VA will attempt to obtain records necessary to make an eligibility determination. **Do not send original documents**; they will not be returned. **Service after September 7, 1980, must be for a minimum of 24 months continuous active duty or be completed under special circumstances, e.g., death on active duty.** Persons who have only limited active duty service for training while in the National Guard or Reserves are not eligible unless there are special circumstances, e.g., death while on active duty, or as a result of training. Reservists and National Guard members who, at time of death, were entitled to retired pay, or would have been entitled, but for being under the age of 60, are eligible; please submit a copy of the Reserve Retirement Eligibility Benefits Letter with the claim. Reservists called to active duty other than training and National Guard members who are Federalized and who serve for the period called are eligible.

WHO CAN APPLY - An "applicant" for a Medallion may be any of the following:

(i)   A decedent's family member, which includes the decedent's spouse or individual who was in a legal union as defined in 38 CFR 3.1702(b)(1)(ii) with the decedent; a child, parent, or sibling of the decedent, whether biological, adopted, or step relation; and any lineal or collateral descendant of the decedent;
(ii) A personal representative, defined as a family member or other individual who has identified himself or herself as the person responsible for making decisions concerning the interment of the remains of or memorialization of a deceased individual;
(iii) A representative of a Congressionally-chartered Veterans Service Organization;
(iv) An individual employed by the relevant state, tribal organization, or local government whose official responsibilities include serving veterans and families of veterans, such as a state or county veterans service officer; or
(v)   Any individual who is responsible, under the laws of the relevant state or locality, for the disposition of the unclaimed remains of the decedent or for other matters relating to the interment or memorialization of the decedent.

PRESIDENTIAL MEMORIAL CERTIFICATE - A Presidential Memorial Certificate (PMC) is an engraved paper certificate, signed by the current sitting president, to honor the memory of Veterans discharged under other than dishonorable conditions. If the Veteran is eligible for a headstone, marker, or medallion, one PMC will automatically be provided unless otherwise specified. Additional PMCs may be requested by indicating how many in block 18 of this form.

HOW TO SUBMIT A CLAIM

FAX VA Form 40-1330M and supporting documents to: **1-800-455-7143**.
IMPORTANT: If faxing more than one claim - fax each
claim package *(claim plus supporting documents)* individually
(disconnect the call and redial for each submission).

MAIL claims to: **Memorial Products Service (41B)**
Department of Veterans Affairs
5109 Russell Road
Quantico, VA 22134-3903

A VA medallion may be furnished only upon receipt of a fully completed and signed claim with required supporting documentation.

SIGNATURES REQUIRED - The claimant signs in block 19; the cemetery or other responsible official in block 24. If there is no official on duty at the cemetery, the signature of the person responsible for the property listed in block 23 is required. Entries of "None," "Not Applicable," or "NA" will not be accepted.

ASSISTANCE NEEDED - If assistance is needed to complete this claim, you may contact our Applicant Assistance Unit toll free at: 1-800-697-6947, or via e-mail at mps.headstones@va.gov. If additional assistance is needed to complete this claim, contact the nearest VA Regional Office, national cemetery, or a local Veterans' organization. No fee should be paid in connection with the preparation of this claim. For more information regarding medallion eligibility, affixing procedures, and sizes, visit our website at www.cem.va.gov.

DELIVERY - The medallion is shipped without charge to the name/address designated in Block 21 of the claim. The Government is not responsible for costs associated with affixing the medallion to the privately purchased headstone or marker. Appropriate affixing adhesives, hardware and instructions are provided with the medallion.

CAUTION - To avoid delays in the production and delivery of the medallion, please check carefully to be sure you have accurately furnished all required information and documents before faxing or mailing the claim. The Government is not responsible for costs associated with affixing the medallion to the privately purchased headstone or marker. Medallions furnished remain the property of the United States Government and may not be used for any purpose other than to be affixed to the privately purchased headstone or marker of an eligible deceased Veteran buried in a private or local Government cemetery.

DETACH AND RETAIN THIS GENERAL INFORMATION SHEET FOR YOUR RECORDS.

VA FORM
DEC 2017 **40-1330M**   ALL PREVIOUS VERSIONS OF THIS FORM ARE OBSOLETE

Form approved, OMB No. 2900-0222
Expiration Date: Dec. 31, 2020
Respondent Burden: 15 minutes

VA Department of Veterans Affairs

CLAIM FOR GOVERNMENT MEDALLION FOR PLACEMENT IN A PRIVATE CEMETERY

IMPORTANT: Please read the General Information Sheet before completing this claim. Type or print clearly all information except for signatures. Illegible printing could result in incorrect delivery of the medallion. Failure to complete each block may result in delayed processing. **PLEASE INCLUDE MILITARY DISCHARGE DOCUMENTS.**

1. DID VA PREVIOUSLY DETERMINE ELIGIBILITY FOR BURIAL AT A VA NATIONAL CEMETERY?
   ☐ YES   ☐ NO   ☐ UNSURE

2. NAME OF DECEASED VETERAN

FIRST *(Or Initial)*	MIDDLE *(Or Initial)*	LAST	SUFFIX

3. THERE MUST BE A SET HEADSTONE, MAUSOLEUM, OR CRYPT IN PLACE TO AFFIX THE MEDALLION. IS THE GRAVE CURRENTLY MARKED?   ☐ YES   ☐ NO

4. RACE OR ETHNICITY *(You may select more than one. Information will be used for statistical purposes only.)*
☐ AMERICAN INDIAN OR ALASKA NATIVE ☐ NATIVE HAWAIIAN OR OTHER PACIFIC ISLANDER
☐ BLACK OR AFRICAN AMERICAN ☐ WHITE
☐ HISPANIC OR LATINO ☐ OTHER *(Specify)* _____

5. GENDER *(Information will be used for statistical purposes only.)*
☐ MALE
☐ FEMALE

6. AGE AT TIME OF DEATH

VETERAN'S SERVICE AND IDENTIFYING INFORMATION *(Use numbers only, e.g., 05-15-1941)*

7. VETERAN'S SOCIAL SECURITY NO. OR SERVICE NO.

SSN: SVC. NO.:

8. PLACE OF BIRTH *(City and State or Country)*

PERIODS OF ACTIVE MILITARY DUTY

9A. DATE OF BIRTH			9B. DATE OF DEATH			10A. DATE(S) ENTERED			10B. DATE(S) SEPARATED		
MONTH	DAY	YEAR	MONTH	DAY	YEAR	MONTH	DAY	YEAR	MONTH	DAY	YEAR

11. BRANCH OF SERVICE (BOS) *(Check applicable box(es))* **NOTE:** *If one BOS is selected, it will be spelled out on the medallion, i.e. U.S. ARMY, U.S. AIR FORCE, etc. If more than one BOS is selected, they will be abbreviated on the medallion, i.e. USA, USAF, USN, USMC, USCG, etc.*
☐ ARMY ☐ MARINE CORPS ☐ COAST GUARD ☐ MERCHANT MARINE ☐ NAVY ☐ AIR FORCE ☐ ARMY AIR FORCES (WW II)
☐ OTHER (USAAC, WAAC, etc.) *(Specify)*

12. MEDALLION SIZE REQUESTED *(Check one) (Refer to general information sheet for exact sizes)*
☐ LARGE (M5) ☐ MEDIUM (M3) ☐ SMALL (M1)

13. ARE YOU:
☐ FAMILY MEMBER *(Specify relationship)* _____ ☐ VETERANS SERVICE OFFICER ☐ CEMETERY MANAGEMENT *(where the unclaimed remains are buried)*
☐ PERSONAL REPRESENTATIVE *(Person responsible for decisions concerning burial of decedent; include written authorization)* ☐ FUNERAL HOME MANAGEMENT *(that received the unclaimed remains)*

14. NAME AND MAILING ADDRESS OF CLAIMANT *(No., Street, City, State, and ZIP Code)*

15. DAYTIME PHONE NO. OF CLAIMANT

16. E-MAIL ADDRESS *(Optional)*

17. I WOULD LIKE A PRESIDENTIAL MEMORIAL CERTIFICATE?
☐ YES   ☐ NO

18. IF "YES" HOW MANY?

CERTIFICATION: By signing below I certify the medallion will be affixed to a privately purchased headstone or marker in the cemetery listed in Block 23 at no expense to the Government, and that I (or the party listed in Block 21) have agreed to accept delivery, and all information entered on this claim is true and correct to the best of my knowledge. I also certify, to the best of my knowledge, that the decedent has never committed a serious crime, such as murder or other offense that could have resulted in imprisonment for life, has never been convicted of a serious crime, and has never been convicted of a sexual offense for which he or she was sentenced to a minimum of life imprisonment.

PENALTY: The law provides severe penalties, which include fine or imprisonment, or both, for the willful submission of any statement or evidence of a material fact, knowing it to be false or for the fraudulent acceptance of any benefit to which you are not entitled.

19. SIGNATURE OF CLAIMANT

20. DATE *(MM/DD/YYYY)*

21. NAME AND DELIVERY ADDRESS FOR MEDALLION *(No., Street, City, State, and ZIP Code); (If same as applicant, please enter SAME)*

22. DAYTIME PHONE NO. *(Include Area Code)*

23. NAME AND ADDRESS OF CEMETERY WHERE PRIVATELY PURCHASED HEADSTONE IS IN PLACE OR A MAUSOLEUM, OR CRYPT TO AFFIX THE MEDALLION MARKER OF THE DECEASED VETERAN IS LOCATED *(No., Street, City, State, and ZIP Code)*

CERTIFICATION: By signing below I certify the size medallion indicated above is permitted in the cemetery.

24. SIGNATURE OF CEMETERY OFFICIAL

25. DATE *(MM/DD/YYYY)*

VA FORM DEC 2017 **40-1330M**   ALL PREVIOUS VERSIONS OF THIS FORM ARE OBSOLETE

Form 7: Application for United States Flag for Burial

Department of Veterans Affairs   **APPLICATION FOR UNITED STATES FLAG FOR BURIAL PURPOSES**

PRIVACY ACT NOTICE: VA will not disclose information collected on this form to any source other than what has been authorized under the Privacy Act of 1974 or Title 38, Code of Federal Regulations 1.576 for routine uses (i.e., civil or criminal law enforcement, congressional communications, epidemiological or research studies, the collection of money owed to the United States, litigation in which the United States is a party or has an interest, the administration of VA programs and delivery of VA benefits, verification of identity and status, and personnel administration) as identified in the VA system of records, 58VA21/22/28, Compensation, Pension, Education, and Vocational Rehabilitation and Employment Records - VA, published in the Federal Register. Your obligation to respond is required to obtain or retain benefits. Giving us the veteran's SSN account information is voluntary. Refusal to provide the veteran's SSN by itself will not result in the denial of benefits. VA will not deny an individual benefits for refusing to provide his or her SSN unless the disclosure of the SSN is required by a Federal Statute of law in effect prior to January 1, 1975, and still in effect. The requested information is considered relevant and necessary to determine entitlement to benefits under the law. The responses you submit are considered confidential (38 U.S.C. 5701). Information submitted is subject to verification through computer matching programs with other agencies.

RESPONDENT BURDEN: We need this information to determine eligibility for issuance of a burial flag to a family member or friend of a deceased veteran (38 U.S.C. 2301). Title 38, United States Code, allows us to ask for this information. We estimate that you will need an average of 15 minutes to review the instructions, find the information, and complete this form. VA cannot conduct or sponsor a collection of information unless a valid OMB control number is displayed. You are not required to respond to a collection of information if this number is not displayed. Valid OMB control numbers can be located on the OMB Internet Page at www.reginfo.gov/public/do/PRAMain. If desired, you can call 1-800-827-1000 to get information on where to send comments or suggestions about this form.

IMPORTANT - Postmaster or other issuing official: Submit this form to the nearest VA regional office. Be sure to complete the stub at the bottom.

INFORMATION ABOUT THE DECEASED VETERAN *(Complete as much as possible)*
(Information provided is considered essential when applying for other VA benefits.)

1. FIRST, MIDDLE, LAST NAME OF VETERAN *(Print or type)*	2. MAIDEN NAME OR OTHER NAME(S) VETERAN USED WHILE ON ACTIVE DUTY *(Print or type)*		

3. VA FILE NUMBER	4. SOCIAL SECURITY NUMBER	5. MILITARY SERVICE NUMBER/SERIAL NUMBER

6. BRANCH OF SERVICE *(Check box)*
☐ ARMY ☐ NAVY ☐ AIR FORCE ☐ MARINE CORPS ☐ COAST GUARD ☐ SELECTED SERVICE ☐ OTHER *(Specify)*

7. DATE ENTERED ACTIVE DUTY *(or Selected Reserve)*	8. DATE RELEASED FROM ACTIVE DUTY *(or Selected Reserve)*	9. DATE OF BIRTH	10. DATE OF DEATH

11. DATE OF BURIAL	12. PLACE OF BURIAL *(Name of cemetery, city, and State)*

13. HAS DOCUMENTATION BEEN PRESENTED OR ATTACHED THAT SHOWS THE VETERAN MEETS THE ELIGIBILITY CRITERIA? *(See Paragraphs C, D, and E of the "Instructions")*
☐ YES ☐ NO *(If "No," explain in Item 15, "Remarks" (See paragraph E of the "Instructions"))*

INFORMATION ABOUT THE FLAG RECIPIENT AND APPLICANT

14A. NAME OF PERSON ENTITLED TO RECEIVE FLAG	14B. RELATIONSHIP OF DECEASED VETERAN *(See Paragraph F of the "Instructions")*

14C. ADDRESS OF PERSON ENTITLED TO RECEIVE FLAG *(Number and street or rural route, city or P.O., State and ZIP Code)*	14D. TELEPHONE NUMBER

15. REMARKS

I CERTIFY that the statements made in this document are true and complete to the best of my knowledge. I further certify that the deceased veteran is eligible, in accordance with the attached instructions, for issue of a United States flag for burial purposes, and such flag has not been previously applied for or furnished.

16. SIGNATURE OF APPLICANT *(Sign in INK)*	17. ADDRESS OF APPLICANT *(Number and street or rural route, city or P.O., and ZIP Code)*	18. RELATIONSHIP TO DECEASED VETERAN	19. DATE SIGNED

PENALTY - The law provides that whoever makes any statement of a material fact knowing it to be false shall be punished by a fine, imprisonment, or both.

ACKNOWLEDGMENT OF RECEIPT OF FLAG (ONLY ONE FLAG MAY BE ISSUED FOR EACH DECEASED VETERAN)

20. SIGNATURE OF PERSON RECEIVING FLAG *(Sign in INK)*	21. DATE FLAG ISSUED	

22. NAME AND ADDRESS OF POST OFFICE OR OTHER FLAG ISSUE POINT	**FOR VA USE**	
	DATE NOTIFICATION FORWARDED TO SUPPLY	STATION NUMBER

VA FORM 27-2008, MAR 2015   SUPERSEDES VA FORM 27- 2008, JUL 2012, WHICH WILL NOT BE USED.

- -

This stub is to be completed by the POSTMASTER or other issuing official. Upon receipt the VA Regional Office will detach and forward it to the appropriate Supply Officer.

NOTIFICATION OF ISSUANCE OF FLAG

DATE FLAG ISSUED	ISSUING POINT TELEPHONE NO.	ADDRESS OF POST OFFICE OR OTHER FLAG ISSUE POINT
SIGNATURE OF POSTMASTER OR OTHER ISSUING OFFICIAL		

VA FORM MAR 2015 **27-2008**   SUPERSEDES VA FORM 27- 2008, JUL 2012, WHICH WILL NOT BE USED.   SEE INSTRUCTIONS

See instructions on next page.

INSTRUCTIONS

A. How can I contact VA if I have questions?

If you have questions about this form, how to fill it out, or about benefits, contact your nearest VA regional office. You can locate the address of the nearest regional office in your telephone book blue pages under "United States Government, Veterans" or call 1-800-827-1000 (Hearing Impaired TDD line 1-800-829-4833). You may also contact VA by Internet at https://iris.va.gov/.

B. How do I apply for a burial flag?

Complete VA Form 27-2008, and submit it to a funeral director or a representative of the veteran or other organization having charge of the funeral arrangements or acting in the interest of the veteran. You may get a flag at any VA regional office or U.S. Post Office. When burial is in a national, State or military post cemetery, a burial flag will be provided.

C. Who is eligible for a burial flag?

Generally, veterans with an other than dishonorable discharge. *Note:* This includes veterans who served in the Philippine military forces while such forces were in the service of the U.S. armed forces under the President's Order of July 26, 1941 and died on or after April 25, 1951, and veterans who served in the Philippine military services are eligible for burial in a national cemetery.

Veterans who were entitled to retired pay for service in the reserves, or would have been entitled to such pay but not for being under 60 years of age.

Members or former members of the Selected Reserve (Army, Air Force, Coast Guard, Marine Corps, or Naval Reserve; Air National Guard; or Army National Guard) who served at least one enlistment or, in the case of an officer, the period of initial obligation, or were discharged for disability incurred or aggravated in line of duty, or died while a member of the Selected Reserve.

D. Who is not eligible for a burial flag?

Veterans who received a dishonorable discharge.

Members of the Selected Reserve whose last discharge from service was under conditions less favorable than honorable.

Peacetime veterans who were discharged before June 27, 1950 and did not serve at least one complete enlistment or incur or aggravate a disability in the line of duty.

Veterans who were convicted of a Federal capital crime and sentenced to death or life imprisonment, or were convicted of a State capital crime and sentenced to death or life imprisonment without parole, or were found to have committed a Federal or State capital crime but were not convicted by reason of not being available for trial due to death or flight to avoid prosecution.

Discharged or rejected draftees, or members of the National Guard, who reported to camp in answer to the President's call for World War I service but who, when medically examined, were not finally accepted for military service.

D. Who is not eligible for a burial flag? *(Continued)*

Persons who were discharged from World War I service prior to November 12, 1918, on their own application or solicitation by reason of being an alien, or any veterans discharged for alienage during a period of hostilities.

Persons who served with any of the forces allied with the United States in any war, even though United States citizens, if they did not serve with the United States armed forces.

Persons inducted for training and service who, before entering such training and service were transferred to the Enlisted Reserve Corps and given a furlough.

Former temporary members of the United States Coast Guard Reserve.

E. What documentation is required in order to receive a burial flag?

Provide a copy of the veteran's discharge documents that shows service dates and the character of service, such as DD Form 214, or verification of service from the veteran's service department or VA. Various information requested, is considered essential to the proper processing of the application. Ensure these areas are completed as fully as possible. *Note:* If the claimant is unable to provide documentary proof, a flag may be issued when a statement is made by a person of established character and reputation that he/she personally knows the deceased to have been a veteran who meets the eligibility criteria.

F. Who is eligible to receive a burial flag?

Only one flag may be issued for each deceased veteran. Generally, the flag is given to the next-of-kin as a keepsake after its use during the funeral service. The flag is given to the following person(s) in the order of precedence listed:

surviving spouse

children, according to age

parents, including adoptive, stepparents, and foster parents

brothers or sisters, including brothers or sisters of half blood

uncles or aunts

nephews or nieces

others, such as cousins or grandparents

When there is no next-of-kin, VA will furnish the flag to a friend making a request for it. If there is no living relative or one cannot be located, and no friend requests the flag, it must be returned to the nearest VA facility.

Note: The flag cannot be replaced if it is lost, destroyed, or stolen. Additionally, a flag may not be issued after burial unless it was impossible to obtain a flag in time to drape the casket or accompany the urn before burial. If the next-of-kin or friend is requesting the flag after the veteran's burial, he or she must personally sign the application and explain in Item 15 "Remarks" the reason that prevented timely application for a burial flag.

VA FORM 27-2008, MAR 2015

Form 8: Presidential Memorial Certificate Request

Form Approved, OMB No. 2900-0567
Expiration Date: Oct. 31, 2020
Respondent Burden: 3 Minutes

VA Department of Veterans Affairs | PRESIDENTIAL MEMORIAL CERTIFICATE REQUEST FORM

RESPONDENT BURDEN: Public reporting burden for this collection of information is estimated to average three minutes per response, including the time to review instructions, search existing data sources, gather the necessary data, and complete and review the collection of information. The obligation to respond is voluntary and not required to obtain or retain benefits. Statutory authority for the Presidential Memorial Certificate (PMC) Program is 38 U.S.C. 112. The information requested is approved under OMB Control Number 2900-0567, and is necessary to allow eligible recipients (next of kin, other relatives or friends) to request PMC.

The National Cemetery Administration does not give, sell or transfer any personal information outside of the agency. The Department of Veterans Affairs (VA) may not conduct or sponsor, and you are not required to respond to this collection of information unless it displays a valid OMB Control Number. Responding to this collection is voluntary. Send comments regarding this burden estimate or any other aspects of this collection of information, including suggestions for reducing this burden, to VA Clearance Officer (005G2), 810 Vermont Avenue NW, Washington, DC 20420. **SEND COMMENTS ONLY.** *Please do not send applications for benefits to this address.*

SECTION I - INSTRUCTIONS FOR COMPLETING VA FORM 40-0247, PRESIDENTIAL MEMORIAL CERTIFICATE REQUEST FORM

Military/Discharge Documents: VA recommends that you attach photocopies of readily available supporting documents so that we can make the determination quickly. Documents may include the most recent discharge document (DD Form 214) showing active duty service records other than for training purposes, or active duty for a minimum of 24 continuous months for enlisted Servicemembers after September 7, 1980; for officers, after October 16, 1981, or the full period for which the person was called to active duty. If you are unable to locate copies of military records, apply anyway, as VA will attempt to obtain records necessary to make a determination.

Name of Veteran: DO NOT include nicknames, military rank or civilian title(s).

Name and Mailing Address of Person Requesting Certificate: Provide the full name and complete mailing address to avoid delays in delivery.

We strongly recommend you complete this form online (http://www.cem.va.gov/pmc.asp) and print and sign before you submit your request.

Complete a new VA Form 40-0247 for each additional address where certificates will be mailed to.

Privacy Act Information: VA considers the responses you submit confidential (38 U.S.C. 5701). VA may only disclose this information outside the VA if the disclosure is authorized under the Privacy Act, including the routine uses identified in the VA system of records, 175VA41A published in the Federal Register.

SECTION II - VETERAN/SERVICEMEMBER INFORMATION

1. NAME OF VETERAN *(First, Middle, Last)*	2. VETERAN SSN OR SERVICE NUMBER OR VA FILE NUMBER *(Required)*

SECTION III - PERSON REQUESTING CERTIFICATE INFORMATION

3. NAME OF PERSON REQUESTING CERTIFICATE	4. MAILING ADDRESS OF PERSON REQUESTING CERTIFICATE
5. HOME OR WORK TELEPHONE NUMBER *(Include area code)*	
6. REQUESTOR EMAIL ADDRESS	7. NUMBER OF CERTIFICATES REQUESTED

SECTION IV - CERTIFICATION AND SIGNATURE

CERTIFICATION: I certify, to the best of my knowledge, that the decedent has never committed a serious crime, such as murder or other offense that could have resulted in imprisonment for life, has never been convicted of a serious crime, and has never been convicted of a sexual offense for which he or she was sentenced to a minimum of life imprisonment.

8. SIGNATURE OF PERSON REQUESTING CERTIFICATE *(Required)*

SECTION V - MAILING ADDRESS AND FAX NUMBER

PLEASE SEND ANY MILITARY DOCUMENTS AND SIGNED FORM TO:

Presidential Memorial Certificates (41B3)
National Cemetery Administration   Or   Fax To: 1 (800) 455-7143
5109 Russell Road
Quantico, VA 22134-3903

(The blocks below are for official use only)

9. CASE MANAGER NAME	10. PMC ID NUMBER	11. CASE MANAGER EMAIL

VA FORM NOV 2017 **40-0247**   ALL VERSIONS OF THIS FORM DATED BEFORE MAY 2013 WILL NOT BE ACCEPTED OR PROCESSED.

Form 9: Certificate of Release or Discharge from Active Duty - DD-214

As was noted in the chapter titled, *Government Benefits and Programs*, this form is issued to military personnel when they are released from active duty in the armed services of the United States. Commonly referred to in the funeral service industry by the current form number, DD-214, the document will clearly state the discharge classification in a section called Character of Service. Prior to 1950, other forms with various form numbers were used by the different armed service branches. An example of a pre-1950 form that was used for honorable discharges is shown on the next page.

CAUTION: NOT TO BE USED FOR IDENTIFICATION PURPOSES	THIS IS AN IMPORTANT RECORD. SAFEGUARD IT.	ANY ALTERATIONS IN SHADED AREAS RENDER FORM VOID

CERTIFICATE OF RELEASE OR DISCHARGE FROM ACTIVE DUTY

1. NAME (Last, First, Middle)	2. DEPARTMENT, COMPONENT AND BRANCH	3. SOCIAL SECURITY NO.

4.a. GRADE, RATE OR RANK	4.b. PAY GRADE	5. DATE OF BIRTH (YYMMDD)	6. RESERVE OBLIG. TERM. DATE
			Year / Month / Day

7.a PLACE OF ENTRY INTO ACTIVE DUTY	7.b HOME OF RECORD AT TIME OF ENTRY (City and state, or complete address if known)

8.a LAST DUTY ASSIGNMENT AND MAJOR COMMAND	8.b STATION WHERE SEPARATED

9. COMMAND TO WHICH TRANSFERRED	10. SGLI COVERAGE — None / Amount: $

11. PRIMARY SPECIALTY (List number, title and years and months in specialty. List additional specialty numbers and titles involving periods of one or more years.)	12. RECORD OF SERVICE	Year(s)	Month(s)	Day(s)
	a. Date Entered AD This Period			
	b. Separation Date This Period			
	c. Net Active Service This Period			
	d. Total Prior Active Service			
	e. Total Prior Inactive Service			
	f. Foreign Service			
	g. Sea Service			
	h. Effective Date of Pay Grade			

13. DECORATIONS, MEDALS, BADGES, CITATIONS AND CAMPAIGN RIBBONS AWARDED OR AUTHORIZED (All periods of service)

14. MILITARY EDUCATION (Course title, number of weeks, and month and year completed)

15.a MEMBER CONTRIBUTED TO POST-VIETNAM ERA VETERANS' EDUCATIONAL ASSISTANCE PROGRAM	Yes	No	15.b HIGH SCHOOL GRADUATE OR EQUIVALENT	Yes	No	16. DAYS ACCRUED LEAVE PAID

17. MEMBER WAS PROVIDED COMPLETE DENTAL EXAMINATION AND ALL APPROPRIATE DENTAL SERVICES AND TREATMENT WITHIN 90 DAYS PRIOR TO SEPARATION	Yes	No

18. REMARKS

Character of Service "Discharge"

19.a MAILING ADDRESS AFTER SEPARATION (Include Zip Code)	19.b NEAREST RELATIVE (Name and address - include Zip Code)

20. MEMBER REQUESTS COPY 6 BE SENT TO — DIR. OF VET AFFAIRS — Yes / No	22. OFFICIAL AUTHORIZED TO SIGN (Typed name, grade, title and signature)
21. SIGNATURE OF MEMBER BEING SEPARATED	

SPECIAL ADDITIONAL INFORMATION (For use by authorized agencies only)

23. TYPE OF SEPARATION	24. CHARACTER OF SERVICE (Include upgrades)

28. NARRATIVE REASON FOR SEPARATION

29. DATES OF TIME LOST DURING THIS PERIOD	30. MEMBER REQUESTS COPY 4 — Initials

DD Form 214, NOV 88 — Previous editions are obsolete.

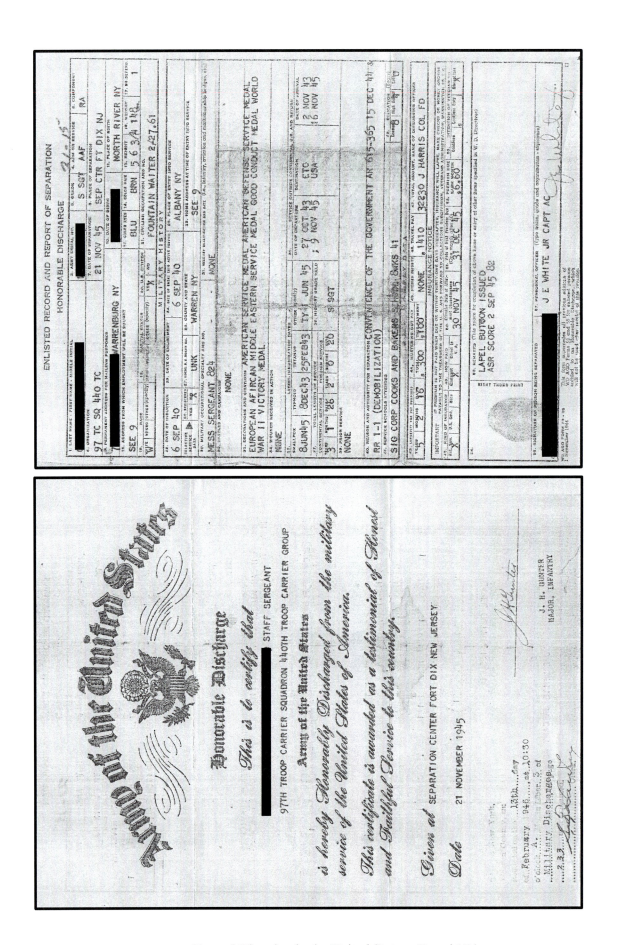

Form 10: VA Before You Call Checklist

National Cemetery Scheduling Office
(800) 535-1117

Before You Call Checklist

To help expedite your call to the National Cemetery Scheduling Office (NCSO), please obtain the information listed in the checklist below.

In advance of the call to schedule services, you may also fax discharge or other documents to (866) 900-6417.

Information Type	Information Details	Response
Cemetery Information		
National cemetery requested	Name of cemetery	
Is this burial a first or second interment *If second (subsequent) interment, previous decedent information is required*	First or second	
Previous Decedent Information		
Previous decedent's full name	First name, middle name, and last name	
Previous decedent's social security number	Social security number	
Previous decedent's date of birth	Date of birth	
Previous decedent's date of death	Date of death	
Veteran Information		
Veteran's full name	First name, middle name, and last name	
Veteran's social security number	Social security number	
Veteran's date of death	Date of death	
Veteran's date of birth	Date of birth	
Veteran's branch of service	Branch of service	
Military rank	Rank	
Marital status	Married/divorced/never married/widowed/other	
Gender of Veteran - Male or Female	Male/female	
Race of Veteran	Race	
Decedent Information		
Relationship to Veteran	Self (Veteran)/spouse/child/other	
Decedent's full name	First name, middle name, and last name	
Decedent's social security number	Social security number	
Date of birth	Date of birth	
Date of death	Date of death	
Decedent address	Address/state/zip code	
Home of record in service area	Home within 75 miles of cemetery	
Decedent Gender	Gender	
Marital status	Married/divorced/never married/widowed/other	
Funeral Home Information		
Funeral home name	Funeral home name	
Funeral home identification number	Funeral home identification number	
Funeral home address	Address/state/zip code	
Funeral home contact full name	First name, middle name, and last name	
Funeral home contact email address	Email address	
Funeral home phone number	Phone number	

Fax discharge documents and death certificate of Veteran and prior decedent, as applicable, to (866) 900-6417
Death certificate of previous decedent is required to validate legal marital status, if documents are not available within NCSO records

Information Type	Information Details	Response
Marital Status and Surviving Spouse Information		
Surviving spouse information	First name, middle name, and last name:	
If no surviving spouse, name of decedent's next of kin	First name, middle name, and last name:	
Relationship to decedent	Spouse/child/other:	
Social security number of spouse	Social security number:	
Date of birth of spouse	Date of birth:	
Veteran status of spouse	Veteran status of spouse:	
Request for set-aside grave	Yes/no:	
Does the Veteran have any adult dependent children, who are mentally or physically disabled	Yes/no:	
Information Type	**Information Details**	**Response**
Adult Dependent Child		
Adult dependent child's full name	First name, middle name, and last name:	
Adult dependent child's social security number	Social security number:	
Adult dependent chiild's date of birth	Date of birth:	
Interment Details		
Type of remains	Casket/urn:	
Liner type	Standard government/private vault:	
Liner size: Small - 60L x 20W x 18D Regular - 86L x 30W x 28D Extra Large - 86L x 38W x 28D Oversized - 88L x 34W x 27D Jumbo - 98L x 44W x 30D	Small/regular/ extra large/oversized/jumbo:	
Urn dimensions: Niche size - 9L x 13W x 18 D	Dimensions:	
Federal Law Information		
Response to the question *"To the best of your knowledge, has the decedent ever **committed** a capital crime?"*	Yes/no:	
Response to the question *"To the best of your knowledge, has the decedent ever been **convicted** of a sexual offense of which he or she was sentenced to a minimum of life in prison?"*	Yes/no:	
Military Honors Information		
Request for military honors	Yes/no:	
Branch of service requested	Branch of service:	
Request for committal service	Yes/no:	
Emblem of Belief Information		
Request for a religious emblem of belief for the marker	Yes/no/not at this time:	
Selection of the emblem of belief	Selection:	
Scheduling Information		
Method of delivery to cemetery	Funeral home/family:	
Name of individual who is scheduling military honors	Name:	
Preferred date and time of the scheduled service	Date/time:	

Fax discharge documents and death certificate of Veteran and prior decedent, as applicable, to (866) 900-6417
Death certificate of previous decedent is required to validate legal marital status, if documents are not available within NCSO records

Form 11: Case Checklist and Worksheet

As described in the chapter titled, *Preparing for Funeral Events*, every death case should have a master checklist and worksheet enumerating the actions and activities that must take place to prepare for a funeral. These provide a single-source location for staff members to record assigned tasks have been completed and a quick-reference snapshot of the progress being made as the work proceeds.

There should be only one master list kept in a specific central location where all staff members regularly update their progress to keep everyone current.

A Case Checklist and Worksheet form is shown on the next page.

Case Checklist and Worksheet

Decedent _____ Case No. _____ Lead Director _____

Dates, times and locations

Calling hours1:_____

Calling hours2:_____

Funeral: _____

Cemetery: _____

After-service _____

Merchandise Selected (describe all items fully)

Casket/Urn: _____

Vault: _____

Flowers: _____

Prayer cards: _____

Thank-you:_____

Donation cards: _____

Register book: _____

Add'l 1:_____

Add'l 2:_____

Immediate Actions (specify newspapers)

Update website   Complete _____

Update social media sites   Complete _____

Create customer account   Complete _____

Send obituary 1 _____   Complete _____

Send obituary 2 _____   Complete _____

Notifications (add name & contact number)

Clergy:_____   Notified _____

Hairdresser:_____   Notified _____

Cemetery: _____   Notified _____

Add'l 1:_____   Notified _____

Add'l 2:_____   Notified _____

Paperwork for case file

Statement (contract)   ☐ Complete _____

Final billing w/any changes to contract   ☐ Complete _____

Cremation authorization   ☐ Complete _____

Embalming report   ☐ Complete _____

Removal report   ☐ Complete _____

Staff assignments   ☐ Complete _____

Car list   ☐ Complete _____

Obituaries   ☐ Complete _____

Casket/urn invoice   ☐ Complete _____

Vault invoice _____   ☐ Complete _____

Body receipt _____   ☐ Complete _____

Add'l 1 _____   ☐ Complete _____

Add'l 2 _____   ☐ Complete _____

Add'l 3 _____   ☐ Complete _____

Staff Tasks

Death certificate filed   ☐ Complete _____

Burial/transit permit placed in case file   ☐ Complete _____

Clergy record forwarded   ☐ Complete _____

Prayer cards printed   ☐ Complete _____

Register book prepared   ☐ Complete _____

Thank-you cards prepared   ☐ Complete _____

Donation envelopes   ☐ Complete _____

Temporary cemetery marker   ☐ Complete _____

Checks printed

   Local registrar - $ _____   ☐ Complete _____

   Cemetery - $ _____   ☐ Complete _____

   Clergy - $ _____   ☐ Complete _____

Notification of death sent to SSA   ☐ Complete _____

VA burial allowance forms prepared   ☐ Complete _____

VA monument/marker forms prepared   ☐ Complete _____

VA interment application submitted   ☐ Complete _____

VA presidential memorial certs. requested   ☐ Complete _____

American flag application   ☐ Complete _____

American flag picked up from USPS   ☐ Complete _____

Spring burial worksheet   ☐ Complete _____

Add'l 1 _____   ☐ Complete _____

Add'l 2 _____   ☐ Complete _____

Add'l 3 _____   ☐ Complete _____

Add'l 4 _____   ☐ Complete _____

Add'l 5 _____   ☐ Complete _____

Notes _____

_____

_____

_____

_____

_____

INITIAL AND DATE ALL NOTIFICATIONS AND COMPLETIONS!

Form 12: Staff Assignments

As described in the chapter titled, *Preparing for Funeral Events*, the lead director should prepare staff assignments with respect to carrying out the visitation and calling hours; funeral or memorial service; final dispositions; and other planned events, such as an after-service gathering.

These assignments should be in writing and kept in a central location where staff members may readily view them. Many funeral establishments have taken this one step further and post the assignments on a secure and confidential website where staff members with the proper authority may review them at any time from any computer with internet-access.

In addition to assignments, some funeral establishments include short passages from operation or procedure manuals to reinforce certain duties and responsibilities, such as the responsibility of a company driver to ensure an assigned vehicle has sufficient fuel for any trip they are assigned to make for an event.

A Staff Assignments form is shown on the next page.

Staff Assignments

General Information

Decedent _____ Case No. _____ Lead Director _____

Locations: Calling hours _____ Funeral _____ Disposition _____

Calling Hours Staff ("*Notified by*" *must be dated and initialed by person notifying the staff member of their assignment*)

Date: _____ From _____ to _____	Date: _____ From _____ to _____
Family expected arrival at _____	Family expected arrival at _____
1. _____ Notified by _____	1. _____ Notified by _____
2. _____ Notified by _____	2. _____ Notified by _____

Funeral Staff (in addition to lead director) ("*Notified by*" *must be dated and initialed by person notifying the staff member of their assignment*)

1. Name _____ Assemble at _____ Arrive by _____ **Notified by** _____

   Assignments _____ Driver of _____

2. Name _____ Assemble at _____ Arrive by _____ **Notified by** _____

   Assignments _____ Driver of _____

3. Name _____ Assemble at _____ Arrive by _____ **Notified by** _____

   Assignments _____ Driver of _____

4. Name _____ Assemble at _____ Arrive by _____ **Notified by** _____

   Assignments _____ Driver of _____

5. Name _____ Assemble at _____ Arrive by _____ **Notified by** _____

   Assignments _____ Driver of _____

6. Name _____ Assemble at _____ Arrive by _____ **Notified by** _____

   Assignments _____ Driver of _____

Notes - _____

_____

_____

Duties as described in Operation Manual:

Lead director - The sole responsibility of the lead director is to care for and respond to the immediate family. They should be in close proximity to them at all times; escort them in and out of the funeral home, churches, and other venues; escort them to and from the gravesite; assist in getting them into and out of vehicles; and explain any delays or activities taking place, as needed.

Casket transporter - Supervise all movement and transportation of casketed remains into and out of all venues and disposition locations; supervise all movement of casketed remains within venues, including gravesite locations; organize and instruct pallbearers; ensure casket exterior is clean and presentable after each movement; place or remove items on the casket, e.g., religious pall, cross, or U.S. Flag; and coordinate with military honor guards and other graveside organizations as needed.

Drivers - Ensure assigned vehicle has sufficient fuel for the round-trip and is clean, inside and out. Support passengers in entering and exiting the vehicle by opening and closing doors. Assist disabled or mobility challenged individuals in all respects, including when necessary transportation of personal support devices, such as walkers and wheelchairs.

Form 13: Spring Burial Worksheet

As described in chapter titled, *Post-Funeral Follow-up and Aftercare*, funeral establishments complete a spring burial worksheet to record interments that are going to take place after winter has passed and weather is conducive to digging graves and performing outdoor committals and ceremonies.

These worksheets are generally kept in a three-ring binder for ease of use when it comes time to start scheduling and planning the spring services. As this period of time is usually the two months immediately prior to Memorial Day weekend (April and May), funeral establishments can expect to be inundated with requests to have spring burials completed in time for Memorial Day events.

This, combined with requests to have these burials on a week-end so as to not necessitate family members taking additional time off from work, usually results in a very busy spring schedule. Many funeral establishments handle multiple spring burials every Saturday and Sunday for these two busy months.

A Spring Burial Worksheet form is shown on the next page.

XYZ Funeral Home
SPRING BURIAL WORKSHEET
(file in three-ring binder)

Case Info
Deceased _____ DOD _____ DOB _____ Case # _____

Cemetery/Location in Spring
❐ XYZ Cemetery   ❐ ABC Cemetery   ❐ Other _____

Current Location of Remains & Containers
❐ Town Vault   ❐ Prospect Hill Vault   ❐ Funeral Home   ❐ Other _____

❐ <u>Casket</u>   ❐ <u>Urn</u>   Description _____

❐ <u>Vault</u>   Description _____

Contact Info
Family1 _____ Relation _____ Phone1) _____ 2) _____

Family2 _____ Relation _____ Phone1) _____ 2) _____

Clergy _____ Phone1) _____ 2) _____

B U R I A L   S C H E D U L E

Burial Date: _____ *Burial Time:* _____

❐ Family confirmed   ❐ Clergy confirmed   ❐ Cemetery confirmed   ❐ Burial permit corrected/amended, as needed

❐ Vault company confirmed for: ❐ grass   ❐ tent   ❐ device   ❐ other _____

Headstone lettering?   ❐Yes ❐No   If yes, details: _____

Temporary marker?   ❐Yes ❐No   If yes, details: _____

Veteran's flag?   ❐Yes ❐No   If yes, details: _____

Veteran's plaque?   ❐Yes ❐No   If yes, ❐ Bronze or ❐ Granite? Details _____

Military honors?   ❐Yes ❐No   If yes, details: _____

Short obituary?   ❐Yes ❐No   If yes, details: _____

Flowers?   ❐Yes ❐No   If yes, details: _____

Notes: _____

_____

_____

_____

Guide 1: Environmental Protection Agency (EPA)
Burial at Sea Instructions

Source: Environmental Protection Agency website; retrieved online August 2019.

Instructions for Burial at Sea

The EPA has issued a general permit under the Marine Protection, Research and Sanctuaries Act (MPRSA) to authorize the burial of human remains at sea. The general permit is published in the federal regulations at 40 CFR 229.1.

The following activity is not allowed under the MPRSA general permit for burial at sea:

- Placement of human remains in ocean waters within three nautical miles from shore, i.e., the ordinary low water mark or a closing line drawn on nautical charts across the openings of bays and rivers.

- Placement of non-human remains (such as pet remains).

- Placement of materials which are not readily decomposable in the marine environment, such as plastic or metal flowers and wreaths, tombs, tombstones, gravestones, monuments, mausoleums, artificial reefs, etc.

Preparation for Burial at Sea

Human remains shall be prepared for burial at sea and buried in accordance with accepted practices and requirements as may be deemed appropriate and desirable by the United States Navy, United States Coast Guard or civil authority charged with the responsibility for making such arrangements. In addition, state and/or local requirements may apply to the transportation of human remains on land, for example, to locations other than cemeteries.

Non-cremated, non-casketed remains
If no casket is used, EPA recommends wrapping a natural fiber shroud or sail cloth around the body and adding additional weight, such as a steel chain, to aid in rapid sinking.

Non-cremated casketed remains
If using a casket, plastic materials should be removed from the casket before burial at sea because plastic materials do not degrade and may create unacceptable marine debris. A metal casket, as used by the United States Navy, should be considered. EPA recommends that:

- a minimum of twenty 2-inch (5 cm) holes be drilled into the casket to facilitate rapid flooding and venting of air. The holes should be evenly spaced on the top (8 holes), bottom (8 holes) and head and foot ends (2 holes each) of the casket. The holes may be covered with a porous material like cloth or paper so that the remains are not visible, as long as plastic-containing adhesives like tape are not used;

- to aid rapid sinking, additional weight, such as sand or concrete (but not lead), be added to the casket to achieve a total weight of at least 300 pounds (136 kg)

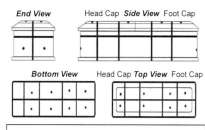

Recommended casket preparations to aid rapid, permanent, and intact sinking: twenty 2-inch holes, six bands and a total weight of at least 300 pounds.
Diagram from the United States Navy Burial at Sea Program, *Guidelines for Casket Preparation* (2010).

to offset the buoyancy of both the body and the casket. Weighing the foot end of the casket facilitates feet-first sinking; and

- the casket should be banded with at least six durable stainless-steel bands, chains, or natural fiber ropes in order to ensure rapid and permanent sinking of the intact casket. One band should be placed over each of the two lengthwise axes of the casket (top-to-bottom and head-to-foot), as well as four bands at evenly spaced intervals along the narrow axis of the casket. The latter is important for caskets with separate head and foot caps. Commercial shipping straps are likely to deteriorate rapidly in the marine environment and should not be used.

Disposal Location and Measures

Non-cremated remains
The MPRSA general permit authorizes burial at sea of non-cremated human remains at locations at least three nautical miles from land and in ocean waters at least 600 feet deep. In certain areas, specifically east central Florida, the Dry Tortugas, Florida and west of Pensacola, Florida to the Mississippi River Delta, such at sea burials are only authorized in ocean waters at least 1,800 feet deep. Refer to 40 CFR 229.1(a)(2) for details. All necessary measures must be taken to ensure that the remains sink to the bottom rapidly and permanently.

Cremated remains
Cremated remains shall be buried in or on ocean waters of any depth provided that such burial takes place at least three nautical miles from land.

Decomposable flowers and wreaths
Flowers and wreaths consisting of materials that are readily decomposable in the marine environment may be placed at the burial site. Plastic flowers or synthetic wreaths would not be expected to decompose rapidly.

Notice to EPA within 30 days
You must notify EPA of the burial at sea within 30 days following the event. All burials at sea conducted under the MPRSA general permit must be reported to the EPA Region from which the vessel carrying the remains departed.

A burial at sea of non-cremated and cremated human remains may be reported to EPA using the Burial at Sea Reporting Tool. The Burial at Sea Reporting Tool enables individuals or companies that have conducted a burial at sea to enter information into a simple online form and report the burial directly to EPA. For information about the Burial at Sea Reporting Tool including instructions for reporting, please see the Burial at Sea Reporting Tool Fact Sheet. Please note that you do not need to submit documentation, such as a Certificate of Death, to EPA when reporting a burial at sea.

To report a burial of human remains by other means, please contact the EPA Region where the vessel carrying the remains departed. To identify the appropriate EPA Regional contact, please see EPA's Regional Offices Contact List.

Guide 2: Typical Christian Church Interior Design

<u>Guide Definitions and Terminology</u>

Altar - an elevated place or structure on which sacrifices are offered or at which religious rites are performed; in the Christian faith, a table on which the Eucharist or Holy Communion is offered.

Chancel - the portion of the church surrounding the altar, usually enclosing the clergy; area behind the altar or communion rail.

Epistle side - In western Christianity, the side of a church from where an epistle (religious writing) is read. As viewed from the nave, it is on the right-hand side of the altar [by Author].

Foyer (narthex, vestibule) - the entry way into a church, funeral establishment, or other public building; entrance hall.

Gospel side - In western Christianity, the side of the church from where the gospel (Bible verses) is read. As viewed from the nave, it is on the left-hand side of the altar [by Author].

Nave - the seating or auditorium section of a church.

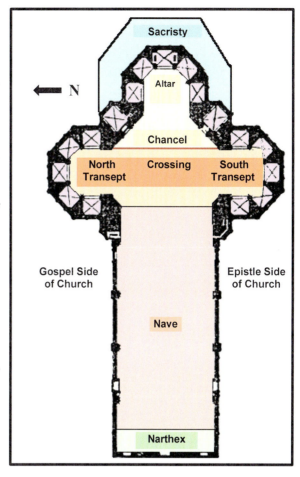

Sacristy - a room, usually located behind the altar, of a church, where clergy members prepare for services and ceremonies; may hold clergy vestments and other items of worship [by Author].

Sanctuary - the part of the church surrounding the altar, inside the chancel.

Transepts - wings of the main part of the church which may serve as small chapels for baptism, weddings, and even small funeral services.

Guide 3: Proper Way to Turn a Casket Around in a Church

↓ **Starting position**: Casket is perpendicular to the altar with the feet closest to the altar.

↓ **Step 1**: Push the casket forward and to the left in front of the pews on the left side of the church. Wait for the clergy and other officials (if any) to get into position in the aisle.

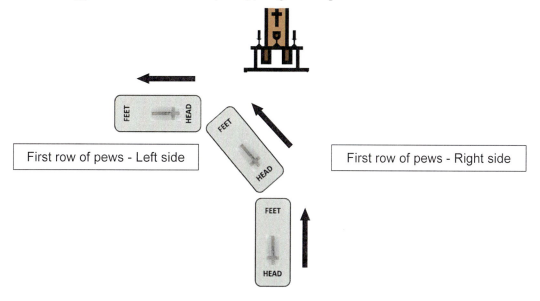

↓ **Step 2**: Push the casket all the way back across the aisle and in front of the pews on the right side of the church.

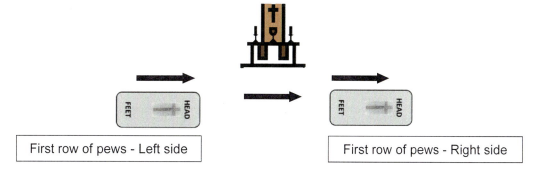

↓ Step 3: Push the casket forward and to the left to get positioned in the aisle with the feet facing the congregation. Wait for the church officials to start the procession and then follow the officiant.

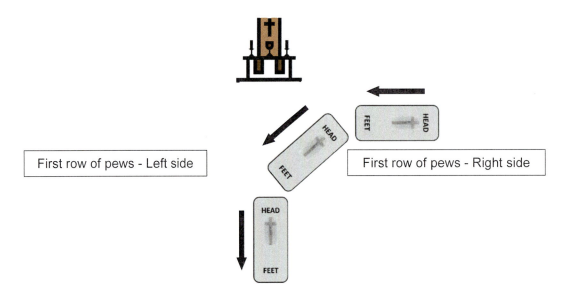

Note: When the decedent is an ordained clergy member, the casket position is reversed so the head comes into the church first. This has the decedent facing the congregation, as they would be when standing at the altar.

Guide 4: USPS Shipping Guidelines for Cremated Remains

These are the guidelines found in USPS Publication 139 as it was released in September 2019.

How to Package and Ship Cremated Remains

The United States Postal Service® offers Priority Mail Express® and Priority Mail Express International® service for shipping human or animal cremated remains domestically and internationally. Whether you are shipping the remains of a loved one or a pet to or between family members or to an artisan to incorporate the remains into blown glass or other works of art, this publication is designed to provide the necessary preparation and packaging requirements that will aid in protecting this special mailing during transit.

General Instructions

Cremated remains are permitted to be mailed to any domestic address when the package is prepared as described below and in the referenced postal manuals.

Cremated remains are permitted to be mailed to an international address when the designating country does not prohibit the contents and when Priority Mail Express International service is available to that country. You can verify this by checking the Individual Country Listing in the *Mailing Standards of the United States Postal Service,* International Mail Manual (IMM®).

Packaging

You will need a primary inner sift-proof container, cushioning material, and an outer shipping package.

Note: A sift-proof container is any vessel that does not allow loose powder to leak or sift out. There are many options available to store cremated remains - from simple wooden boxes to decorative urns. USPS® recommends consulting with a licensed funeral director to help you select the best container.

Inner Primary Container

- **Domestic Shipping:** The inner primary container must be strong, durable, and constructed in such a manner as to protect and securely contain the contents inside. It must be properly sealed and sift-proof.

- **International Shipping:** A funeral urn is required as the inner primary container. It must be properly sealed and sift-proof.

Seal and Address the Inner Primary Container

In the event the shipping label becomes detached from the outer container, the Postal Service™ recommends that you put the sift-proof container in a sealed plastic bag. Then, attach a label with the complete return address and delivery address on the sealed plastic bag and the wording "Cremated Remains."

Cushioning Material

For both domestic and international shipping, place sufficient cushioning all around the inner primary sift-proof container to prevent it shifting inside the outer shipping package during transit and to absorb any shock to prevent breakage.

Outer Shipping Package

For both domestic and international shipping, cremated remains must be shipped by USPS Priority Mail Express or Priority Mail Express International Service utilizing either a USPS-produced or customer-supplied shipping package. If using a customer-supplied shipping package, it must be strong and durable to withstand transportation handling.

For convenience, the Postal Service has a Priority Mail Express Cremated Remains box that may be used for domestic or international shipments using the applicable Priority Mail Express service. The Priority Mail Express Cremated Remains box can be ordered online at the Postal Store on USPS.com® and is available as part of a kit.

Before closing and sealing the shipping package, the Postal Service recommends adding a slip of paper with both the sender's and recipient's address and contact information inside the package. This extra step will help to identify the sender and receiver in the event the shipping label becomes detached.

Labeling and Markings

To increase the visibility of mail pieces containing cremated remains, the outer shipping box (USPS- produced or customer-supplied) containing cremated remains must be marked with Label 139, *Cremated Remains,* affixed to each side (including top and bottom). Label 139 is available at the Postal Store on USPS.com or can be obtained at a retail Post Office™ location.

Address Your Package

Domestic Shipping:

- A complete return address and delivery address must be used. The address format for a package is the same as for an envelope. Write or print address labels clearly. Use ink that does not smear and include the addresses and ZIP Codes™ for you and your recipient.

- Double check the mailing address, especially the ZIP Code. You can use Look Up a ZIP Code™ on USPS.com.

- Mailers may generate single-ply Priority Mail Express labels through Click-N-Ship® or other USPS-approved methods.

International Shipping:

A complete return address and delivery address must be used. The mailer must indicate the identity of the contents (Cremated Remains) on the required applicable customs declaration form. To determine the applicable required customs form, see IMM Section 123.61.

Note: If available, the cremation certificate should be attached to the outer box or made easily accessible. The sender is responsible for adherence to any restrictions or observances noted by the designating country.

Guide 5: Typical Airline Shipping Requirements

Note: The information in this guide was copied directly from *American Airlines* website in January of 2019. The information is, in the opinion of the author, representative of typical airline shipping requirements as they relate to the shipment of human remains and cremated remains.

Shipping Guidelines

Uncremated remains
When shipping uncremated remains, please provide a physician's or health officer's certificate or a burial transit permit. It is required by local, state, government, and international regulations. Shipping cadavers for research purposes does not require a burial transit permit. Please contact the state or country officials both at the origin and destination for full details on all regulations and document requirements.

Minimum packaging requirements for uncremated remains
Please secure the remains in a casket (or hermetically sealed casket as required) or alternative container (approved metal container or combination unit) in order to prevent shifting and the escape of strong odors. Caskets and alternative containers must be enclosed in an outer container (airtray) made of wood, particle board, corrugated fiberboard, plastic, or other water repellent material, and must have at least six handles and sufficient rigidity and padding to protect the inner container and contents from damage by ordinary care and handling. Please use new airtrays; used airtrays are not permitted. With certain types of combination units or cremation containers, airtrays may not be required. Containers should be clearly labeled with the following information: Air Waybill number, name of the deceased and the destination.

Unembalmed remains
Dry ice is not necessary to pack unembalmed remains. When using dry ice, remember that it will be subject to dangerous goods shipping regulations. Please secure unembalmed remains in a casket or combo unit or metal container in order to prevent shifting and the escape of strong odors. Please contact the state or country officials both at the origin and destination for full details on all regulations and document requirements.

Cremated remains
When transporting cremated remains, please keep in mind that the acceptance guidelines are slightly different compared to that of uncremated remains. Unless the remains are destined for a burial service, you will not need a burial transit permit. Please contact the state or country officials both at the origin and destination for full details on all regulations and document requirements.

Minimum packaging requirements for cremated remains
- Cremated remains must be contained in a five-millimeter polyurethane bag within cardboard outer packaging.

- A metal container or urn is the preferred method of inner packaging.

- Minimum size requirements (12"x12"x12") apply.

- Cremation containers are not acceptable for the transportation of human remains.

- Outer containers should be labeled with the following information:

  - Air Waybill number

  - Name of the deceased

  - Destination

Due to security requirements, no personal items may travel inside of the casket with the remains. All personal effects must be shipped separately. Please ensure the casket is checked before sealing and delivering.

Airtray information
Airtrays and combinations units must be new. For your convenience, we sell paperboard and adult-sized airtrays (87"x32"x23") which meet the requirements for an outside shipping container. Please note that reusing airtrays is not allowed. We do not offer infant airtrays for sale. The cost of an adult-sized airtray is $90 USD.

Airtrays are available for purchase through TLC. Our specialists will verify availability at your originating city and assist with the purchase at the time of your booking.

International guidelines
Caskets and outer containers (airtrays or wooden boxes depending on the country) are required for all international shipments of human remains. Please ensure you are providing the correct container based on your country of destination.

All international paperwork must be easily accessible by American Airlines and the receiving party. Paperwork must move with the remains in a document pouch on the outside of the container and cannot travel with the family escorting the remains nor be attached to the inside or outside of the casket.

For uncremated remains, please secure the remains in a hermetically sealed casket or an approved metal container. Combination units are not accepted to international destinations (with the exception of Canada).

Glossary

Acknowledgment cards - thank you cards. (Chapter 3)

Acolyte - an altar attendant. (Chapter 12)

Adaptive funeral rite - a funeral rite that is adjusted to the needs and wants of those directly involved. (Chapter 7)

Aftercare - those appropriate and helpful acts of counseling, personal and/or written contact that come after the funeral. (Chapter 13)

Air tray - a transfer container consisting of a wooden tray with a cardboard covering for the casket. (Chapter 16)

Alkaline hydrolysis - a process that uses water, alkaline chemicals, heat and sometimes pressure and agitation to accelerate natural decomposition, leaving bone fragments. (Chapter 4)

Altar - an elevated place or structure on which sacrifices are offered or at which religious rites are performed; in the Christian faith, a table on which the Eucharist or Holy Communion is offered. (Chapter 12 and Guide 2)

Alternative container - an unfinished wood box or other non-metal receptacle or enclosure, without ornamentation or a fixed interior lining, which is designed for the encasement of human remains and which is made of fiberboard, pressed-wood, composition materials (with or without an outside covering) or like materials. (Chapter 7)

Apostille - certification/legalization of a document for international use (under terms of the 1961 Hague Convention). (Chapters 14 and 15)

Arrangement conference - the meeting between the funeral practitioner and the client family during which funeral arrangements are discussed; may refer to preneed or at-need situations. (Chapters 2 and 3)

At-need cases - when a death has occurred. (Chapters 1 and 9)

Beneficiary - means the named individual for whom a preneed agreement is purchased. The beneficiary may also be the purchaser [by Author]. (Chapters 9 and 10)

Block - a subdivision of a cemetery containing several lots. (Chapter 4)

Burial (interment) - the act of placing a dead human body in the ground. (Chapter 4)

Burial-transit permit (disposition permit) - a legal document, issued by a governmental agency, authorizing transportation and/or disposition of a dead human body. (Chapter 5)

Calling hours - (visitation, visiting hours) - time set aside for friends and relatives to pay respect for the deceased prior to the funeral service. (Chapters 11 and 12)

Cash advance - any item of service or merchandise described to a purchaser as a 'cash advance,' 'accommodation,' 'cash disbursement,' or similar term. A cash advance item is also any item obtained from a third party and paid for by the funeral provider on the purchaser's behalf. Cash advance items may include but are not limited to: cemetery or crematory services; pallbearers; public transportation; clergy honoraria; flowers; musicians or singers; nurses; obituary notices; gratuities; and death certificates. (Chapter 3)

Casketbearer (pallbearer) - one who actively bears or carries the casket during the funeral service and at the committal service. (Chapters 3 and 12)

Cause of death - diseases, injuries, or complications that resulted in death [by Author]. (Chapter 5)

Celebrant - a person who designs and officiates a personalized ceremony or rite; the officiant who celebrates the Mass in the Roman Catholic Church. (Chapter 7)

Celebrant funeral - a funeral service not focused on any specific religion, belief, faith, or rite; officiated by a trained and qualified, non-clergy official [by Author]. (Chapters 7 and 11)

Cemetery - an area of ground set aside and dedicated for the final disposition of dead human remains. (Chapters 4 and 11)

Cemetery tent - a portable shelter employed to cover the grave area during the committal. (Chapter 11)

Certified copy of a death certificate - a legal copy of the original death certificate. (Chapters 3 and 5)

Church truck - a wheeled collapsible support for the casket used in the funeral home, church, or home. (Chapter 11)

Chancel - the portion of the church surrounding the altar, usually enclosing the clergy; area behind the altar or communion rail. (Guide 2)

Chapel - a building or designated area of a building in which services are conducted. (Chapter 12)

Columbarium - a structure, room or space in a mausoleum or other building containing niches or recesses used to hold cremated remains. (Chapter 4)

Combination case (AKA combo case) - a transfer container for uncasketed remains consisting of a particle board tray with a cardboard cover. (Chapter 16)

Committal service - that portion of the funeral conducted at the place of disposition of dead human bodies. (Chapter 12)

Common carrier - any carrier required by law to convey passengers or freight without refusal if the approved fare or charge is paid (airline, train, etc.). (Chapters 14 and 15)

Contract - a legally enforceable agreement [FSL term]. (Chapter 9)

Coroner - usually an elected officer without medical training whose chief duty is to investigate questionable deaths. (Chapter 1)

Cot - a portable stretcher commonly employed in a transfer vehicle for the moving of the deceased. (Chapter 2)

Couch crypt - a crypt in which the casket likes parallel to the crypt face [MM term]. (Chapter 4)

Cremated remains – the result of the reduction of a dead body to inorganic bone fragments by intense heat. (Chapters 4 and 7)

Cremation - the reduction of a dead human body to inorganic bone fragments by intense heat in a specifically designed retort or chamber. (Chapter 4)

Crematory - a furnace or retort for cremating dead human bodies; a building that houses a retort. (Chapter 11)

Crucifer or crossbearer - one who carries the crucifix/cross during an ecclesiastical procession. (Chapters 12 and 16)

Crypt - a chamber in a mausoleum, of sufficient size, generally used to contain the casketed remains of a deceased person. (Chapter 4)

Death certificate - a legal document containing vital statistics, disposition, and final medical information pertaining to the deceased. (Chapters 2, 3 and 5)

Death notice - a newspaper item publicizing the death of a person and giving service details. In some parts of the United States, can contain the same information as an obituary. (Chapter 3)

Deceased - a dead human body. (Chapter 1)

Dentures - false teeth. (Chapter 2)

Department of Veterans Affairs or VA (previously known as Veterans Administration) - a federal agency that administers benefits provided for veterans of the armed forces. (Chapter 6)

Direct cremation - disposition of human remains by cremation, with no formal viewing, visitation, or ceremony with the deceased present. (Chapter 7)

Direct disposition - any method of disposition of the human remains without formal viewing, visitation, or ceremony with the deceased present. (Chapter 7)

Dismissal - procedures or invitation intended to facilitate an organized departure. (Chapter 12)

Disposition permit - see burial-transit permit. (Chapter 5)

Due diligence - the attention reasonably expected from, and ordinarily exercised by, a person who seeks to satisfy a legal requirement or to discharge an obligation. (Chapter 8)

Ecumenical - representing a number of different Christian churches [by Author]. (Chapter 13)

Entombment - the placing of remains in a crypt in a mausoleum. (Chapter 4)

Epistle side - In western Christianity, the side of a church from where an epistle (religious writing) is read. As viewed from the nave, it is on the right-hand side of the altar [by Author]. (Guide 2)

First call - when the funeral establishment receives notification of death. (Chapter 1)

First viewing (preview) - a private time for the family to view the deceased before public visitation begins. (Chapter 12)

Forwarding remains - one of the categories required to be itemized on the GPL (if the funeral provider offers the service). This involves services of the funeral provider in the locale where death occurs and preparation for transfer to another funeral provider as selected by the family (consumer). Funeral Rule requires package pricing of this service with a description of the components included. (Chapter 15)

Foyer (narthex, vestibule) - the entry way into a church, funeral establishment, or other public building; entrance hall. (Chapter 12 and Guide 2)

Fraternal - relating to a social organization. (Chapter 11)

Funeral coach (hearse) - specialty vehicle designed to transfer casketed remains. (Chapters 2 and 12)

Funeral goods - means all products sold directly to the public in connection with funeral services [by FTC]. (Chapters 3, and 7)

Funeral procession - the movement of vehicles from the place of the funeral to the place of disposition. (Chapter 12)

Funeral service - the rites held at the time of disposition of human remains, with the deceased present. (Chapter 12)

Funeral services - means services used to care for and prepare bodies for burial, cremation, or other final disposition; and services used to arrange, supervise, or conduct the funeral ceremony or final disposition of human remains [by FTC]. (Chapters 3 and 7)

General price list (GPL) - a printed list of goods and services offered for sale by funeral providers with retail prices. The GPL is considered the keystone of the Funeral Rule. (Chapter 2)

Gospel side - In western Christianity, the side of the church from where the gospel (Bible verses) is read. As viewed from the nave, it is on the left-hand side of the altar [by Author]. (Guide 2)

Gratuity - gift or small sum of money tendered (tip) for a service provided. (Chapter 11)

Grave - an excavation in the earth as a place for interment; interment space. (Chapter 4)

Graveside service - a ceremony or ritual, religious or otherwise, conducted at the grave. (Chapter 7)

Green burial - disposition without the use of toxic chemicals or materials that are not readily biodegradable. (Chapters 4 and 7)

Green cemetery - a place of interment that bans the use of metal caskets, toxic embalming, and concrete vaults and may also require the use of aesthetically natural monuments. (Chapters 4 and 7)

Green funeral - death care that minimizes the use of energy in service offerings/products and that bans the use of toxic/hazardous materials. (Chapter 7)

Guaranteed contract - an agreement where the funeral establishment promises that the services and merchandise will be provided at the time of need for a sum not exceeding the original amount of the contract plus any accruals, regardless of the current prices associated with providing the services and merchandise at the time of the funeral. (Chapter 9)

Hearse - see funeral coach. (Chapters 2 and 12)

Home funeral - one that takes place within the residence of the deceased as was commonly done in the United States until the mid-20th century. (Chapter 7)

Honorarium - compensation or recognition for services performed. (Chapter 12)

Honorary casketbearers (Honorary pallbearers) - friends of the family or members of an organization or group who act as an escort or honor guard for the deceased. They do not carry the casket. (Chapters 3 and 12)

Humanist funeral - a funeral rite that is in essence devoid of religious connotation. (Chapter 7)

Immediate burial - disposition of human remains by burial, with no formal viewing, visitation, or ceremony with the deceased present, except for a graveside service. (Chapter 7)

Informant - one who supplies vital statistics information about the deceased. (Chapter 5)

Initial notification of death - the first contact a funeral establishment receives regarding a death. (Chapter 1)

Inter - to bury in the ground. (Chapter 4)

Inurnment - placing cremated remains in an urn or placing cremated remains in a niche or grave. (Chapters 4 and 7)

Irrevocable contract - an agreement for future funeral services which cannot be terminated or canceled prior to the death of the beneficiary. (Chapter 9)

Kneeler - (prayer rail, prie dieu) - a small bench placed in front of the casket or urn to allow a person to kneel for prayer. (Chapter 11)

Lot - a subdivision in a cemetery which consists of several graves or interment spaces. (Chapter 4)

Malpractice - failure to perform a professional service with the ability and care generally exercised by others in the profession [FSL term]. (Chapter 8)

Manner of death - the mode of death, such as accident, homicide, natural, or suicide [by Author]. (Chapter 5)

Mausoleum - a building containing crypts or vaults for entombment. (Chapter 4)

Medical examiner - a forensically-trained physician who investigates questionable or unattended deaths (has replaced the coroner in some jurisdictions). (Chapter 1)

Memorial book (register book) - a book signed by those attending a visitation or service. (Chapters 3 and 11)

Memorial folder (service folder) - a pamphlet made available at the funeral service giving details about the deceased and the funeral arrangements. (Chapter 3)

Memorial gathering - a scheduled assembly of family and friends following a death without the deceased present. (Chapters 3 and 7)

Memorial park - a cemetery, or section of a cemetery, with only flush to the ground type markers. (Chapter 4)

Memorial service - funeral rites without the remains present. (Chapters 3 and 7)

Metal case (Ziegler case) - a gasketed container, which can be used as an insert in a casket or as a separate shipping container. (Chapter 16)

Narthex (foyer, vestibule) - see Foyer. (Chapter 12 and Guide 2)

National cemetery - a cemetery created and maintained under an act of Congress for burial of veterans of military service and their eligible family members. (Chapter 6)

Nave - the seating or auditorium section of a church. (Guide 2)

Niche - a recess or space in a columbarium used for the permanent placing of cremated remains. (Chapter 4)

Non-guaranteed contract - agreement in which the funeral establishment promises to apply the amount pre-paid plus any accruals to the balance due. However, the cost of the funeral will be based upon the current price for services and merchandise at the time death occurs. (Chapter 9)

Obituary - traditionally, a news item concerning the death of a person which usually contains a biographical sketch. Can appear in media other than newspapers such as online sources and service programs. Is sometimes used interchangeably with death notice or funeral notice. (Chapter 3)

Officiant - one who conducts or leads a service or ceremony. (Chapter 2)

Outer burial container - any container designed for placement in the grave around the casket. (Chapter 4)

Pall - a symbolic cloth placed over the casket. (Chapters 12)

Pallbearer (casketbearer) - see casketbearer. (Chapters 3 and 12)

Perpetual care - an arrangement made by the cemetery whereby funds are set aside, the income from which is used to maintain the cemetery indefinitely. (Chapter 6)

Pouch - a leak resistant, zippered bag designed to contain human remains and any body fluids; used primarily for the removal of human remains from the place of death. (Chapters 3 and 16)

Prayer card - a card with the name of the decedent and a prayer or verse, which may or may not include the dates of birth and death. (Chapters 3 and 11)

Prayer rail (kneeler, prie dieu) - see kneeler. (Chapter 11)

Prefunded funeral arrangements - funeral arrangements made in advance of need that include provisions for funding or prepayment. (Chapters 9 and 10)

Preneed cases - cases where funeral arrangements are made prior to a death occurring, in preparation for use in the future [by Author]. (Chapter 9)

Pre-planned funeral arrangements - funeral arrangements made in advance of need that do not include provisions for funding or prepayment. (Chapter 9)

Preview - see first viewing. (Chapter 12)

Private carrier - those who transport only in particular instances and only for those they chose to contract with (e.g. funeral establishment vehicles and livery). (Chapters 14 and 15)

Prie dieu (prayer rail, kneeler) - see kneeler. (Chapter 11)

Procession/processional - the movement, in an orderly fashion, at the beginning of a service. (Chapter 12)

Purchaser - means the named individual paying for and purchasing a preneed account. The purchaser may also be the beneficiary [by Author]. (Chapters 9 and 10)

Receiving remains - one of the categories required to be itemized on the GPL (if the funeral provider offers the service). This involves services of the funeral provider after initial services have been provided by another firm at the locale of death. Funeral Rule requires package pricing of this service with a description of the components included. (Chapter 15)

Receiving vault - a structure designed for the temporary storage of bodies not to be immediately interred. (Chapter 4)

Recession/recessional - the movement, in an orderly fashion, at the end of a service. (Chapter 12)

Register book (memorial book) - see memorial book. (Chapters 3 and 11)

Registrar - means a public official responsible for keeping official records on births, deaths, and marriages [by Author]. (Chapter 5)

Retort - the burning chamber in a crematory, also referred to as the cremator; the total mechanical unit for the cremation process. (Chapter 4)

Revocable contract - agreement which may be terminated by the purchaser at any time prior to the death of the beneficiary with a refund of monies paid on the contract as prescribed by state law. (Chapter 9)

Sacristy - a room, usually located behind the altar, of a church, where clergy members prepare for services and ceremonies; may hold clergy vestments and other items of worship [by Author]. (Guide 2)

Sanctuary - the part of the church surrounding the altar, inside the chancel. (Guide 2)

Section - the largest subdivision of a cemetery. (Chapter 4)

Service folder - see memorial folder. (Chapter 3)

Social Security Administration - a branch of the U. S. Department of Health and Human Services which provides benefits for retirement, survivors, and disability; and includes Supplemental Security Income (SSI) and Medicare. (Chapter 6)

Survivor(s) - one who outlives another person or event. (Chapter 3)

Temporary container - a receptacle for cremated remains, usually made of cardboard, plastic, or similar materials designed to hold cremated remains until an urn or other permanent container is acquired, or other disposition is made. (Chapter 4)

Third party contracts - agreements which involve the funeral practitioner/funeral establishment because the family being served has contracted with someone else (a third party) for services or merchandise also available from the funeral establishment i.e. caskets, vaults, urns, preneed insurance, etc. (Chapter 10)

Tomb - a general term designating those places suitable for the reception of a dead human body. (Chapter 4)

Transepts - wings of the main part of the church which may serve as small chapels for baptism, weddings, and even small funeral services. (Guide 2)

Transfer container - an enclosure used for the protection of human remains during transportation. (Chapter 16)

Transfer of remains - the moving of the dead human body from the place of death to the funeral establishment or other designated place. (Chapters 1 and 2)

Transfer vehicle - the automobile generally used for transporting the uncasketed dead human body from the place of death to the mortuary. (Chapter 2)

Trust account - account established by one individual to be held for the benefit of another (as a method of payment of funeral expenses); creates a fiduciary responsibility. Money paid to a funeral establishment for future services is placed in an account with the funeral establishment as trustee for the benefit of another. (Chapter 10)

Urn - permanent container for cremated remains meant for decorative or inurnment purposes. (Chapter 4)

Vestibule (foyer, narthex) - see foyer. (Chapter 12 and Guide 2)

Vestments - ritual garments worn by the clergy. (Chapter 12)

Visitation (calling hours, visiting hours) - see calling hours. (Chapters 7 and 12)

Vital statistics - data concerning birth, marriage, divorce, sickness, and death. (Chapters 2, 3 and 6)

Ziegler case - see metal case (represents a specific brand of metal case, but in use have become synonymous terms). (Chapter 16)

Sources Consulted

"A Journey of Compassion." American Airlines Cargo. American Airlines, Inc., 2018, retrieved January 2019.
URL: https://www.aacargo.com/learn/humanremains.html

"Agnostic." Merriam-Webster Dictionary. Merriam-Webster, Inc., retrieved October 2018.
URL: https://www.merriam-webster.com/dictionary/agnostic

American Board of Funeral Service Education. "Funeral Directing and Arranging." Curriculum outline as approved 2016.

"Atheist." Merriam-Webster Dictionary. Merriam-Webster, Inc, retrieved October 2018.
URL: https://www.merriam-webster.com/dictionary/atheist

Bromwich, Jonah Engel. "An Alternative to Burial and Cremation Gains Popularity." *The New York Times*, October 19, 2017, retrieved December 2018.
URL: https://www.nytimes.com/2017/10/19/business/flameless-cremation.html

Budge, E.A. Wallis. *The Mummy: A Handbook of Egyptian Funerary Archaeology*. Kessinger Publishing LLC, 2010.

Burnham, Scott J. *Contract Law for Dummies*. John Wiley & Sons Inc., 2012.

C.G. Labs Inc. "DNA Memorial: Saving the Past for the Future." Thunder Bay, Ontario, Canada; retrieved August 2020.
URL: www.cglabscorp.com/

"Christianity." Merriam-Webster Dictionary. Merriam-Webster, Inc, retrieved October 2018.
URL: https://www.merriam-webster.com/dictionary/Christianity

Cleveland, Larry J. *Funeral Service Marketing and Merchandise: A Guide for Practitioners and Mortuary Science Students*. Hudson Valley Professional Services, 2018.

Cleveland, Larry J. *Funeral Service Law in the United States: A Guide for Funeral Service Students*. Hudson Valley Professional Services, 2019.

Cremation Association of North America. "Support for Members Offering Pet Cremation." Wheeling, Illinois, retrieved August 2020.
URL: https://www.cremationassociation.org/page/PetCremation

DeSmith, Kristy. "What Makes a Contract Invalid?" Law Depot, June 17, 2015, retrieved July 2018.
URL: https://www.lawdepot.com/blog/what-makes-a-contract-invalid/

Global Genetic Health, Inc. "DNA Memorial: Connecting People Across Genetic Histories." Thunder Bay, Ontario, Canada; retrieved August 2017.
URL: https://dnamemorial.com/

Green Burial Council. "Find a Provider." Ojai, California, retrieved March 2017.
URL: http://greenburialcouncil.com/find-a-provider/

Habenstein, Robert Wesley, and William M. Lamers. *The History of American Funeral Directing*, *8th ed*. National Funeral Directors Association, 2014.

"How to Package and Ship Cremated Remains." Government Printing Office. United States Postal Office, September 2019, brochure, retrieved January 2019.
URL: https://about.usps.com/publications/pub139.pdf

Hoy, William G. *Do Funerals Matter? The Purposes and Practices of Death Rituals in Global Perspective*. Routledge, Taylor, and Francis Group, 2013.

Legal Information Institute. "Standard of Care." Cornell Law School; Cornell, New York; retrieved November 2020.
URL: https://www.law.cornell.edu/wex/standard_of_care

Mukhtar, Saqib, et al. "Managing Contaminated Animal and Plant Materials: Field Guide on Best Practices." Texas A&M University, 2012, retrieved August 2017.
URL: http://iiad.tamu.edu/wp-content/uploads/2012/06/ConMat.pdf

Murray, Rachel. "Funeral Home Offers DNA Preservation." Dayton Daily News, Dayton, Ohio, published March 13, 2015; retrieved September 2017.
URL: www.daytondailynews.com/business/funeral-home-offers-dna-preservation/Ll6xmoF3ObBSO5FbHKxCeJ/

National Funeral Directors Association. "2017 Consumer Awareness and Preferences Study." Brookfield, Illinois, press release dated June 22, 2017, retrieved July 2018.
URL: https://www.nysfda.org/index.php/news-events/news/press-releases/704-nfda-consumer-survey-funeral-planning-not-a-priority-for-americans

New York State Department of Health. "New York State Electronic Death Registration System (EDRS)." New York State Government, Bureau of Vital Statistics, Version 2.1, February 2017, retrieved July 2018.
URL: https://www.health.ny.gov/vital_records/edrs/funeral.htm

"Reality of Consent." The Free Dictionary. Farlex, Inc., 2018, retrieved online July 2018.
URL: https://legal-dictionary.thefreedictionary.com/Reality+of+Consent

Stevens, Holly. *Undertaken with Love: A Home Funeral Guide for Families and Community Care Groups*. National Home Funeral Alliance, 2016.

United States, Department of the Army. *Arlington National Cemetery*. United States Government, 2018, retrieved November 2020.
URL: https://www.arlingtoncemetery.mil/

---, Department of Health and Human Services, Centers for Disease Control. "Funeral Directors' Handbook on Death Registration and Fetal Death Reporting." United States Government, 2019 revision, DHHS Publication No. (PHS) 2019-1109.

---, Department of Labor, Federal Trade Commission. "Complying with the Funeral Rule." United States Government, April 2019, retrieved November 2020.
URL: www.ftc.gov/system/files/documents/plain-language/565a-complying-with-funeral-rule_2020_march_508.pdf

---, Department of Labor, Occupational Safety and Health Administration. "Personal Protective Equipment, OSHA 3151-12R." United States Government, 2004, retrieved November 2020.
URL: https://www.osha.gov/Publications/osha3151.pdf

---, Department of Veterans Affairs. "Survivor Benefits." United States Government, January 2018, retrieved July 2018.
URL: https://www.va.gov/family-member-benefits/

---, ---, National Cemetery Administration. "Burial and Memorial Benefits." United States Government, 2018, retrieved July 2018.
URL: https://www.cem.va.gov/burial_benefits/

---, Social Security Administration. "How Social Security Can Benefit You When a Family Member Dies." United States Government, Pub. No. 05-10008, May 2017, retrieved July 2018.
URL: https://www.ssa.gov/pubs/EN-05-10008.pdf

---, Social Security Administration. "Survivors Benefits." United States Government, Pub. No. 05-10084, March 2018, retrieved July 2018.
URL: https://www.ssa.gov/pubs/EN-05-10084.pdf

Webster, Lee. *Essentials for Practicing Home Funeral Guides.* National Home Funeral Alliance, 2015.

West's Encyclopedia of American Law, 2nd ed. "Malpractice." Thomas/Gale Publishers, Detroit, Michigan, Vol. 6, pg. 409, 2005.

"What is a U.S. Embassy?" Discover Diplomacy. U.S. Diplomacy Center, United States Department of State, retrieved January 2019.
URL: https://diplomacy.state.gov/discover-diplomacy

Illustrations

1. **Image - Passenger Vans for Transfer of Remains**
    Illustrations and information courtesy of Tribute Enterprises
    Long Beach, California, April 2018
    URL: http://www.tributeenterprises.org/

2. **Illustrations - Crypt Types**
    Illustrations and information courtesy of North Bay Roman Catholic Cemeteries
    North Bay, Ontario, Canada, August 2017
    URL: http://www.nbrcc.ca/
       -and-
    Carrier Mausoleums Construction, Inc.
    Saint-Laurent, Quebec, Canada, August 2017
    URL: http://www.cmc-carrier.com/

3. **Images - Natural Burial Containers/Methods**
    Illustrations and information courtesy of Northwoods Casket Company
    Beaver Dam, Wisconsin, March 2017
    URL: http://www.northwoodscasket.com/

4. **Images - Transportation and Shipping Containers**
    Illustrations and information courtesy of AMA Containers
    Kingwood, Texas, February 2017
    URL: http://www.airtrayman.com/

5. **Images - Personalized Traditional Goods and Themed Funerals**
    Illustrations and information courtesy of Wilson Funeral Home
    Norwich, New York, September 2017
    URL: http://wilsonfh.com/

6. **Image - Monogrammed Overlay**
    Illustrations and information courtesy of Mathews International
    Pittsburgh, Pennsylvania, April 2017.
    URL: http://matw.com/

    --- All Matthews International images are copyright protected and may not be reproduced or copied for any purpose without the written permission of Matthews International. ---

7. **Image - Executive Coaches**
    Illustration and information courtesy of Premier Plus Travel and Tours
    Queensbury, New York, November 2016.
    URL: http://www.premierplustours.com/

8. **Image - DNA Preservation**
    Illustration and information courtesy of DNA Memorials (C.G. Labs Inc.)
    Thunder Bay, Ontario, Canada, July 2020.
    URL: http://dnamemorialorder.com/

Index

A4A 146
ABFSE 9, 11, 45
Aftercare 129
Air pressure on flights 149
Air trays 146
Airlines for America 146
Airlines, checked/carry-on bags 134
Alkaline hydrolysis disposition 50
Allied professionals 105
American Board of Funeral Service
    Education .... *See* ABFSE
American Disabilities Act 112
Apostille 136, 142
Arlington National Cemetery 67
Arrangement conference 32
Attending physicians 53
Balloon releases 79
Beneficiary, preneed 97
Blocks, cemetery 46
Body bag .... *See* Pouches
Bridges, toll 125
Bug stamp 148
Burial platforms 84
Burial transit permits 55
Car lists 124
Carry-on bags, airlines 135
Case files 90
Case worksheets 105
Cash advances 40
Cause of death 53
CBD payments 39
Cemeteries in national parks 69
Centers for Disease Control 54
Certified copies of death certificate ... 37
Checked baggage, airlines 134
COD payments 39
Columbarium walls 45
Combination units 150
Common carriers 134, 140
Companion crypts 48
Contract, void or voidable 100
Coroner 17, 53
Couch crypts 49
Credit 39

Credit card surcharges 39
Cremated remains
    Shipping 133
    Transportation 133
Cremation disposition 44
Cryonics disposition 50
Crypts 46
    Companion 48
    Couch 49
Customized goods 107
CWO payments 39
Death case files 90
Death certificate, fetal 55
Death certificates 37
Death notice 36
Death, cause of 53
Death, manner of 53
Department of Veteran Affairs 58
DHL shipping 133
Direct aftercare 130
Disaster bags 22
Disaster pouches 150
Discharges, military 63
Disclaimer 12
Dispositions
    Alkaline hydrolysis 50
    Burial (interment) 45
    Cremation 44
    Cryonics 50
    Donation 49
    Entombment 46
    Green burial 49
    Natural burial 49
DNA preservation 76
Domestic shipping
    Cremated remains 133
    Human remains 139
Dress codes 23
Due diligence 87, 196
E-coffins, or green coffins 83
Electronic death certificates 54
Embalm, permission to 28
Embassies 135, 141
Emblems of belief 60, 163

Entombment disposition 46
Environmental Protection Agency 49, 183
Environmentally friendly containers 83
EOM payments 39
Escorts 125
Express contracts 95
Federal Trade Commission 14, 28, 33, 82
   Third-party caskets 85
FedEx shipping 133
Fetal death certificates 55
First call 13
Flowers 37
Food and beverages 77
Funeral equipment 109
Funeral events, inspecting 112
Funeral goods
   Innovative 78
   Traditional 78
Funeral services
   Innovative 74
   Traditional 72
General price list
   At arrangements 39
   For preneeds 98
General price list, at removals 30
Gold star lapel pin 61
Government embassies 135, 141
Graves, cemetery 46
Green burial
   Containers 83
   Conveyances 84
   Disposition 49
Guaranteed funeral contracts 96
High altitude air pressure 149
Home funerals 80
Indirect aftercare 131
Innovative
   Funeral goods 78
   Funeral services 74
Inspecting funeral event sites 112
Insurance assignments 39
International Plant Protection 148
International shipping
   Cremated remains 135
   Human remains 141
Interstate highways 126

Irrevocable funeral contracts 96
Known shippers 144
Landau bars 20
Lead director concept 103
Lots, cemetery 46
Manner of death 53
Medallions 60
Medical examiner 17, 53
Metal shipping case 149
Military discharges 63
Military funeral honors 62
MOM payments 39
Monogramming 79
Mortician 11
Mortuary bags 22
Mortuary pouches 150
National Board Examination 11
National cemeteries in NYS 63
National Cemetery Administration 64
National Cemetery Scheduling Office 66
National Funeral Directors Assoc. 93, 132
National park cemeteries 69
Natural burial
   Containers 83
   Conveyances 84
   Disposition 49
Newspaper notice 36
NFDA 93, 132
Niches 45
Non-declinable fees 40
Notification of death 13
Nurse practitioners 53
Obedience to traffic rules 125
Obituary 36
OSHA 22
Outer burial container 45
Payment terms, retail sales 38
Permission to embalm 28
Personal protective equipment 22
Personalized goods 107
Photo presentations 77
Physician assistants 53
Pouches 22, 150
PPE 22
Preneed funeral arrangements 93, 97
Prepaid funeral arrangements 39

Preservation of DNA 76
Presidential memorial certificate 61
Private carriers 140
Processions, vehicle 126
Public assistance 70
Purchaser, preneed 97
Registrar 53
Removal pouches 150
Removals 27
Revocable funeral contracts 96
Right-of-way 125
Roads, toll 125
Sealer caskets 149
Sections, cemetery 46
Shipping case, metal 149
Shipping crates, wooden boxes 148
Shipping labels 133
Shipping, domestic
    Cremated remains 133
    Human remains 139
Shipping, international
    Cremated remains 135
    Human remains 141
Sky candles 79
Social Security Administration 57
Social services 70
Spring burials 130
Tapestry 79
Telephone etiquette 15
Themed funerals 75, 108

Third-party caskets 85
Toll roads and bridges 125
Tort claims 87
Tracking priority mail 134
Traditional funeral goods 78
Traditional funeral services 72
Traffic rules 125
Training (for transfers) 24
Transfer containers 145
Transfer of remains 17, 19
Transfer vehicles 19
Transportation Security Admin 134, 144
TSA 134, 144
U.S. Flag 61
Undertaker 11
United Parcel Service 133
United States Postal Service .... *See* USPS
USPS Publication 139 189
USPS shipping 133
Vault 45
Vehicle processions 126
Video programs 77
Void a preneed contract 100
Walls, columbarium 45
Website broadcasts 74
Welfare services 70
Wheat stamp 148
Wooden boxes, shipping crates 148
Worksheets, case 105
Ziegler case 149

Hudson Valley Professional Services
~ Educating the Funeral Service Industry ~